MOTIVATIONS FOR MISSION: A RELATIONAL-COVENANTAL PERSPECTIVE

ENOCH WAN & CHRISTOPHER M. SANTIAGO

Relational Paradigm Series of CDRR

Motivations for Mission:
A Relational-Covenantal Perspective

Enoch Wan &
Christopher M. Santiago

Copyright @ 2022 by Western Academic Publishers

Cover designed by Blake Kidney

ISBN: 978-1-954692-00-8

All rights reserved. Except for brief quotations in critical publications or reviews, no part of this book may be reproduced in any manner without prior written permission from the publisher or author

Scripture quotations are from the ESV® Bible (The Holy Bible, English Standard Version®), copyright © 2001 by Crossway, a publishing ministry of Good News Publishers. Used by permission. All rights reserved.

CDRR (Center of Diaspora & Relational Research) @
https://www.westernseminary.edu/outreach/center-diaspora-relational-research

Foreword to
Motivations for Mission: A Relational-Covenantal Perspective

This book explores the mysterious, often-elusive motives that undergird the Christian Church's commitment to mission, which includes the proclamation of the gospel, personal and corporate evangelism, planting new churches near and far, revitalizing existing congregations, and positively impacting cultures, economies, and ecologies with the energy of God's transforming grace. The value of this book, dedicated as it is to cracking the code of sustained missionary engagement, is manifestly apparent to every pastoral leader who has sought to fan the fires of gospel fervor in the hearts and lives of God's people. Missionary fervor, it would seem, is subject to the second law of thermodynamics: when missionary ardor is released into cooler, gospel-deprived environs, the ardor itself cools as it warms these spaces. While it is not impossible for entropy to decrease in such instances – in this case by maintaining or even increasing evangelistic zeal while infusing the vacuum of the world's need with the power of the gospel – this phenomenon cannot occur without a corresponding transfer of energy from another source (or Source). This provides at least a partial explanation for the evident waxing and waning of Christianity's missionary engagements throughout the sum of the Church's history.

I experienced the phenomenon of increasing entropy in a personal way shortly after I began full-time ministry in 1982. Like many newly minted pastors, I was thrilled to have an impact on the church and community. My first assignment was as "minister of evangelism," and the primary goal of my work was to motivate members of the congregation to join the mission of Jesus in making disciples of every nation, starting with family, friends, neighbors, and expanding outward from there. However, I soon discovered that personal zeal was not sufficient to inspire action in others. Members of the church were, in a word, *unmotivated*…or so it seemed. I wrongly assumed that most Christians *wanted* to make Jesus known to the world. All they needed was a little help to organize their efforts. I employed every creative tactic I could think of, but the congregants remained unimpressed and, for the most part, unengaged. Over time, my evangelistic zeal flagged, and I found solace in the work of daily church life: teaching high school classes, writing articles for the bi-weekly church newsletter, visiting church members in the hospital, doing premarital counseling, and performing weddings (and funerals). While my enthusiasm for missions served to raise the overall temperature of the congregation, the heat in me was largely dissipated.

There are, of course, ways to recover the Church's missionary zeal, and leaders have enacted a variety of strategies to achieve that end. Our authors, Wan and Santiago, have highlighted the works of numerous scholars who have devoted their energies to explicating the Church's motivations for mission throughout the centuries. There are, as they note, recurring instances of several noble motives, such as desiring to honor and glorify God, seeking to obey Jesus' Great Commission, pursuing the best for humankind, etc. But these lofty motives have at times coalesced with less-than-noble motives, such as the pursuit of political dominance, racial or cultural hegemony, economic advantage, etc. In this book, Wan and Santiago have also put their finger on a crucial area of inquiry that has remained underexplored: *the analysis of missionary motivations that are rooted in a covenant relationship with the living God.*

For Wan and Santiago, this underemphasized theme turns out to be a key theological datum without which the Church's missionary enterprise is more susceptible to the recurring turns to less-than-noble motives and/or the mingling of pure and impure motives. When individuals and churches are deeply rooted in a covenant relationship with the living God, such persons and faith communities are rightly oriented toward God's mission in the world. There is, in other words, an undeniable correlation between robust spirituality and upright motivations for mission. Moreover, those who are rightly related to God experience in unmediated fashion "the love of Christ" (vis-à-vis 2 Corinthians 5:14, 15 and Ephesians 3:14-21), which produces a life-embracing zeal for God and God's purposes for the Church and world. Finally, viewing God's mission through a relational-covenantal lens helps both the motivators of missions and the missionally motivated to attend to God's mission with a set of priorities that protect them from the corrupting influences of those less-than-noble motives.

To return to our metaphor of entropy, we learn from the second law of thermodynamics that heat does not transfer energy from colder to hotter objects in a local system. The hotter object will warm the colder object, but it will lose heat as it does so. Similarly, the Church, on its own accord, will lose missionary zeal as it infuses its environment with the warmth of God's transforming grace. But the second law of thermodynamics includes an essential caveat that is analogous to Wan and Santiago's appeal to covenant relationship as the principal locus of missionary motivation: *energy coming from another source can decrease the entropy of local systems* (e.g., the sun can provide energy that decreases the entropy of a local system on Earth). Accordingly, when the Church is appropriately connected to its ultimate Power Source via covenant relationship, it receives the necessary energy to sustain its missional engagement with its surrounding environments with sustained and even increasing energy – precisely because it is drawing on God's never-ending provision.

Now to him who is able to do immeasurably more than all we ask or imagine, according to his power that is at work within us, to him be glory in the church and in Christ Jesus throughout all generations, for ever and ever! Amen.
(Ephesians 3:20, 21)

Charles J. Conniry, Jr.
Epiphany, 2022

TABLE OF CONTENTS

LIST OF FIGURES ix
LIST OF TABLES xi
ACKNOWLEGEMENTS xiii
LIST OF ABBREVIATIONS xv
CHAPTER 1 INTRODUCTION 1
    Purpose of the Book 1
    Background of the Book 1
    The Researchers 1
    Areas of Concern 2
    Key Questions 5
    Definition of Key Terms 5
    Potential Significance of the Book 8
    Organization of the Book 8
CHAPTER 2 EXPLORE MOTIVATIONS FOR MISSION
    THEOLOGICALLY 11
    Introduction 11
    Analysis Based on Biblical Theology 13
    Analysis Based on Systematic Theology 34
    Analysis Based on Historical Theology 95
    Summary 116
CHAPTER 3 EXAMINE MOTIVATIONS FOR MISSION WITH
    MOTIVATIONAL THEORIES 117
    Introduction 117
    Survey of Motivational Theories 119
    Evaluate the Motivational Theories 123
    Integrate Motivational Theory into the Relational-
        Covenantal Lens 131
    Examine Motivations for Mission with an Augmented
        Relational-Covenantal Lens 138
    Summary 138

CHAPTER 4 MISSIOLOGICAL IMPLICATIONS FROM RELATIONAL-COVENANTAL MOTIVATIONS FOR MISSION 139
    Introduction 139
    Personal Implications 139
    Pastoral and Ecclesiastical Implications 144
    Intercultural Implications 147
    Summary 162
CHAPTER 5 CONCLUSION 163
APPENDIX DETAILED OUTLINE OF BOOK CONTENTS 165
BIBLIOGRAPHY 171

LIST OF FIGURES

Figure 1. Surrounding 2 Corinthians 5:14, 15 literary analysis..........................17
Figure 2. Covenantal assurance and motivations for mission connection 71
Figure 3. Parts of the Relational-Covenantal Lens 72
Figure 4. Relational-Covenantal Lens 73
Figure 5. Creator and creatures in relation to each other................................148
Figure 6. Relationships within intercultural ministries....................................150
Figure 7. Three-culture model of communication..151
Figure 8. Framework for understanding intercultural communication 152
Figure 9. Collectivistic-dependency cultures and Individualistic-independency cultures 154

LIST OF TABLES

Table 1. Covenantal Triperspectivalism and motivational stimuli 75

Table 2. Covenantal Relational Paradigm and motivational dimensions 76

Table 3. Basic Relational-Covenantal Culture motivational responses for mission 77

Table 4. Hiebert's Critical Contextualization Model 124

Table 5. Relational-Critical Contextualization Model 126

Table 6. Integrating motivational theory into the Relational-Covenantal Lens 137

Table 7. Suggestions in addressing areas of deficiencies in relational-covenantal worldview 147

Table 8. Suggestions for interculturally communicating RCC motivations for mission 159

Table 9. Comparing Hiebert's Critical Contextualization Model with Relational-Covenantal Motivations 161

ACKNOWLEGEMENTS

We want to first express our gratitude to our Triune God for his grace in allowing us to publish this book together. We are thankful to our families for their on-going prayers and support of our ministries. We are grateful to all who helped edit the manuscript. We also express thanks to various colleagues and classmates at Western Seminary for their help and encouragement through this project.

LIST OF ABBREVIATIONS

ANE	Ancient Near East
GC	Great Commission
NC	New Covenant
NT	New Testament
OC	Old Covenant
OT	Old Testament
RCC	Relational-Covenantal Culture
RCL	Relational-Covenantal Lens
RCM	Relational-Covenantal Motivations
WCF	Westminster Confession of Faith
WSC	Westminster Shorter Catechism

CHAPTER 1

INTRODUCTION

In Matthew 28:18-20, Jesus as the King of the Kingdom of God commanded his people to "make disciples of all the nations."[1] In Acts 1:8, Jesus also said his people would be his witnesses to the world. Over the centuries since Jesus spoke these words, the Church has been inconsistently motivated to be on mission with her Lord and King.[2] The topic of *motivations for mission* has been addressed throughout the centuries. The prescribed motivations for engaging in mission have been as varied as the people who have written about this topic. We seek in this book to contribute to the research about the motivations for mission from a *relational-covenantal perspective*.

Purpose of the Book

The purpose of this book is to explore motivations for mission from a covenantal perspective within a relational framework in three steps: exploring the topic theologically, examining it theoretically, and deriving missiological implications.

Background of the Book

This book is our attempt at condensing and simplifying material I, Chris, wrote for my doctoral dissertation in the Doctor of Intercultural Studies program at Western Seminary in Portland, Oregon. Enoch Wan contributed greatly in advising, supervising, and directing my doctoral research and writing. I have been interested in this subject for almost twenty years. I wrote my master's thesis on a similar issue. In my doctoral dissertation, I deepened and expanded my previous research on this topic.

The Researchers

Enoch Wan is Research Professor of Intercultural Studies, Director of the Doctor of Intercultural Studies program, and Director of the Doctor of Education in Intercultural Education program at Western Seminary in Portland, Oregon. He was also the Founding Director of the PhD Intercultural Studies Program at Reformed Theological Seminary in Jacksonville,

---

[1] All Scripture quotations in this book are from the English Standard Version.
[2] In chapter 2, in the section entitled the *Great Commission*, we point out that besides the important command of Jesus in Matthew 28:19 to "make disciples of all the nations," the Church's understanding of its mission must also include other important passages in the Bible.

Mississippi. He is a past president of the Evangelical Missiological Society. He has written extensively on many missiological topics.

I, Chris, have been actively engaged in cross-cultural service for almost twenty years. I have been involved with evangelism and church planting, as well as teaching and mentoring local church leaders. I earned a master's degree from Reformed Theological Seminary in Charlotte, North Carolina. I completed a doctorate degree from Western Seminary in Portland, Oregon. My home church is Gateway Church in Livermore, California.

Areas of Concern

For over two thousand years, the Church has faced the challenge of maintaining a steady missionary zeal that is based on scriptural motivations. At times, the Church has been consumed with holy passion to proclaim the gospel and establish local churches. At other times, it has been sluggish to engage in its God-given mission. The Church moreover has often had a mixture of pure and impure motives for its mission work.

Various books that generally survey the Church's mission history, as well as studies that specifically study mission motivations, often reveal the Church's difficulty in sustaining mission enthusiasm that is founded on pure motives. In the course of time, the Church has seen the waxing and waning of missionary fervor throughout Church history. Stephen Neill[3] points out that the Spirit-filled first-century Church was a "genuinely missionary Church."[4] The Book of Acts and other writings testify to its missionary zeal. John Terry and Robert Gallagher[5] believe that the Early Church Christians[6] also maintained a tremendous "Christian zeal" with great sacrifice for the faith, and this contributed greatly to the remarkable spread of Christianity in those years.[7] There were, however, times when the Church seemed to cool in its ardor to see the propagation of the gospel into new areas. For instance, as

---

[3] Stephen Neill was a missionary for twenty years in India and became Bishop of Tinnevelly. Later, he held various teaching positions including Professor of Missions and Ecumenical Theology at the University of Hamburg. From 1979 until his death in 1984, Neill was the Assistant Bishop in the Diocese of Oxford. See Stephen Neill, *A History of Christian Missions*, Second ed. (New York: Penguin Putnam Inc., 1986; reprint, 1990), 1.

[4] Neill, 21.

[5] John Terry is department chair and professor of missions at Mid-America Baptist Theological Seminary, and Robert Gallagher is department chair and associate professor of intercultural studies at Wheaton College. See John Mark Terry and Robert L. Gallagher, *Encountering the History of Missions (Encountering Mission): From the Early Church to Today*, Google Books ed. (Baker Academic, 2017), Back cover.

[6] By this title, Terry and Gallagher mean the Church between the years 100 and 500 A.D.

[7] Terry and Gallagher, 14.

David Bosch[8] notes, "very little happened by way of a missionary outreach during the first two centuries after the Reformation."[9] Those in the Reformation appeared to have but "little time for thought of missions."[10] And there has also been in Church history the mixture of pure and impure motives for mission. J. H. Bavinck[11] said, "The history of missions discloses a motley mixture of motives which have inspired missionary work."[12] Often there were several motives inciting the missionaries. There were the lofty motives of God's glory, obedience to Jesus' command, and the good of man, yet sometimes mixed in were the less noble motivations of the spread of cultural dominance, colonialism, and exerting political influence.[13] Verkuyl[14] has also found in his research the Church sometimes had a combination of "pure motives" as well as "impure motives" that compelled it in its mission activities.[15]

Many of the researchers that have studied the Church's motivations for mission have done so from a historical perspective. Their approach is very necessary and helpful. For instance, in Green's[16] important study, he

---

[8] David Bosch was a very influential Protestant missiologist in South Africa and Professor of Missiology at the University of South Africa. See David J. Bosch, *Transforming Mission: Paradigm Shifts in Theology of Mission*, 20th Anniversary, Kindle ed. (ORBIS, 2011), Kindle locations 185-195.

[9] Bosch, 234. We should note that Bosch agrees with modern scholarship that finds a developing mission theology in the Protestant Reformers like Luther and Calvin. As a result, Bosch is more understanding as to why there was little missionary outreach in the Protestant Reformation, and he attributes the causes to "serious practical obstacles" such as leaders' focus on reforming the domestic churches first, and the "battle for sheer survival." See Bosch, 234.

[10] Neill, 185. Like Bosch, Neill seeks to be understanding of the Reformers' difficult situation that distracted them from greater engagement in the work of worldwide mission. However, Neill still criticizes the Reformers for not being more zealous for foreign mission when he writes, "Yet, when everything favourable has been said that can be said, and when all possible evidences from the writings of the Reformers have been collected, it all amounts to exceedingly little." See Neill, 189.

[11] Johan Herman Bavinck was a Dutch Reformed missionary to Indonesia. He later became the first Professor of Missions at both the Theological University of Kampen and the Free University of Amsterdam. See "Bavinck, Johan Herman (1895-1964) | History of Missiology," http://www.bu.edu/missiology/missionary-biography/a-c/bavinck-johan-herman-1895-1964/ (21 September 2018).

[12] J. H. Bavinck, *Inleiding in De Zendingswetenschap (An Introduction to the Science of Missions)*, trans., David H. Freeman (Kampen: J. H. Kok, 1954; reprint, Phillipsburg, NJ: Presbyterian and Reformed Publishing Co., 1962), 278.

[13] Bavinck, 3, 278.

[14] Johannes Verkuyl was a Dutch Reformed missionary to Indonesia. He later became Professor of Missions at the Free University of Amsterdam. See "Verkuyl, Johannes (1908-2001) | History of Missiology," http://www.bu.edu/missiology/missionary-biography/t-u-v/verkuyl-johannes-1908-2001/ (21 September 2018).

[15] Johannes Verkuyl, *Contemporary Missiology: An Introduction*, trans., Dale Cooper (Grand Rapids, MI: Eerdmans, 1978), 164-175.

[16] Michael Green is a British theologian and former Principal of London College of Divinity.

investigated many aspects of the Early Church's evangelism including its mission motivations.[17] In Van Den Berg's[18] classic study on the motives for mission, he studied the evangelical missionary motives between the years 1698 to 1815.[19] There are also Beaver's[20] research of missionary motivations before the American Revolution[21] and Varg's[22] investigation of Protestant motives for mission from 1890-1917.[23] *Though all these historically-oriented studies are necessary and important; yet, there is a deficiency in the missiological literature in studying motivations for mission from a relational-covenantal perspective.*

There are several potential benefits a relational-covenantal study of mission motivations could have for the Church. Such a study would contribute an *underrepresented perspective* to the missiological research on motives for mission. Additionally, Western Christianity's increased interest in the importance of *relationships* due to epistemological shifts,[24] such a study could increase awareness of mission motives and encourage greater zeal for mission. Also, with the trend of the more *relationally-minded* and collectively-oriented "majority world"[25] Church becoming more active in mission work,[26] such a study might again prove helpful in stimulating deeper understanding of mission motives as well as stimulate more fervor for mission.

---

[17] Michael Green, *Evangelism in the Early Church*, Revised edition, Kindle ed. (Grand Rapids, MI: Wm. B. Eerdmans Publishing, 2003), Kindle locations 3068-3384.

[18] Johannes Van Den Berg's book was originally his doctoral dissertation. Van Den Berg later became a church historian.

[19] Johannes Van Den Berg, *Constrained by Jesus' Love: An Inquiry into the Motives of the Missionary Awakening in Great Britain in the Period between 1698 and 1815* (Kampen: J.H. Kok, 1956).

[20] R. Pierce Beaver was Professor of Mission at the University of Chicago Divinity School and a former director of the Overseas Ministries Study Center.

[21] R. Pierce Beaver, "American Missionary Motivation before the Revolution," *Church History* 31, no. 2 (1962).

[22] Paul A. Varg was an American historian and former Dean of the College of Arts and Letters at Michigan State University.

[23] Paul A. Varg, "Motives in Protestant Missions, 1890-1917," *Church History* 23, no. 1 (1954).

[24] Bosch, 339-353; Paul G. Hiebert, *Missological Implications of Epistemological Shifts: Affirming Truth in a Modern/Postmodern World*, ed. Alan Neely, H. Wayne Pipkin, and Wilbert R. Shenk, Christian Mission and Modern Culture (Harrisburg, PA: Trinity Press International, 1999), 68-116; Enoch Wan, "The Paradigm of 'Relational Realism,'" *Occasional Bulletin* 19, no. 2 (Spring 2006): 1-2.

[25] "Majority world" is now the preferred title for what used to be called the "third world" or the "developing world" or "global south." See Enoch Wan, "Introduction," in *Missions from the Majority: Progress, Challenges, and Case Studies*, ed. Enoch Wan and Michael Pocock, Evangelical Missiological Society Series (Pasadena, CA: William Carey Library, 2013), i-ii.

[26] M. David Sills, *Changing World, Unchanging Mission: Responding to Global Challenges*, iBooks ed. (Downers Grove, IL: InterVarsity Press, 2015), 306.

Key Questions

Given the focus of this book, the following are our key questions:
1. How do the biblical covenants motivate God's people to engage in mission?
2. What are some aspects of motivational theories that correspond with covenantal motivations for mission?
3. What are some missiological implications that come from this study?

Definition of Key Terms

In order to foster clear communication of what we do in this book, we offer here some definitions of key terms.

Archival research – A type of research that exclusively uses secondary sources of documents and published works.

Biblical theology – A way of studying the Scriptures in which one pays attention to the progressive historical development of a particular theme throughout redemptive history.

Covenant – A biblical and divine covenant is a special love relationship between God and humans involving his solemn promises, mutual obligations, and an oath-bound commitment.[27]

Covenant people – This refers to the people who enter into one of the scriptural covenants with God. In the Bible, the central covenantal promise he reiterated many times in his various covenants was that he would have a special people who would be in covenant relationship with him.[28]

---

[27] This is our composite definition after considering several works on the biblical covenants. See Peter J. Gentry and Stephen J. Wellum, *Kingdom through Covenant: A Biblical-Theological Understanding of the Covenants*, Kindle ed. (Wheaton, Illinois: Crossway, 2012), Kindle locations 1068 1080, 3124-3151, 3046-3059; Peter Golding, *Covenant Theology: The Key of Theology in Reformed Thought and Tradition* (Tain, Ross-shire: Christian Focus Publications, 2004), 75-79; Fred A. Malone, *The Baptism of Disciples Alone: A Covenantal Argument for Credobaptism Versus Paedobaptism* (Cape Coral, FL: Founders Press, 2003), 60-62; David McKay, *The Bond of Love: God's Covenantal Relationship with His Church* (Tain, Ross-shire: Christian Focus Publications, 2001), 11-14; Greg Nichols, *Covenant Theology: A Reformed and Baptist Perspective on God's Covenants* (Vestavia Hills, AL: Solid Ground Christian Books, 2011), 117; O. Palmer Robertson, *The Christ of the Covenants* (Phillipsburg: Presbyterian and Reformed Publishing, 1980), 4-15; J. R. Williamson, *From the Garden of Eden to the Glory of Heaven* (United States: Calvary Press Publishing, 2008), 19; Paul R. Williamson, *Sealed with an Oath: Covenant in God's Unfolding Purpose* (Downers Grove, IL: IVP Academic, 2007), 43.

[28] A basic form of this central promise is *"I will be your God, and you shall be my people."* See Gen. 17:7; Exod. 29:45-46; Lev. 26:12; Jer. 31:33; Ezek. 36:28; Rev. 21:3.

Covenantal perspective – Broadly speaking, when we use the term "covenantal," we mean something having to do with the divine covenants[29] found in the Scriptures. Narrowly speaking, we mean something having to do with *the special interpersonal dynamics between the Lord and his people* given the unique oath-bound relationship they have with one another. This narrow meaning is our most common usage of the term covenantal.

Covenantal Triperspectivalism – A theological framework based on a recurring three-fold pattern found in God's covenantal lordship. The three-fold pattern includes God's *authority*, *control*, and *presence*. By applying these, one can extend them into three "perspectives" – *normative* (authority), *situational* (control), and *existential* (presence).[30]

Culture – We adopt an abbreviated form of Wan's definition for culture – "patterned interaction of personal Beings/beings."[31]

Historical theology – The study of the Christian Church and the development of its doctrines.

Missio Dei – This refers to the plan and work of God in the Church and world to glorify his name by establishing his kingdom through reconciling all things to himself through Jesus Christ.[32]

---

[29] The major historical divine covenants we find explicitly mentioned in the Bible are the covenant with Adam (Adamic covenant; see Gen. 1-3; Hosea 6:7), the covenant with Noah (Noahic covenant; see Gen. 9:11), the covenant with Abraham (Abrahamic covenant; see Gen. 12:1-3, 15:1-21, 17:1-27), the covenant with Moses (Mosaic covenant and also referred to as the Old Covenant; see Exod. 19-24), the covenant with King David (Davidic covenant; see 2 Sam. 7), and finally the New Covenant (see Jer. 31:34; Luke 22:20).

[30] John M. Frame, *The Doctrine of the Knowledge of God*, 4 vols., A Theology of Lordship, vol. 1 (Phillipsburg: P&R Publishing, 1987), 17, 73-75; John M. Frame, *The Doctrine of the Christian Life*, 4 vols., A Theology of Lordship, vol. 3 (Phillipsburg: P&R Publishing, 2008), 19-37. We should add that in Frame's writings he does not explicitly use the descriptor "covenantal" in front of his model of triperspectivalism. This is our addition in calling it covenantal triperspectivalism. We have done this to take what is implicit in his model and make it explicit. In Frame's writings about this model, he clearly affirms the connection it has with the covenants of the Bible. For instance, at the center of his triperspectival model is the lordship of God over his people. And according to Frame, "lordship is a *covenantal* [italics ours] concept." See Frame, *The Doctrine of the Knowledge of God*, 12.

[31] Enoch Wan, "A Critique of Charles Kraft's Use/Misuse of Communication & Social Sciences in Biblical Interpretation & Missiological Formulation," in *Missiology and the Social Sciences: Contributions, Cautions, and Conclusions*, ed. Edward Rommen and Gary Corwin, Evangelical Missiological Society Series (Pasadena, CA: William Carey Library, 1996), 122.

[32] Henry T. Blackaby and Avery T. Willis, "On Mission with God," in *Perspectives on the World Christian Movement: A Reader*, ed. Ralph D. Winter and Steven C. Hawthorne (Pasadena:

Mission* and *missions – Mission is the Christian individually and the Church institutionally at both levels continuing on and carrying out the *missio Dei* of the Triune God spiritually, socially, for redemption, reconciliation, and transformation.[33] Missions (plural) refers to the Church's many and various activities as it participates in the *missio Dei*, especially as the Church takes Christianity cross-culturally in order to make the nations disciples of Jesus Christ.[34]

Missiological implications – Likely consequences of something upon the Church's mission.

Missiology – A simple definition is that it is the study of Christian mission. A more detailed description is that it is an integrative study of mission using a multi-disciplinary approach which includes such things as theology, Christian history, intercultural studies, behavioral science theory, and mission methods.[35]

Motivations for mission – Internal drives that incite the Christian individually and the Church institutionally to continue on and carry out the *missio Dei* of the Triune God.[36] We use "motivations" and "motives"

William Carey Library, 1999), 55. We modified the insights in Blackaby's and Willis' article to flow better in one sentence.

[33] This is based on a definition for mission found in the chapter by Enoch Wan, "'Mission' and *Missio Dei*: Response to Van Engen's 'Mission Defined and Described,'" in *Missionshift: Global Mission Issues in the Third Millennium*, ed. David Hesselgrave and Ed Stetzer (Nashville, TN: B&H Academic, 2010), 46. I simplify it here.

[34] David Bosch makes a helpful differentiation between the singular (mission) and plural (missions) terms when he wrote, "We have to distinguish between *mission* (singular) and *missions* (plural). The first refers primarily to the *missio Dei* (God's mission), that is, God's self-revelation as the One who loves the world, God's involvement in and with the world, the nature and activity of God, which embraces both the church and the world, and in which the church is privileged to participate. *Missio Dei* enunciates the good news that God is a God-for-people. *Missions* (the *missiones ecclesiae*; the missionary ventures of the church), refer to particular forms, related to specific times, places, or needs, of participation in the *missio Dei*." See Bosch, Kindle locations 594-605.

[35] Gerald H. Anderson, "Introducing Missiology," *Missiology* 1, no. 1 (1973).

[36] Modified from a definition for motivation, "The drive that produces goal-directed behavior." See "Motivation," in *The Gale Encyclopedia of Psychology*, ed. Jacqueline L. Longe, *Gale Virtual Reference Library* (Gale, 2016). http://link.galegroup.com.westernseminary.idm.oclc.org/apps/doc/CX3631000520/GVRL?u=s4556763&sid=GVRL&xid=51e456a4. (accessed 8 May 2019). Additionally, in chapter 2, in the section entitled the *Great Commission*, we point out that in addition to the command "make disciples of all the nations" from Matthew 28:19, the Church must also include other biblical passages to derive her understanding of her mission.

interchangeably. Also, motivations include both motivational stimuli and motivational responses. There can be both extrinsic as well as intrinsic motivational stimuli. These stimuli foster the responses in a believer to engage in mission.[37]

Relational-covenantal culture – We are coining a term, "relational-covenantal culture" (RCC). It is the relational-covenantal dynamics in patterns of behavior, values, beliefs, and fundamental allegiance that we see working between the Persons of the Trinity as well as between the Triune God and his covenant people.

Relational Paradigm – A theological framework based on the inter-Trinitarian relationship between the Father, Son, and Holy Spirit and its outworking in vertical (i.e., God with humans) and horizontal relationships (i.e., humans with humans).[38]

Spirituality - "A state of deep relationship with God."[39]

Systematic theology – A way of studying the Scriptures in a thematic or topical way.

Potential Significance of the Book

We believe the book is significant in two ways. One is theological, and the other is practical. First, theologically, motivations for mission have been studied from many angles, though studying this topic from the relational-covenantal perspective appears to be rare. As a result, this book could perhaps add to the theological literature on motivations for mission from a much-needed perspective. Second, practically, the implications of this book could help the Church to develop new relational ways using the relational-covenantal framework to help motivate God's people to engage in mission.

Organization of the Book

We have organized the book into five chapters. Chapter 1 is our introduction. In chapter 2 we theologically explore the topic using biblical, systematic, and historical theologies. In chapter 3 we examine the topic using

---

[37] See "Motivation," in *The Gale Encyclopedia of Psychology*.
[38] Enoch Wan and Mark Hedinger, *Relational Missionary Training: Theology, Theory, and Practice*, ed. Kendi Howells Douglas and Stephen Burris, Urban Ministry in the 21st Century (Skyforest, CA: Urban Loft Publishers, 2017), 17-60.
[39] J. M. Houston, "Spirituality," in *Evangelical Dictionary of Theology*, ed. Walter A. Elwell (Grand Rapids: Baker Academic, 2001).

motivational theories. We also evaluate these theories from a scriptural perspective. In chapter 4, we derive from our study six implications for motivations for mission. In chapter 5 we offer a conclusion. We also provide the reader with an *Appendix* that shows a detailed outline of all the sections of the book.

CHAPTER 2

EXPLORE MOTIVATIONS FOR MISSION THEOLOGICALLY

Introduction

Our first key question is, "*How do the biblical covenants motivate God's people to engage in mission?*" Here in this chapter we answer that question. We explore this question using separate analyses in *biblical theology*, *systematic theology*, and *historical theology*.

A few qualifying statements are in order before we begin our theological exploration in this chapter. There are two kinds of statements we would like to make. The first are assumptions we want to make explicit. The second are statements that act like delimiters for this study. We offer these statements with minimal elaboration.

There are ten *assumptions* we want to explicitly state. First, the Scriptures of the Old Testament (OT) and New Testament (NT) are God's inerrant and infallible word, and thus they are our supreme authoritative rule for faith and practice. Second, the Persons of the Trinity are in covenant relationship with one another,[40] and their interaction with each other can be considered a "culture."[41] We use the term relational-covenantal culture (RCC).[42] Third, God

---

[40] Wan and Hedinger, 27-32; Louis Berkhof, *Systematic Theology*, New combined ed. (Grand Rapids: Eerdmans, 1996), 265ff; Robertson, 54; Robert L. Reymond, *A New Systematic Theology of the Christian Faith* (Nashville: Thomas Nelson Publishers, 1997), 502; Wayne Grudem, *Systematic Theology: An Introduction to Biblical Doctrine* (Grand Rapids: Zondervan, 1994), 518-519; *London Baptist Confession of Faith*, (1689), 7.3.

[41] This is so because the covenant relationship that the Persons of the Trinity enjoy with each other has interaction patterns, and culture, as Enoch Wan succinctly defines it, is "patterned interaction of personal Beings/beings." See Wan, "A Critique of Charles Kraft's Use/Misuse of Communication & Social Sciences in Biblical Interpretation & Missiological Formulation," 122. It is beyond the scope of this book to delve into a justification of this statement that the Persons of the Trinity have "interaction patterns." Suffice it to say, many theologians have long observed that the Scriptures reveal these patterns of interaction between the Persons of the Trinity. For instance, Ralph Smith believes there is a covenantal mutual love, faithfulness, and righteousness the Persons display in their relationship with one another. See Ralph Smith, *Paradox and Truth: Rethinking Van Til on the Trinity* (Moscow, ID: Canon Press, 2002), 85; quoted in Wan and Hedinger, 27.

[42] Among the three Persons of the Trinity, they enjoy a *perfect Trinitarian relational-covenantal culture* (RCC). In studying the relational dynamics of the covenants God established with his *people* in the Scriptures, we term these patterns of behavior, values, beliefs, and fundamental allegiances also a RCC, but it is a *God-to-human RCC*. Unless we specify otherwise, from here forward when we mention the RCC, we mean the God-to-human RCC. Within the RCC, there are patterns of how God motivates his people and patterns of what kinds of motives he expects from his people.

uses covenants to establish and guide *the special relationship* he and his covenant people enjoy with each other. Therefore, within the framework of these covenants, we can expect to find *relational dynamics and principles*. These *relational-covenantal dynamics and principles* have a bearing on the motivation of his covenant people. Fourth, God's covenant people are from various cultures. The relational-covenantal principles affect them regardless of the culture to which they belong, and this is because they are in a covenant relationship with the Triune God. Fifth, because God has been pleased to let the human writers of Scripture use aspects of their culture to communicate his truth, it is helpful to study these cultural artifacts, like Ancient Near East (ANE) covenant forms and features, to gain insight into biblical covenantal faith and life. Sixth, covenants are about a deep special relationship between God and his people. Therefore, part of our exploration includes understanding a *covenantal spirituality*. Seventh, sin is a reality in humankind's current existence. Sin can mar human awareness of covenantal motivational stimuli as well as proper responses to them. Eighth, there are *general* patterns of covenantal motivations in the OT. These general patterns of covenantal motivations help us in identifying key covenantal "motivations for mission" in the NT.[43] Ninth, John Frame's[44] Covenantal Triperspectivalism and Enoch Wan's Relational Paradigm are scriptural.[45] And finally tenth, there are creative ways to synthesize Covenantal Triperspectivalism, the Relational Paradigm, and other covenantal truths into a *relational-covenantal "lens"* (RCL).

The second group of statements are seven *delimiters* to our theological exploration. First, we study motivations for mission exclusively from the

---

[43] There are relational-covenantal principles that transcendent time and carry over from Old Covenant (OC) to New Covenant (NC). It is beyond the scope of this book to give a full hermeneutical justification for this. We will simply suffice it to say we are following a recognized evangelical hermeneutic when we identify these relational-covenantal truths as "timeless," "transcultural," and "universal" principles that are applicable to God's people in the OC and NC. See Gentry and Wellum, Kindle locations 7625 and 11914, 13746-13779, 14140-14155; William W. Klein, Craig L. Bloomberg, and Robert L. Hubbard, Jr., *Introduction to Biblical Interpretation*, Revised and Expanded ed. (Nashville: Thomas Nelson Publishers, 2004), 485-498; Sidney Greidanus, *The Modern Preacher and the Ancient Text: Interpreting and Preaching Biblical Literature* (Grand Rapids: Eerdmans, 1988), 169-173; R. C. Sproul, Jr., *Knowing Scripture*, Second ed. (Downers Grove: InterVarsity Christian Fellowship, 1977; reprint, Downers Grove: InterVarsity Press, 2009), 120-127.

[44] John M. Frame, author of the *A Theology of Lordship* series of theological books, taught at Westminster Theological Seminary in California, as well as teaching systematic theology and philosophy at Reformed Theological Seminary in Orlando, Florida, until retirement.

[45] Covenantal Triperspectivalism and the Relational Paradigm are *theological* concepts or frameworks. Frame elaborates on Covenantal Triperspectivalism in several of his volumes in the *A Theology of Lordship* series. See for instance Frame, *The Doctrine of the Knowledge of God*, 73-75. Likewise, when Wan and Hedinger write about the Relational Paradigm, it is under the "Part One: *Theology* [italics ours]" section of their book. See Wan and Hedinger, 3.

relational-covenantal perspective. However, we do recognize that there are other legitimate ways to research these motivations. Second, in the *Analysis Based on Biblical Theology* and *Analysis Based on Systematic Theology* sections, we concentrate on selected texts from the Apostle Paul's writings. Third, though we may research relevant features of ANE covenants that have a bearing on the historic biblical covenants, yet we primarily concentrate on the features of the historic covenants that are recorded in the Scriptures. Fourth, we do not restate or critique the historic and classic Reformed formulations of Covenant Theology[46] as articulated in places like the Westminster Confession of Faith (WCF) or the 1689 London Confession of Faith. Our focus is on *researching covenant-related interpersonal dynamics* so as to better understand motivations for mission. Fifth, although there are various precious and interesting elements of the biblical covenantal relationship, yet we merely touch on these elements and seek instead to center on those elements relevant to understand covenantal motivations. Sixth, we concentrate on exploring the "ideal" relational-covenantal motivations (RCM) categories. We do not explore sin-tainted motivations for mission. And finally seventh, the book primarily focuses on the special relationship between God and his covenant people. Though the Scriptures inform us that there are three spheres of personal beings (i.e., Triune God, spirits [angels, Satan, demons], and humans),[47] and important relational dynamics between them, yet this book concentrates solely on the relational-covenantal dynamics between God and his people.

Analysis Based on Biblical Theology

In this section we analyze several biblical passages that seem to demonstrate a positive correlation[48] between spirituality and missionary zeal. We believe Gordon Smith has correctly observed, "The dynamic relationship between spirituality and mission is obvious in the Book of Acts. . . . It is also

---

[46] "Covenant Theology" is a system of theology that arose from Reformed theologians who identified the covenants in the Scripture as a major means by which God is unfolding his redemptive plan through history. It seeks to describe the overarching structures (i.e., the divine covenants) and inter-relatedness of those structures so as to better understand God's redemptive work. It also focuses on the federal headship of Christ over his people. J. I. Packer called Covenant Theology an important "hermeneutic" for interpreting the Bible. See Golding, 10-11. As Reformed believers, we agree with much of Covenant Theology, but it is beyond the scope of this book to integrate classic Covenant Theology in our investigation of motivations for mission.

[47] Wan, "A Critique of Charles Kraft's Use/Misuse of Communication & Social Sciences in Biblical Interpretation & Missiological Formulation," 122-123, 132-133.

[48] By "positive correlation" we mean when spirituality *increases* then there is also a corresponding *increase* in mission zeal. Contrariwise, when spirituality *decreases* there is also a *decrease* in zeal to engage in mission.

evident in the life of Jesus . . . And in the apostle Paul we see a dynamic connection . . ."[49]

Covenants are about a special relationship between God and his people. Spirituality as defined by Houston is "a state of deep relationship with God."[50] Therefore, part of our exploration includes understanding a covenantal spirituality. This assumption, we trust, gives clarity as to why in a book focusing on motivations for mission from a covenantal perspective we feel the need to study the connection between spirituality and mission motivations.

Selection Criteria for Texts

There are several criteria we have used to select passages we will consider. First, we wanted to *limit the scope to Paul's life*. After all, Paul is the prototype missionary given to us in the Book of Acts. His epistles are excellent first-hand sources to understand what this prototypical missionary's theology, behavior, and methods were. Helpful missiological works such as Ramsay's[51] and Reymond's[52] focus on Paul's missionary history, theology, and travels. Other works like Allen's[53] and Hesselgrave's[54] seek to dissect Paul's missionary methodology and apply it to contemporary mission endeavors. The scope of this book would simply have been too large had we sought to do a more thorough biblical theology analysis on spirituality,[55] missionary zeal,[56] and their apparent positive correlation. It would have been fascinating to expound passages in the OT that seem to indicate this principle of correlation

---

[49] Gordon T. Smith, "Spirituality," in *Evangelical Dictionary of World Missions*, ed. A. Scott Moreau, Harold Netland, and Charles Van Engen (Grand Rapids: Baker Reference Library, 2000), 904.

[50] Houston.

[51] William M. Ramsay, *St. Paul the Traveller and Roman Citizen* (London: Hodder & Stroughton, 1907). Sir William Michell Ramsay was an archaeologist as well as a classical and New Testament scholar.

[52] Robert L. Reymond, *Paul: Missionary Theologian* (Tain, Ross-shire: Christian Focus Publications, 2000). Robert Lewis Reymond was a Christian theologian who taught at Covenant Theological Seminary and Know Theological Seminary.

[53] Roland Allen, *Missionary Methods: St. Paul's or Ours?* (Grand Rapids, MI: Wm B. Eerdmands Publishing Co., 1962; reprint, 2002). Roland Allen was a missionary and missionary strategist.

[54] David J. Hesselgrave, *Planting Churches Cross-Culturally: North America and Beyond*, Second ed. (Grand Rapids: Baker Books, 2002). David J. Hesselgrave was professor of mission at Trinity Evangelical Divinity School in Deerfield, Illinois. He served as a cross-cultural missionary in Japan and as executive director of the Evangelical Missiological Society.

[55] Adam has done a wonderfully helpful biblical theology on spirituality that takes into account numerous OT and NT passages. Peter Adam, *Hearing God's Words: Exploring Biblical Spirituality*, ed. D.A. Carson, New Studies in Biblical Theology (Downers Grove: InterVarsity Press, 2004).

[56] Kostenberger and O'Brien have surveyed OT and NT to put together a penetrating biblical theology on mission. See Kostenberger, Andreas J., and Peter T. O'Brien. *Salvation to the Ends of the Earth: A Biblical Theology of Mission*. Vol. 11, New Studies in Biblical Theology, 2001.

between deep assurance and fervor to obey God,[57] yet again it would have been beyond the scope of this work. Secondly, we selected text within the Pauline corpus in which Paul *more clearly states, or the context clearly indicates, some aspect of his spirituality and/or missionary zeal.* Though we have tried to be objective in our selection, yet there was a measure of subjectivity in striving to use our criteria.[58]

2 Corinthians 5:14, 15

> For the love of Christ controls us, because we have concluded this: that one has died for all, therefore all have died; and he died for all, that those who live might no longer live for themselves but for him who for their sake died and was raised.

Original context, structure, and meaning

To better understand 2 Corinthians 5:14, 15, we first need to take a look at the greater historical *context* of Paul's interaction with the Corinthians as well as the immediate context to reconstruct the historical situation. Second, we need also to look briefly at the literary *structure* of this passage. Then thirdly, keeping the context and structure in mind, we will seek to understand Paul's *meaning* in this passage.

First, let us consider the *broader historical context.* Paul faced "opposition both external and internal"[59] in Corinth. Luke's record of Paul's first contact with the Corinthians in Acts 18:1-18 clearly documents the *external* opposition Paul experienced with the obstinate Jews. After he leaves Corinth he goes to Ephesus, then on to Antioch, and then back to Ephesus (Acts 18:19-19:1). Paul toils on in Ephesus for more than two years (Acts 19:10). While in Ephesus, he had more dealings with the Corinthian church both by letter and in person. This forms the important historical backdrop for Second Corinthians.[60]

As Paul labored on in Ephesus, he became aware of *internal* opposition in the church against him. There were at least two delegations from Corinth that visited Paul in Ephesus. There was the delegation made up of Stephanus,

---

[57] For instance, in Ps. 51:10-13 the psalmist states that the sense of God's presence motivates him to declare God's salvation to others. Also, Dan. 11:32 appears to correlate knowing God (that is, a deep personal relationship) and zeal to obey him.

[58] There are other helpful passages such as Rom. 12:1-2 and Titus 2:11-14, 3:4-8, that indicate elements of Paul's spirituality and mission zeal. However, we did not feel they were as "clear" in bringing out the elements we wanted to study, nor did we feel we had space and time to include them in this book. Hence, they will not be part of our analysis.

[59] J. Knox Chamblin, "Pauline Epistles," (Charlotte, NC: Reformed Theological Seminary-Virtual Campus, 2003), 75.

[60] Colin G. Kruse, *2 Corinthians: An Introduction and Commentary*, ed. Leon Morris, Tyndale New Testament Commentary, vol. 8 (Downers Grove: InterVarsity Press, 1987), 22.

Fortunatas, and Achaicus (1 Cor. 16:15-18). They apparently were delivering an official letter from the Corinthian believers asking for Paul's advice on topics such as marriage and divorce, food offered to idols, conduct of worship, spiritual gifts, the resurrection, and the collection (1 Cor. 7:1a).[61] Paul addresses these concerns in 1 Corinthians 7-16. However, the other delegation of "Chloe's people" (1 Cor. 1:11), perhaps an "unofficial delegation,"[62] informs Paul of a growing factionalism in the Corinthian church even against him (1 Cor. 1:12). Subsequently, Paul separately dispatched Timothy (1 Cor. 4:17, 16:10-11) and Titus (2 Cor. 2:13-14, 7:14-16, 8:16-9:5) on several trips to Corinth to ascertain the situation in the church.[63] Paul also again made a personal trip to Corinth (2 Cor. 1:15-16) to remedy the situation, but it was a painful trip and he changed his original plans so as to spare them of another painful encounter (2 Cor. 1:23-2:1).

The identity of the people and issues of the *internal* opposition against Paul is complex.[64] From various statements in First and Second Corinthians, one of the main contentions of Paul's opponents was to contrast Paul's apparent weakness (in appearance, doctrine, speech, experience in ministry, etc.) with their inflated displays of strength.[65] Their desire was to discredit Paul's apostolic authority so as to gain a following for themselves among the Corinthian Christians.[66]

It seems apparent by the plain reading of the text of Second Corinthians that there is a clear shift in Paul's tone between chapters 1-9 and chapters 10-13. In the first nine chapters, Paul is more affirming and enthusiastic. However, in the last four chapters, Paul appears more combative and forceful. It appears Paul wrote the letter in "stages."[67] It is likely he wrote the first nine chapters after receiving a wonderful encouraging report from Titus at how opposition was dying down and the Corinthians were responding favorably to Paul (2 Cor. 2:12-13, 7:6-15).[68] Later, at another stage in his writing the epistle, he receives another report of the situation in Corinth deteriorating again because of a resurgence of the internal opposition. It is at this point he

---

[61] Kruse, 22; Chamblin, 74.

[62] Chamblin, 74.

[63] Kruse, 23; Chamblin, 75.

[64] Paul W. Barnett, "Opponents of Paul," in *Dictionary of Paul and His Letters*, ed. Gerald F. Hawthorne, Ralph P. Martin, and Daniel G. Reid (Downers Grove: InterVarsity Press, 1993), 644.

[65] The following passages are examples of this opposition: 1 Cor. 1:18-2:16; 2 Cor. 2:14-17, 3:1-3, 4:1, 16, 10:12-14, 11:5-6, 23.

[66] Simon J. Kistemaker and William Hendriksen, *Exposition of the Second Epistle to the Corinthians*, New Testament Commentary, vol. 19 (Grand Rapids: Baker Book House, 1953-2001), 4.

[67] Kistemaker and Hendriksen, 4-5.

[68] Kruse, 24-25; Chamblin, 76; Ralph P. Martin, *Word Biblical Commentary: 2 Corinthians*, ed. David A. Hubbard et al., Second ed., Word Biblical Commentary, vol. 40 (Dallas: Word, Incorporated, 1998), xxxv.

writes the latter four chapters of the letter that have a more combative and defensive tone.[69]

Secondly, we want to consider briefly the surrounding literary *structure* of this passage. We agree with Kistemaker that Second Corinthians can be divided into five major parts: introduction (1:1-11), the apostle's ministry (1:12-7:16), the collection (8:1-9:15), a defense of Paul's apostolic authority (10:1-13:10), and a conclusion (13:11-14).[70] Chamblin's outline of the letter closely coincides with this structure as well.[71] Both identify the main body of the letter from 1:12-13:10. Additionally, Chamblin's literary analysis of the structure immediately surrounding 2 Corinthians 5:14, 15 is insightful. We reproduce it in Figure 1 with only slight modifications:[72]

FIRST MAIN SECTION (1:12-7:16): THE APOSTLE AND THE CHURCH

Sub-Sec. 1 (1:12-2:13): PAUL AND THE CORINTHIANS

Sub-Sec. 2 (2:14-6:13): PAUL, GOD, AND THE CORINTHIANS

A. (2:14-17) Apostolic Ministry: Introduction
B. (3:1-4:5) The Apostolic Calling: Ministers of the New Covenant
C. (4:6-18) The Apostolic Life-in-Death
D. (5:1-10) The Apostolic Hope: Life Beyond Death
E. (5:11-6:2) The Apostolic Appeal: Ministry of Reconciliation
F. (6:3-13) The Apostolic Suffering

Sub-Sec. 3 (6:14-7:1): THE CORINTHIANS AND GOD

Sub-Sec. 4 (7:2-4): TRANSITION BACK TO THE THEME OF 1:12-2:13 (hint of transition also in 6:11-13)

Sub-Sec. 5 (7:5-16): PAUL AND THE CORINTHIANS

Figure 1. Surrounding 2 Corinthians 5:14, 15 literary analysis

The passage is couched in a structure from 1:12-7:16 where Paul described core characteristics of his apostolic ministry (2:14-6:13) especially among the Corinthians. Given the context that we briefly surveyed above, Paul

---

[69] Kruse, 25-26; Chamblin, 76; Martin, xxxv.
[70] Kistemaker and Hendriksen, 5.
[71] Chamblin, 122.
[72] Chamblin, 122.

did this apparently to further solidify the Corinthians' renewed "affection and loyalty"[73] to him as an apostle (e.g., 6:11-13). He did this to further counter the negative impressions left in the minds of the Corinthians as a result of his opponents' slander against him (e.g., 5:12, 6:8-10).

Thirdly, having considered the broader context and structure of the passage, we want to look at the *narrower literary context and meaning* of the passage itself. Paul here is still continuing the defense of his apostolic ministry. In particular, he is seeking to address the apparent slander of his opponents against the *motives*[74] *of his missionary ministry*. Kruse believes Paul is more focused on justifying his "style" of ministry.[75] We think that choice of words is unfortunate because it only muddles the interpretation of the passage. At the end of his exposition of 5:11-15, Kruse himself summarized the passage as Paul elaborating and justifying the "motivation for [his] ministry."[76]

In v. 11, Paul's "therefore" ties it to the previous topic in vv. 9, 10 about the "judgment seat of Christ." Paul is saying that one of the motives he[77] has in his ministry is the sober realization that he is accountable to Jesus Christ, the Judge. As a result, he seeks to "persuade others." There appears to be a "double flavor"[78] meant in this. One flavor, Paul could mean that knowing Christ is his Judge in ministry, he is motivated to have integrity in fulfilling his evangelistic ministry of calling people to salvation. This would go well with the following evangelistic appeal of the "ministry of reconciliation" in v. 20. However, the other flavor, the general context and the immediately following verse (v. 12), tell us that Paul is still defending his apostolic ministry from the unjust criticism of opponents. Thus, we could understand Paul to be saying he wants to persuade his Corinthian opponents that contrary to what they say, he really is motivated by the holy fear of God in his ministry. Then, like an echo from 2 Corinthians 4:2, Paul goes on to say in v. 11 that his pure motives for ministry are "known to God" and that he hopes the Corinthians' "conscience" would also be persuaded of this.

In v. 12 Paul, reflecting what he expressed in 2 Corinthians 3:1, is ever aware that his self-defense here of his ministry motives could give more fuel

---

[73] Kruse, 24.
[74] Martin, 116ff; Kistemaker and Hendriksen, 182ff; Kruse, 117ff.
[75] Kruse, 117.
[76] Kruse, 122.
[77] We are aware that Paul in 2 Cor. 5:11 and through the rest of the passage often uses the plural pronouns "we" and "us." The exact antecedent of these pronouns is not clear. We tend to think that Paul may have had his apostolic co-workers like Timothy (2 Cor. 5:11) and Titus (2 Cor. 8:23) in mind. But in any case, Paul includes himself as is evident when in v. 11 he switches to the singular pronoun "I." Given this, we will concentrate our exegesis on how Paul applies the truths he brings up to his personal apostolic ministry. See also Martin, 122-123.
[78] Martin, 121.

to his opponents in Corinth to accuse him of pride and selfishness. However, he clarifies that the reason he is justifying the integrity of his motives in ministry is so that those who are for him in the Corinthian church "may be able to deal with the criticisms of those men."[79] Paul's opponents loved to emphasize the importance of the externals of their ministries – letters of commendations that they kept with them to show others (3:1), eloquence (10:10, 11:16), Jewish pedigree (11:22), visions and revelations (12:1).[80] Yet Paul wanted his opponents and his supporters in Corinth to know he was not proud and selfish like them. Rather, he was one who emphasized what God emphasized, the humble and selfless motives of a pure heart.

In v. 13, Paul's words seem to be a complete enigma. He appears to say something that has no apparent connection to any of his preceding statements. However, when we recall that Paul in v. 12 had contrasted his opponents' blameworthy preoccupation with the "outward appearance" of things compared to his praiseworthy focus on "heart" matters, we may have a clue to his meaning. In v. 13, his usage of the verb we translate "beside ourselves" may point back to the ecstatic experiences he had experienced since becoming a Christian (e.g., trance in the temple [Acts 22:17-18], tongues speaking [1 Cor. 14:18], heavenly vision [2 Cor. 12:7]).[81] If so, then what Paul may be saying is consistent with the last part of v. 12. Namely, Paul is contrasting how different his proud opponents handle their claims to ecstatic experience compared with how he handles them. The way Paul handles these powerful things "is for God," that is, they are between him and God and not to be paraded around before the Corinthians. When he ministers to the people at Corinth, he does so with the motive of humility and with the method that "is for you," that is, in a way where he can communicate to their minds. Thus again, Paul is defending his motives and methods in ministry against his opponents' criticism.

In v. 14, we have Paul continuing his self-defense of his motives in ministry against the wicked accusations his opponents in Corinth have hurled at him. Previously in v. 11, he said that the "fear of the Lord" motivated him to faithfully persuade others of the gospel and of his integrity in the apostolic ministry. In v. 12, Paul said that his ministry was motivated by unselfish humility of the heart. Now, here, Paul emphatically announces to his readers in Corinth another powerful "selfless" motive that drives his apostolic ministry, the "love of Christ."[82]

---

[79] Kruse, 119.
[80] Kistemaker and Hendriksen, 185.
[81] Kistemaker and Hendriksen, 186; Martin, 127.
[82] Martin, 131-132.

Paul's use of "love of God" or "love of Christ" in his epistles is often ambiguous.[83] So it is here in v. 14. Is he writing intending an objective genitive, that is, our love to God or Christ? Or is he writing using a subjective genitive, that is, God's or Christ's love for us? The deciding factor must be the context. When we consider v. 14b-15 where Paul highlights Christ's death on the cross, it becomes clear that it is *the love of Christ for Paul* that was demonstrated on the cross that Paul has in his mind.[84] Paul similarly wrote in Romans 5:8, "But God showed his love for us in that while we were still sinners, Christ died for us."

Yet what effect did the love of Christ have on Paul? Paul says it "controls" or "compels" him. The present tense of the verb "emphasizes the continuous nature of the pressure upon Paul."[85] This "overpowering sense of Christ's love is one of the chief driving forces in Paul's own life."[86] Martin says that for Paul this love of Christ was the "dominating force in his life."[87]

How did this love of Christ exert such a compelling force upon Paul's life? Paul says this was so "because we have *concluded* [italics ours]" something about the love of Christ. That is, Paul thought and meditated upon the cross of Christ's love.[88] And this led in his heart to a rational conviction. Kruse rightly points out, "It was not the bare fact of Christ's death on the cross that moved Paul, it was the death of Christ understood in a particular way."[89]

What was this rational conclusion or conviction that Paul came to while thinking about the love of Christ for him on the cross? In the rest of vv. 14b, 15, he spelled it out. He concluded that, "One [Christ] died for all. . . ." There has been much debate on whether to interpret this "for" with a "substitutionary" or "representative" meaning.[90] Though we fully believe that Paul teaches elsewhere in his epistles the substitutionary nature of Christ's cross (e.g., Rom. 3:23-26; 1 Cor. 15:3; 2 Cor. 5:21; 1 Tim. 2:6), yet in v. 14b the context causes us to think that Paul is referring in this case to the representative aspect of Christ's cross.[91] As Paul expounded the representative nature of the cross in Romans 6:1-11, here in v. 14b he seems

---

[83] R. Mohrlang, "Love," in *Dictionary of Paul and His Letters*, ed. Gerald F. Hawthorne, Ralph P. Martin, and Daniel G. Reid (Downers Grove: InterVarsity Press, 1993), 575.

[84] Hulitt Gloer, "2 Corinthians 5:14-21," *Review & Expositor* 86, no. 3 (1989): 397; Martin, 128; Kruse, 120-121; Kistemaker and Hendriksen, 187.

[85] Kruse, 120.

[86] Mohrlang, 576.

[87] Martin, 129.

[88] Martin, 129.

[89] Kruse, 121.

[90] Martin, 129-131; Gloer, 397-398.

[91] If a substitute dies for others, then the others do not die. But Paul immediately says, "therefore all have died." This indicates to us he does not have the idea of substitute in his mind in v. 14. Rather, like in Rom. 6:1-11, Paul seems to be emphasizing the representative aspect of Christ's death on the cross.

to be emphasizing the same.[92] Paul is saying that those who have been united to Christ by faith benefit from Christ's unselfish representative work on the cross. Namely, Christ's death is also their death to the penalty as well as the power of selfish sin. When Paul contemplated the unselfish love of Christ on the cross, which by union to Christ set him free from sin's curse and selfish power, this deeply motivated him.

Even so, what did Christ's love for Paul on the cross compel or motivate him to do? In v. 15, he said that it motivated him not to live for himself but to live for Christ who died for him. In v.15b, Paul said his love "answers" Christ's love with love in kind. Chamblin writes, "References to loving God and Christ are not lacking in Paul. Yet his emphasis lies on God's love for his children and their answering love for other people, both within and beyond the church."[93]

For Paul, the *indicatives* of Christ's cross-based love drove the *imperative* of a cross-like life.[94] At the cross, Christ loved Paul by dying for him. Christ's dying love was Paul's death to slavery to self, sin, and Satan. Therefore, this called forth in Paul a life that was dead to sin and self, yet thoroughly alive to Christ.

We should also notice that Paul in v. 15 seems to move beyond a description of the motivational power of Christ's love in *his* own life. He also expects this same appreciated love of Christ to motivate his *readers*. Kruse and Gloer observe:

What kept Paul on the right path, and will keep us there too, is an awareness of the exceptional character of Christ's love for us. We love him and desire to live for him as we realize that he loved us and gave himself for us.[95]

This death and resurrection with Christ is potentially available to all; however, not all have appropriated it by faith. These who have are "the living ones" of verse 15. Theirs is a life controlled by "the love of Christ."[96]

In summary, it is important to remember the continuity of what Paul is doing in this passage. In defense of his apostolic ministry against his critics in Corinth, Paul starting in v. 11 has been emphasizing the unselfish motives and methods of his ministry. He has given his readers the "two poles"[97] of

---

[92] It is interesting that Martin, who favors the substitutionary interpretation for the "for all," surprisingly yet correctly, we believe, sees the "therefore all have died" as clearly having a representative meaning. See Martin, 131. It seems more consistent and more persuasive to us to understand Paul to have the representative aspect of the cross of Christ in mind throughout the whole of v. 14.
[93] J. Knox Chamblin, *Paul and the Self: Apostolic Teaching for Personal Wholeness* (Grand Rapids: Baker Books, 1993; reprint, Eugene, OR: Wipf and Stock Publishers, 2002), 135 n.12.
[94] Herman Ridderbos, *Paulus: Ontwerp Van Zijn Theologie (Paul: An Outline of His Theology)*, Paperback ed. (Kampen: J. H. Kok N. V., 1966; reprint, Grand Rapids: Eerdmans, 1997), 253-258.
[95] Kruse, 122.
[96] Gloer, 398.
[97] Kruse, 122.

motivation for his ministry. The sobering effects of the fear of the Lord motivated Paul to a ministry that is humble, unselfish, and faithful. And the unselfish love of Christ for him, displayed at the cross, drove Paul to a cross-shaped, loving, and self-denying missionary ministry.

Observations on Paul's spirituality

There are two observations we have about Paul's spirituality from 2 Corinthians 5:14, 15. First, as we noticed earlier, Paul in 2 Corinthians 5:11-15 appears to be emphasizing a *cognitive knowledge of Christ's love*. This included the redemptive-historical fact of the cross as well as the redemptive meaning of it. According to v. 14, Paul "concluded" something. This is, he thought. He pondered. He studied. He mused on the historical event of "one has died for all. . . ." And as a result of this meditation upon the cross of Christ, he concluded some things. Martin quotes Hughes as saying that the things Paul "concluded" about the love of Christ were the "rational ground of his security in Christ."[98] First, he concluded that the cross was a supreme display of Christ's love for him. He was *assured* of Christ's love for him on the cross. Secondly, like a chain reaction, he also concluded this assurance of Christ's love should control or compel him and other believers to live loving and self-sacrificing lives for Christ and others. Murray has commented on this spiritual dynamic:

The Holy Spirit is the Spirit of truth and therefore as the Spirit of love he captivates our hearts by the love of God and of Christ to us. In the diffusion of that love there flows also love to one another. "Beloved, if God loved us, we ought also to love one another" (I John 4:11). The biblical ethic knows no fulfilment [sic] of its demands other than that produced by the constraint and claim of Christ's redeeming love (cf. II Cor. 5:14, 15; Galatians 2:20). Our love is always ignited by the flame of Christ's love. And it is the Holy Spirit who sheds abroad in our hearts the igniting flame of the love of God in Christ Jesus. The love that is ignited is the fruit of the Spirit.[99]

So, in summary, there are two observations we have made that are very important spiritual principles in this book. First, *Paul's assurance of Christ's love has a cognitive element.*[100] Second, *Paul's assurance of Christ's love had the spontaneous effect of stirring up mission zeal in him.*

---

[98] P. E. Hughes, *Paul's Second Epistle to the Corinthians*, New International Commentary on the New Testament, vol. 47 (Grand Rapids, MI: Eerdmans, 1962), 193; quoted in Martin, 129.

[99] John Murray, *Principles of Conduct* (Grand Rapids: Eerdmans, 1957; reprint, 1984), 226.

[100] Later in this book, we will explore the biblical doctrine of assurance more fully from a covenantal angle. We do believe in the classic Reformed doctrine of assurance as expressed in the WCF, chapter 18. We believe it is faithful to the Bible when it says that assurance has three critical elements: the promises of God's Word (more cognitive), the evidences of new life (again a bit more cognitive and objective), and the inward witness of the Spirit (more experiential and subjective).

Galatians 2:20

I have been crucified with Christ. It is no longer I who live, but Christ who lives in me. And the life I now live in the flesh I live by faith in the Son of God, who loved me and gave himself for me.

Original context, structure and meaning

The language of the first few verses of Paul's letter to the Galatians immediately paints for us a *context* of serious trouble and urgency. With passion and abruptness, Paul even omits the customary thanksgiving part of his letter[101] and immediately attacks the problem head on. He says with palpable dissatisfaction in Galatians 1:6-7 that "trouble-makers"[102] have entered the church and the Galatian Christians were so quickly duped by them. Paul says the problem is so serious because it involves nothing less than an attack on the gospel of grace. Many scholars agree with this understanding of the general urgency of the situation in Galatians. However, what exactly the problem was that the "trouble-makers" brought to the church is a matter of much debate.

We are aware that since the early 1980s with the publication of E. P. Sander's work[103] fierce debate has raged in a reexamination of "Paul's theology of the law and the Jewish people."[104] It is beyond the scope of this book to enter into this debate.[105] Suffice it to say, we are still persuaded by the traditional Reformation view that the problem in the church at Galatia was in large part "Judaizers"[106] who had come preaching a "different gospel" which was not the true gospel. They taught a works righteousness, a keeping of the Mosaic law in order for one to be justified. We disagree with Sanders, and others who came after him to refine his arguments,[107] that legalistic Judaism was not the problem, rather, the problem was *wholly* a "covenantal nomism"[108] that Paul sought to counter. Nevertheless, there do appear to be some helpful insights from their research. This covenantal nomism seems to

---

[101] D. A. Carson and Douglas J. Moo, *An Introduction to the New Testament*, Second ed. (Grand Rapids: Zondervan, 2005), 456.

[102] F. F. Bruce, *Paul: Apostle of the Heart Set Free*, Paperback ed. (Grand Rapids: Eerdmans, 2000), 179.

[103] E. P. Sanders, *Paul and Palestinian Judaism: A Comparison of Patterns of Religion* (Philadelphia: Fortress, 1977).

[104] Chamblin, "Pauline Epistles," 25.

[105] We have found Water's critique of the "new perspective on Paul" very helpful in seeing the many flaws in this movement. Guy Prentiss Waters, *Justification and the New Perspective on Paul: A Review and Response* (Phillipsburg, NJ: P&R Publishing Company, 2004).

[106] Reymond, *Paul: Missionary Theologian*, 130.

[107] Especially James D. G. Dunn and N. T. Wright.

[108] Waters, 61-64.

have been *part* of the problem Paul was seeking to correct in Galatia. We tend to agree with Longenecker:

> Paul deals with *both* [italics ours] "legalism" (i.e., the attempt to gain favor with God by means of Torah observance) and "nomism" (i.e., the response of faith to a God who has acted on one's behalf by living a life governed by Torah). In 2:15–16 Paul presents in abbreviated form the case against the former; in 2:17–20 he deals with the latter, with 2:21 being a summary conclusion incorporating both.[109]

Chapell similarly observed, "Paul strongly and directly corrects the Galatian Christians, who have begun to look to their own works not only for making them right with God but also for keeping them right with God."[110]

On the one hand, Paul was demolishing the error of legalism, which taught a justification by works. Against this error Paul declared in no uncertain terms in Galatians 2:16, "We know that a person is not justified by works of the law but through faith in Jesus Christ." On the other hand, Paul was also going after the error of a type of nomism. Those troubled by this kind of nomism kept the law out of gratitude for saving grace, which is right and biblical covenantal living. However, the problem came when this tended to make some proud[111] of their moral achievements and mistaken in their reliance upon their law-keeping rather than upon faith in the grace of Christ. To this error Paul forcefully declared, "I have been crucified with Christ. It is no longer I who live, but Christ who lives in me. And the life I now live in the flesh I live by faith in the Son of God, who loved me and gave himself for me." According to Paul, the law in itself has no power to justify or to sanctify.

The text of Galatians 2:20 is nested in the *structure* of Galatians 2:15-21. This passage has been rightly recognized as the main *propositio* or thesis of the letter.[112] The structure is "a speech with an original audience (Cephas) and a new audience – all those in Galatia."[113] This is a record of words of admonishment that Paul publicly spoke to Peter on an occasion in Antioch when Peter appeared to back-peddle on the gospel of grace due to the appearance of Judaizing Christians from Jerusalem (see vv. 11-14).

---

[109] Richard N. Longenecker, *Word Biblical Commentary: Galatians*, ed. David A. Hubbard et al., Word Biblical Commentary, vol. 41 (Dallas: Word, Incorporated, 2002), 95.

[110] Bryan Chapell, *Holiness by Grace: Delighting in the Joy That Is Our Strength* (Wheaton: Crossway Books, 2001), 52.

[111] Thomas R. Schreiner, *Paul, Apostle of God's Glory in Christ: A Pauline Theology* (Downers Grove: InterVarsity Press, 2001), 116-122.

[112] Longenecker, 95; Michael J. Gorman, *Apostle of the Crucified Lord: A Theological Introduction to Paul & His Letters* (Grand Rapids: Eerdmans, 2004), 200.

[113] Gorman, 200.

We have already touched lightly on the *meaning* of Galatians 2:20 when dealing with the context of the passage. To recall, Paul is dealing with two big problems - a Jewish legalism toward justification and a Jewish nomism toward the Christian life/sanctification. Paul in v. 16 deals with the former error. Works of the law will never justify, because justification is only by faith in Christ. Then, in a parallel way,[114] Paul beginning in v. 19 deals with the latter error. Just as faith in Christ results in justification, so too faith in Christ results in life. In vv. 19, 20, Paul uses the very vivid imagery of death to make his point. Gorman explaining this imagery of death says, "It is a severance from the Law as one's hope for justification and life – the very things most Jews found in the Law."[115]

Galatians 2:20 appears to be epexegetical of v. 19.[116] That is, Paul takes this imagery of death to the law by faith in Christ and expands on it. He continues the very personal tone of address using "I."[117] For Paul, these doctrines were not abstract theology but very personal truths. Setting himself as an example, Paul says, "I have been crucified with Christ. It is no longer I who live, but Christ who lives in me." Paul was a proud self-righteous Pharisee who was seeking by a works righteousness to be justified and live life (see also Phil. 3:5-6). However, when he heard the gospel of grace and "believed in Christ Jesus," he was put in union with Christ (see Gal. 2:16). This union with Christ linked him marvelously to Christ's crucifixion. And Paul's "co-crucifixion," was his death to his old self and old works-righteousness and nomistic way of life (see also Gal. 5:24, 6:14; Rom. 6:1-14).[118] In this way dying to the law through faith union to Christ's cross, he is justified and has power for life. Paul further says, "And the life I now live in the flesh I live by faith in the Son of God. . . ." That is, Paul being dead to the law through the cross no longer relies upon his law-keeping to persuade God to keep accepting and loving him. Rather, Paul's life/sanctification is energized by his on-going dependence upon the "Son of God" who is his life. Finally, Paul says, "who loved me and gave himself for me." For Paul, the cross was never an old dusty historical fact. Paul always saw it as an event that was the most glorious display of Christ's love "for me," and this affected his whole heart – mind, emotions, and will.

---

[114] Gorman, 204.

[115] Gorman, 204.

[116] Longenecker, 93.

[117] Hendriksen points out in the Greek that in just three verses, vv. 18-20, Paul used the personal pronoun "I" twelve times! Simon J. Kistemaker and William Hendriksen, *Exposition of Galatians*, New Testament Commentary, vol. 8 (Grand Rapids: Baker Book House, 1953-2001), 106.

[118] Gorman, 204.

Observations on Paul's spirituality

There are two observations we would like to make about Paul's spirituality as displayed in Galatians 2:20.

First, *Paul's understanding of union and communion with Christ is deeply personal and relational.* For Paul, his doctrine of union with Christ, of believers being "in Christ," was not simply some abstract theological construct. It was full of relational and emotional blessings. This union is key to communion with God. This communion is deeply rooted in a biblical "Christian mysticism" as Longnecker says in his comments on Galatians 2:20:

"Christian mysticism." Mysticism, of course, frequently conjures up ideas about the negation of personality, withdrawal from objective reality, ascetic contemplation, a searching out of pathways to perfection, and absorption into the divine—all of which is true for Eastern and Grecian forms of mysticism. The mysticism of the Bible, however, affirms the true personhood of people and all that God has created in the natural world, never calling for negation or withdrawal except where God's creation has been contaminated by sin. Furthermore, the mysticism of biblical religion is not some esoteric searching for a path to be followed that will result in union with the divine, but is always of the nature of a response to God's grace wherein people who have been mercifully touched by God enter into communion with him without ever losing their own identities. It is, as H. A. A. Kennedy once called it, "that contact between the human and the Divine which forms the core of the deepest religious experience, but which can only be felt as an immediate intuition of the highest reality and cannot be described in the language of psychology" (*The Theology of the Epistles*, 122).[119]

Paul's spirituality acknowledged this real intimacy a Christian can enjoy with his Savior and God.

Second, *Paul's contemplation and experience of Christ's love at the cross attracted his on-going faith.* Chapell writes about Galatians 2:20b, "These words first express Christ's attitude toward Paul and, then, describe an action that springs from it."[120] As the love of Christ on the cross motivated Paul in 2 Corinthians 5:14, so in Galatians 2:20 does the love of the "Son of God" attract his faith. Henry has observed, "Those who have true faith live by that faith; and the great thing which faith fastens upon is Christ's loving us and giving himself for us."[121]

---

[119] Longenecker, 92-93.
[120] Chapell, 54.
[121] Matthew Henry, *Matthew Henry's Commentary on the Whole Bible: Complete and Unabridged in One Volume* (Peabody: Hendrickson, 1996). See comments on Gal. 2:20.

Ephesians 3:14-21

14 For this reason I bow my knees before the Father, 15 from whom every family in heaven and on earth is named, 16 that according to the riches of his glory he may grant you to be strengthened with power through his Spirit in your inner being, 17 so that Christ may dwell in your hearts through faith—that you, being rooted and grounded in love, 18 may have strength to comprehend with all the saints what is the breadth and length and height and depth, 19 and to know the love of Christ that surpasses knowledge, that you may be filled with all the fullness of God. 20 Now to him who is able to do far more abundantly than all that we ask or think, according to the power at work within us, 21 to him be glory in the church and in Christ Jesus throughout all generations, forever and ever. Amen.

Original context, structure, and meaning

One significant way in which the historical *context* of Paul's letter to the Ephesians differs from his other letters is that there are no pressing problems he is specifically addressing.[122] He shares general truths that will help all believers. For example, he speaks about the breath-taking spiritual identity of believers "in Christ" (1:3-14) and the ramifications it should have on life (e.g., unity [4:1-3], mutual submission [5:8ff], etc.).

A simple analysis of the literary *structure* of Ephesians reveals a basic twofold division. Chapters 1-3 are filled with doctrinal indicatives, and chapters 4-6 are filled with practical imperatives stemming from the indicatives.

The general flow of the letter up to our passage of 3:14-21 is approximately as follows. In chapter 1, Paul rehearses for his readers the great blessings from the Father through the Son to Christians. 1:3 captures his main theme in this chapter, "Blessed be the God and Father of our Lord Jesus Christ, who has blessed us in Christ with every spiritual blessing in the heavenly places. . . ." In chapter 2, Paul rehearses the blessings of the gospel in Christ to both Jew and Gentile. And Paul particularly "praises God for his sovereign grace in bringing lost Jews and lost Gentiles together into one new humanity, one new community."[123] He concludes in 2:19-22 by using the powerful metaphor of a *spiritual temple* to describe this new community.

Then something very curious happens in 3:1. Paul begins a prayer, then suddenly stops it mid-sentence. It really seems that Paul is distracted from his prayer. He is distracted by the truth about his apostolic ministry and its

---

[122] Peter T. O'Brien, *The Letters to the Ephesians*, The Pillar New Testament Commentary (Grand Rapids: Eerdmans 1999), 49; Harold W. Hoehner, *Ephesians: An Exegetical Commentary* (Grand Rapids: Baker Academic, 2002; reprint, 2007), 97.

[123] D. A. Carson, *A Call to Spiritual Reformation: Priorities from Paul and His Prayers* (Grand Rapids: Baker Academic, 1992), 199.

connection to the gospel and the church. So, in 3:2-13, he describes this truth.[124] Then in 3:14 he uses the same phrase he did in 3:1, "For this reason I. . . ." What is Paul doing? It appears he is restarting his prayer that he began in 3:1. Seeing this connection is important because it will greatly help us to understand the "reason" for Paul's prayer in vv.14-19. If 3:14 and 3:1 are part of the same prayer, then the reason he is pointing to for his prayer must be found before 3:1, in 2:19-22. What "reason" do we find? Carson suggests the following, "Paul prays for this reason, namely, that God's declared purpose in creating this new humanity is to bring the people in it to the kind of *spiritual maturity* [italics ours] portrayed in the extended metaphor of the 'holy temple in the Lord . . . a dwelling in which God lives by his Spirit.'"[125] O'Brien sees Paul's reason to pray similarly when he says, "Now he intercedes with the Father that they might be strengthened by his power in order to know and experience Christs [sic] love which surpasses knowledge. By this they will come to full *spiritual maturity* [italics ours]."[126]

Having briefly considered the context and structure leading up to 3:14-21, we now want to enter Paul's prayer and explore its meaning. O'Brien says, "The solemn introduction of vv. 14 and 15 gives great weight to the prayer." In vv. 16-17a, Paul records his first petition. In vv. 17b-19, Paul records his second petition. Then in vv. 20-21, he has a closing doxology.

In vv. 16-17a, Paul is praying that the Spirit would work in his readers' hearts to *spiritually mature* them. The phrase, "you to be strengthened with power through his Spirit" is similar to a phrase he used in Colossians 1:10, 11 to indicate his desire for the spiritual maturity of believers.

In vv. 17b-19, Paul's second petition is amazingly a prayer for the Father to give these Christians a power to grasp at an *experiential* level the incredible love of Christ. As Hoehner observes, "He now prays that they may be united *experientially* [italics ours] in Christ's love."[127] Paul certainly wants these Christians to use their intellect, their mind to "know" the love of Christ. For instance, he says to them that they are "rooted and grounded in love." Earlier in 1:4ff he explained things so their minds could understand the love of God to them was rooted in his sovereign electing love. Also, in 3:18 he says he prays they may "comprehend" the dimensions (height, depth, length, breadth) of the amazing love of God in Christ for them. However, what Paul prays for is not simply an intellectual knowledge of the love of Christ. In v. 19 he also prays that God would give them the blessing "to know the love of Christ that surpasses knowledge." This is a paradox. According to Paul the love of Christ passes *knowledge*, yet Paul is seriously praying for his readers to really *know*

---

[124] Carson, 199.
[125] Carson, 199.
[126] O'Brien, 266.
[127] Hoehner, 471.

this limitless love. How do we solve this paradox? How are we to understand this petition of Paul? We believe with Carson that Paul is "asking God that they might have the power to grasp the dimensions of that love in their *experience* [italics ours]."[128] The Greek word "to know" often means to understand something intellectually or cognitively, though it can also mean to grasp something by means of *personal intimate experience.*[129] We believe this is how Paul is using it here.

Observations on Paul's spirituality

There are two observations about spirituality we would like to make from Paul's prayer in Ephesians 3:14-21. Both have an important bearing on understanding the apparent correlation between spirituality and mission zeal.

Our first observation is that *Paul's spirituality included subjective experience.* He was not shy to talk about it, in fact he prayed for others to also share in this experience. Carson, in commenting on Ephesians 3:17-19, said it well:

> Because some wings of the church have appealed to experience over against revelation, or have talked glibly about an ill-defined "spirituality" that is fundamentally divorced from the gospel, some of us have *overreacted* [italics ours] and begun to view all mention of experience as suspicious at best, perverse at worst. *This overreaction must cease* [italics ours]. The Scriptures themselves demand that we allow more place for experience than that.[130]

What, however, is the nature of this experience? We desire to understand what this experience is for which Paul is praying. We will seek to do so by considering what it is *not*, and then what it possibly *is.*

First, what this experience is not. Paul is not advocating some unbridled and unbiblical "mystical" experience. He is not advocating an "anything-goes" type of spiritual experience. For Paul, the love of Christ was supremely displayed in history at the cross of Christ. For Paul, the love of Christ is always tied to the cross and to the gospel of that cross (e.g., 2 Cor. 5:14, 15; Gal. 2:20). Also, Paul is not saying Christians need to "seek an experience for experience sake." This experience of grasping the love of Christ in the affections by the Spirit's empowerment accompanies *truth* and is not apart from truth. Furthermore, Paul is not praying for a "second blessing-type" experience that will make his readers real Christians. Paul already considered them true Christians. In 1:1, he addresses them as "the saints who are in Ephesus, and

---

[128] Carson, 191.

[129] James Swanson, "1182 Γινώσκω (Ginōskō)," in *Dictionary of Biblical Languages with Semantic Domains : Greek (New Testament)* (Oak Harbor: Logos Research Systems, Inc., 1997).

[130] Carson, 191.

are faithful in Christ Jesus." In 3:17, he considers them to be already "rooted and grounded in love." Lastly, Paul is not praying for a self-centered "spirituality" or self-absorbed emotional experience. Rather, Paul in 3:18 prays that "with all the saints" they corporately would know in their affections such a deep experience of God's love for them.

Secondly, what this experience likely is. It is an experience that involves both the *intellectual* aspect of the heart as well as the *emotional* aspect of the heart. Paul in chapters 1-2 fills the intellects/minds of his readers with the love of God in election, the love of God in regeneration, the love of God on the cross, the love of God in the gospel, and the love of God in making a new community. However, in 3:19 he says he prays for a grasp of this love that "surpasses knowledge." Additionally, it is a Spirit-empowered experience that other parts of Scripture talk about (e.g., Ps. 16:11; Rom. 5:5, 15:13). J. I. Packer is correct when he writes, "The distinctive, constant, basic ministry of the Holy Spirit under the new covenant is so to *meditate Christ's presence* to believers-- that is, to give them such knowledge of his presence with them as their Savior, Lord, and God . . ."[131]

Also, it is an experience that is part of the biblical *assuring* work of the Spirit. There is in the Scriptures a doctrine of assurance of salvation. The *Spirit*, working with the believer's faith in the *promises* of the gospel and the *obedience* of the saint, testifies to a believer he/she is saved and is a Christian. The Spirit's assuring work includes giving Christians *a deep sense of Christ's love* for them.[132] Furthermore, it is an experience that God promised would be part of the NC. The heart, core, and chief blessing of the covenants are that God and his people would be restored to an intimate, personal loving relationship. Jeremiah 31:33-34 reads as follows:

> 33 For this is the covenant that I will make with the house of Israel after those days, declares the Lord: I will put my law within them, and I will write it on their hearts. And *I will be their God, and they shall be my people* [italics ours]. 34 And no longer shall each one teach his neighbor and each his brother, saying, "*Know* [italics ours] the Lord," for they shall all *know* [italics ours] me, from the least of them to the greatest, declares the Lord. For I will forgive their iniquity, and I will remember their sin no more.

Lastly, Paul prays for an experience that must be understood by the "already" and "not yet" tension of the Kingdom of God.[133] Christ at his first

---

[131] J. I. Packer, *Keep in Step with the Spirit: Finding Fullness in Our Walk with God*, Revised and Enlarged ed. (Grand Rapids: Baker Books, 1984; reprint, 2005), 43.

[132] As we noted earlier, the classic Reformed formulation of this can be found in the WCF, chapter 14.

[133] Brian S. Borgman, *Feelings and Faith: Cultivating Godly Emotion in the Christian Life* (Wheaton, IL: Crossway Books, 2009), 77-78; Adam, 147.

coming did inaugurate his "kingdom," that is, his rule and reign. As a result, the *experience* of those promised kingdom blessings of intimacy with God through his Spirit have "already" begun to flow to Christians. However, the full *experience* of this personal communion with God is still "not yet." Paul in the "love chapter" in 1 Corinthians 13:12 captures this "already"/"not yet" tension in which we now live when he writes, "For *now* [italics ours] we see in a mirror dimly, but *then* [italics ours] face to face. *Now* [italics ours] I know in part; *then* [italics ours] I shall know fully, even as I have been fully known."

Our second observation from Ephesians 3:14-21 about spirituality is that Paul knew the powerful motivating force the experiencing of Christ's love has, so he prayed earnestly for God to grant this same experience to his young converts.[134] Earlier we observed that according to the immediate context of Paul's prayer in Ephesians 3, his "reason" for praying for them in that way was for their spiritual maturity. However, as we consider the broader context of Paul's prayer, another important reason emerges.

In chapters 1-3, Paul is building up to things he wants to say in chapters 4-6. In chapters 1-3, Paul rehearses the staggering blessings Christians have in Christ and his prayer for power to mature and to experience God's love. Then, in chapters 4-6, he calls the Christians to obedience. In 4:1 he writes, "I *therefore*, a prisoner for the Lord, urge you to walk in a manner worthy of the calling to which you have been called. . . ." So simply put, in keeping with his overall structure in the letter, *Paul is praying for God to give them power to experience deep communion with Christ in order that they may also obey Christ.* Paul modeled in his own life this connection between communion with God and obedience (e.g., 2 Cor. 5:14, 15; Gal. 2:20). It is a small step to see the implications this spiritual dynamic has for increasing mission zeal.

Romans 15:14-24

> [14] I myself am satisfied about you, my brothers, that you yourselves are full of goodness, filled with all knowledge and able to instruct one another. [15] Yet on some points I have written to you very boldly by way of reminder, because of the grace given me by God [16] to be a minister of Christ Jesus to the Gentiles in the priestly service of the gospel of God, so that the offering of the Gentiles may be acceptable, sanctified by the Holy Spirit. [17] In Christ Jesus, then, I have reason to be proud of my work for God. [18] For I will not venture to speak of anything except what Christ has accomplished through me to bring the Gentiles to obedience—by word and deed, [19] by the power of signs and wonders, by the power of the Spirit of God—so that from Jerusalem and all the way around to Illyricum I have fulfilled the ministry of the gospel of Christ; [20] and thus I make it my

---

[134] Mohrlang, 576.

ambition to preach the gospel, not where Christ has already been named, lest I build on someone else's foundation, **21** but as it is written,

"Those who have never been told of him will see, and those who have never heard will understand."

22 This is the reason why I have so often been hindered from coming to you. **23** But now, since I no longer have any room for work in these regions, and since I have longed for many years to come to you, **24** I hope to see you in passing as I go to Spain, and to be helped on my journey there by you, once I have enjoyed your company for a while.

Original context, structure, and meaning

The general *context* is that Paul has completed the main body of his letter with all of its gospel-filled teaching. *Structurally*, this section begins the conclusion of his letter. In this section, he returns to his relationship with the Roman believers (though they likely have never met physically) and to his missionary work.[135] This return in focus to his relationship with them and his mission work appears to be a "bracketing"[136] to what he said in Romans 1:8-15 when he mentioned his "missionary plans."[137]

In 15:14-16, Paul tactfully and graciously complements the Roman believers' spiritual maturity much as he did earlier in 1:8. In verse 15, Paul refers to the main theological content of his letter as "boldly" reminding them of gospel truths. Yet, as Morris says, it was more than simply a reminder: "Paul was enlarging their horizons but he was also reminding them of things they already knew."[138] Then he gives the reason why he was so bold in his letter to them. It was because of the "grace" God gave to him in his calling as a "minister of Christ Jesus to the Gentiles." Paul's *faith* in Christ's clear call on him as the apostle to the Gentiles appears to have consistently and powerfully motivated him on his mission.[139] Paul no doubt took very seriously his calling to the Gentiles and even likened it to "priestly service" to God. The Gentiles were figuratively a sacrifice offered up by him to God. As such Paul, by his

---

[135] Gorman, 401; James D. G. Dunn, *Word Biblical Commentary: Romans 9-16*, ed. Bruce M. Metzger et al., Word Biblical Commentary, vol. 38b (Dallas: Word, Incorporated, 2002), 856.

[136] Dunn, 856.

[137] Chamblin, "Pauline Epistles," 136, 136a.

[138] Leon Morris, *The Epistle to the Romans*, The Pillar New Testament Commentary (Grand Rapids: Eerdmans 1988), 510.

[139] Evidence of this can be seen in the numerous times Paul recounted to various audiences about his dramatic conversion and then calling as a missionary to the Gentiles (e.g., Acts 22:1-21, 26:12-23; Gal. 1:1-17). See also James E. Cummings, "Paul's Theological Motivation for Mission" (Th.M. thesis, Fuller Theological Seminary, 1974), 15-45.

bold and faithful teaching in this letter, wanted to "insure that the Gentiles are an acceptable and holy sacrifice to God..."[140]

In 15:17-24, the "therefore" connects Paul's thoughts about being a called minister to the Gentiles with the amazing list of Christ's gospel work through him. Paul rightly gives the glory to Christ Jesus (15:17) for the stunning success that attended his mission of "word and deed" (15:18) to those to whom he ministered the gospel. Hendriksen and Kistemaker observe that the "best commentary" of the amazing results of Paul's preaching and deeds by the power of the Spirit is found in the book of Acts.[141] Paul's *faith* in Christ, who so obviously was working through Paul's word and deed ministry prior to this letter, no doubt bolstered Paul's motivation to press on in his mission. In 15:22-24, Paul looks with *hope* to the future of his missionary work. With such blessings from Christ on his previous ministry in the eastern Mediterranean, Paul is motivated by *hope* in Christ's ongoing blessing on his mission plans in the western Mediterranean. Gorman writes:

Feeling that his mission to the region east of Italy was complete, Paul now expresses a desire to pass through Rome on his way to Spain, the western edge of the empire (15:24, 28). His goal is not merely a bit of preaching and fellowship,...but also a sending by them (15:24), which suggests the provision of a mission base, financial support, and perhaps companions.[142]

Observations on Paul's spirituality

We see here in this text that *faith* and *hope* in Christ and his promises were also part of Paul's spirituality. These virtues appear to also be motivating factors in Paul's missionary activities. According to Frame, in the Scriptures, motives and Christian virtues are closely aligned.[143] Frame also says the classic Christian virtues of faith, hope, and love are intertwined. Regarding faith and love he says, "Faith includes hope, for hope is faith directed to God's promises for the future." [144] It should not be surprising, therefore, to see from this passage that the faith and hope the Spirit worked in Paul's heart incites him in his missionary labors.

---

[140] Gorman, 402.
[141] William Hendriksen and Simon J. Kistemaker, *Exposition of Paul's Epistle to the Romans*, New Testament Commentary, vol. 12-13 (Grand Rapids: Baker Book House, 1953-2001), 487. For Paul's *preaching*, see for instance Acts 13:42–44, 48, 49; 16:5, 14, 15, 32–34; 17:4, 11, 12; 18:4, 8, 27, 28. For Paul's *deeds*, see for instance Acts 13:6–12; 14:1–3; 14:8–10; 16:16–18; 16:25 f.; 19:11–16.
[142] Gorman, 402.
[143] Frame, *The Doctrine of the Christian Life*, 324-325.
[144] Frame, *The Doctrine of the Christian Life*, 27.

Summary of Biblical Theology Analysis

In summary, we have used *biblical studies* to analyze our topic. We have seen that Paul, the prototype Christian missionary, indicated in several places in his writings a positive correlation between spirituality and mission zeal. In particular, we have seen that Paul's experience of *love, faith,* and *hope* were powerful stimuli in moving him to engage in mission.

Analysis Based on Systematic Theology

As with the *Analysis Based on Biblical Theology* section of this chapter, here we look once more at the Apostle Paul's motivations for mission, though this time we use the tools of *systematic theology*. Our perspective in studying mission motivations is covenantal. In this section, we *first* attempt to integrate John Frame's Covenantal Triperspectivalism, Enoch Wan's Relational Paradigm, and other covenantal truths into a synthesized *RCL*. We *second* use this lens to explore various texts from our previous section to understand Paul's motivations for mission found in those texts from a covenantal perspective.

Considering Relational-Covenantal Truths

In this section, we begin to look more closely at Covenantal Triperspectivalism, the Relational Paradigm, and other covenantal truths. However first, we would like to broadly review some important literature regarding the covenants in general.

In studying the covenants, Robertson's,[145] Murray's,[146] and Nichol's[147] works on the covenants are very helpful in understanding the structure and redemptive historical development of the divine covenants in the Bible.[148] These are all Reformed theologians, and they are in substantial agreement. Nichols, being a credo-baptist,[149] also brings this helpful perspective to bear in his analysis of the covenants. Golding's[150] work on the covenants gives very

---

[145] O. Palmer Robertson is a theologian and scholar and has taught at Reformed Theological Seminary, Westminster Theological Seminary, Covenant Theological Seminary, and Knox Theological Seminary.

[146] John Murray was a professor of systematic theology at Princeton Theological Seminary and Westminster Theological Seminary.

[147] Greg Nichols is a pastor in Grand Rapids, Michigan and former professor at Trinity Ministerial Academy.

[148] Robertson, 61-63; John Murray, *The Covenant of Grace* (London: Tyndale Press, 1954; reprint, Phillipsburg, NJ: Presbyterian and Reformed Publishing Company, 1988), 12-30; Nichols, 103-122.

[149] A *credo-baptist* is one who believes only those professing saving faith in Jesus should be baptized. This is in contrast to *paedo-baptists*.

[150] Peter Golding pastored at Hayes Town Congregational Chapel and has served on the Board of Governors at the London Theological Seminary since 1984.

important information on the development of traditional Covenant Theology in Church history.[151] Williamson's[152] work shows the importance of the covenants for biblical theology and how the covenants are instrumental in unfolding God's eternal purposes.[153] In McKay's,[154] Waldron's,[155] Barcellos',[156] and Murray's[157] separate works, the authors concentrate on acknowledging and then applying the teaching of Scripture on the covenants to address various theological and practical issues in the Christian life.[158] As touching upon evangelical mission ministry, works such as Kostenberger[159] and O'Brien's,[160] Foster's,[161] and Van Gelder's,[162] helpfully stress the covenantal nature of the Church's mission work.[163]

Many of the works cited above could be characterized as part of classic Covenant Theology that came out of the sixteenth century Protestant Reformation and formed the substantial part of the Reformed tradition's biblical theology.[164] But within Protestantism, there have been other more recent theological positions that have also emphasized the importance of the biblical covenants as part of their system. For instance, Progressive

---

[151] Golding, 13-142.
[152] Paul R. Williamson is Lecturer in Old Testament and Hebrew at Moore Theological College.
[153] Paul R. Williamson, 11.
[154] David McKay is Professor of Systematic Theology, Ethics and Apologetics at the Reformed Theological College.
[155] Samuel Waldron is President and Professor of Systematic Theology at Covenant Baptist Theological Seminary.
[156] Richard Barcellos is Visiting Professor of New Testament Studies at Covenant Baptist Theological Seminary.
[157] Andrew Murray was a South African Christian teacher, writer, and pastor.
[158] McKay, 29-307; Samuel E. Waldron and Richard G. Barcellos, *A Reformed Baptist Manifesto: The New Covenant Constitution of the Church* (Palmdale, CA: Reformed Baptist Academic Press, 2004), 9-79; Andrew Murray, *The Believer's New Covenant* (Minneapolis: Bethany House Publishers, 1984), 34-107.
[159] Andreas J. Kostenberger is Research Professor at Midwestern Baptist Theological Seminary.
[160] Peter T. O'Brien is Senior Research Fellow in New Testament and Vice-Principal of Moore Theological College.
[161] Stuart J. Foster is an evangelical missionary with Serving in Mission (SIM) and a Bible translation consultant.
[162] Craig Van Gelder was professor of domestic missiology at Calvin Theological Seminary and now is professor of congregational mission at Luther Seminary.
[163] Andreas J. Kostenberger and Peter T. O'Brien, *Salvation to the Ends of the Earth: A Biblical Theology of Mission*, ed. D. A. Carson, New Studies in Biblical Theology, vol. 11 (2001), 36, 42-44, 47, 123, 252; Stuart J. Foster, "The Missiology of Old Testament Covenant," *International Bulletin of Missionary Research* 34, no. 4 (2010): 205-207; Craig Van Gelder, "The Covenant's Missiological Character," *Calvin Theological Journal* 29, no. 1 (1994): 190-197.
[164] Gentry and Wellum, Kindle locations 1025-1038; Golding, 14-35.

Dispensationalism,[165] as championed by people like Craig Blaising,[166] Darrell Bock,[167] and Robert Saucy,[168] wants to take seriously the "unfolding, organic nature of the biblical covenants as they lead to Christ."[169] There is also a contemporary movement called "New Covenant Theology." Wells[170] and Zaspel[171] produced a book by the same title in which they attempted to articulate their position by "something more substantial than fugitive pieces ... on this subject."[172] New Covenant Theology seeks to provide a middle road between traditional Covenant Theology and Dispensational Theology. In part, New Covenant Theology seeks to better understand and articulate the continuity and discontinuity between the OC and NC than does Covenant Theology and Dispensational Theology. Also, in Gentry's[173] and Wellum's[174] co-authored book, they advance the system of *"progressive covenantalism"* which they consider to be a "species of 'new covenant theology.'"[175] Like New Covenant Theology, Progressive Covenantalism is an attempted "via media," or middle way, between classic Reformed Covenant Theology on the one hand and Dispensational Theology on the other.[176]

We have also considered literature about the *relational dynamics of the covenants*. For our research about covenantal motives for mission, we are particularly interested in this type of literature. It is from such studies we see a RCC operating between the Persons of the Trinity and between the Triune God and his covenant people.[177] For instance, in their research of the covenantal relationship, Gentry and Wellum significantly point out that the "divine-human relationship is *essentially* and *fundamentally* covenantal, because covenant is intrinsic to the being of God himself."[178] They also importantly point out the central place of God's "faithful loyal love" in all the

---

[165] Gentry and Wellum, Kindle locations 899-911.

[166] Craig A. Blaising is Executive Vice President and Provost of Southwestern Baptist Theological Seminary.

[167] Darrell L. Bock is Executive Director of Cultural Engagement at The Hendricks Center and Senior Research Professor of New Testament studies at Dallas Theological Seminary.

[168] Robert Saucy was Professor of Systematic Theology at Talbot School of Theology.

[169] Gentry and Wellum, Kindle locations 958-972.

[170] Tom Wells is a pastor of The King's Chapel as well as a Bible teacher and writer.

[171] Fred G. Zaspel is the pastor at Reformed Baptist Church in Franconia, Pennsylvania, as well as adjunct professor of systematic theology at the Southern Baptist Theological Seminary.

[172] Tom Wells and Fred Zaspel, *New Covenant Theology: Description, Definition, Defense* (Frederick, MD: New Covenant Media, 2002), 1.

[173] Peter J. Gentry is professor of Old Testament Interpretation at the Southern Baptist Theological Seminary.

[174] Stephen J. Wellum is professor of Christian theology at the Southern Baptist Theological Seminary.

[175] Gentry and Wellum, Kindle locations 278-291.

[176] Gentry and Wellum, Kindle locations 276-288.

[177] In chapter 2 of our book, we delve more into the RCC.

[178] Gentry and Wellum, Kindle locations 3826-3845.

biblical covenants he makes.[179] They write, "At the heart of covenant, then, is a relationship between parties characterized by faithfulness and loyalty in love."[180] It is a key relational-covenantal dynamic. Other essential dynamics in the covenant relationship are *trust* and *obedience*,[181] though one could argue biblically that loyal love and obedience are closely related. Furthermore, in their study of the relationship between Exodus 19:4 with vv. 5-6, they point out a central motivating dynamic in the covenant relationship. They point out, "Verse 4 shows that the *motivation* [italics ours] for concluding and keeping a covenant with Yahweh is sovereign grace."[182] God's abundant displays of grace to his people in a covenant relationship should motivate his people to respond with *gratitude*. This too is a fundamental dynamic of the RCC.

Also, in Joseph Allen's[183] fascinating book, he makes the case that biblical Christian ethics is based on a relational-covenantal model. According to Allen, an ethical theory always has a model, explicitly stated or implied, on how moral agents are related to one another.[184] Without relationship between persons, the argument for ethical obligation (i.e., what one should or should not do) is unsustainable. He also analyzes moral action. Allen finds three general categories of how relationship with God affects moral action. First, there is a response to God's actions. Second, there is obedience to God's command. And third, there is a patterning after God's being and action.[185] Allen concentrates on the third category to build his thesis for ethics based on the covenants. He sees moral action being patterned after God's being and action in a three-fold way. First, it is patterned after God's being and actions consistent with *covenant love*. Second, humankind's highest expression as "image of God" is our ability to enter into covenant with covenant love for God and others. And third, we should follow our God's being and actions of covenant love.[186] Allen believes covenant love is the supreme moral ethic in relationships.[187]

Allen describes the three main words for love in the Bible - *ahabah* (Hebrew, unconditional love to the elect), *hesed* (Hebrew, faithful covenantal love), and *agape* (Greek, has a combined meaning of both of the other two OT

---

[179] Gentry and Wellum, Kindle locations 3319-3411.
[180] Gentry and Wellum, Kindle locations 3312-3325.
[181] Gentry and Wellum, Kindle locations 4705-4721, 13952-13970.
[182] Gentry and Wellum, Kindle locations 7328-7341.
[183] Joseph L. Allen was professor of Christian ethics at the Perkins School of Theology, Southern Methodist University.
[184] Joseph L. Allen, *Love and Conflict: A Covenantal Model of Christian Ethics* (Nashville: Abingdon Press, 1984), 15.
[185] Allen, 54ff.
[186] Allen, 60.
[187] Allen, 9.

words).[188] Furthermore, Allen gives six characteristics of covenant love.[189] First, it binds us together as members of a covenant community. Second, it affirms the worth of each covenant member. He writes, "It is our *being* as covenant members that matters most fundamentally in God's sight; our being as persons precedes whether we are morally good and whether we are useful."[190] Third, it extends covenant love inclusively. Allen writes, "We can express the highest priority need, the ultimate human need for God's kingdom and God's righteousness, in terms of covenant. What people need, in and beyond every other need, is to live loyally in covenant with God and with one another, to live in that fellowship with God and their fellows in which they can truly be themselves."[191] Fourth, it seeks to meet the need of each member of the covenant community. Fifth, it is steadfast. Stressing this quality of biblical covenant love he writes, "To keep a covenant requires committedness over time: not momentary concern, but enduring loyalty; not occasional beneficence, but dependability."[192] Sixth and finally, it is reconciling.

Daniel Block[193] adds many insights about the RCC. The Ten Commandments are referred to in Hebrew and the Septuagint as the "ten words"[194] or "ten declarations." Block believes the term is best interpreted as, "the ten principles of the covenant relationship."[195] He believes there was a mnemonic reason for ten, that is, it corresponded to the ten fingers so as to facilitate better remembering them as "summarizing the essence of covenant relationship."[196] They are "not as legal code, but as a statement of covenant policy, as guidance for life...[they] create a framework and ethos with which the Israelites were to live."[197] Summarizing the main purpose of the Decalogue, Block writes, "In short, the Decalogue calls on the head of the household to be covenantally committed to YHWH, his household, and his neighbors, so that he will resist seeking his own advantage, and seek instead the interest of others."[198] According to Block, the Decalogue shaped the RCC of the Hebrews at the very core by "creating a worldview that begins by declaring YHWH's past grace in redeeming Israel from bondage..."[199] That is,

---

[188] Allen, 60.
[189] Allen, 31ff.
[190] Allen, 63.
[191] Allen, 71.
[192] Allen, 72.
[193] Daniel I. Block is the Gunther H. Knoedler Professor of Old Testament at Wheaton College, Wheaton, Illinois.
[194] See Exod. 34:28; Deut. 4:13, 10:4.
[195] Daniel I. Block, *How I Love Your Torah, O Lord!: Studies in the Book of Deuteronomy*, Google Books ed. (Eugene, OR: Cascade Books, 2011), 24.
[196] Block, 25.
[197] Block, 26.
[198] Block, 33.
[199] Block, 36.

at the "deep culture" or "worldview" level of the Hebrew RCC are the fundamental *vertical* and *horizontal* assumptions of the Decalogue. And all the other outward layers of values, beliefs, and behaviors of the RCC formed around this core. Block writes, "And herein lies the profound significance of the Decalogue, for in the Torah of Moses the covenantal seed that was planted by YHWH himself has come to full flower."[200]

Block also comments on an important motivational element in covenantal culture. He points out the important motivational purpose of the historical prologue section of ANE covenant documents. It was meant to highlight the suzerain's "gracious actions" to the vassal, and to illicit the vassal's loyalty to the lord as the "appropriate response" of a "redeemed people."[201] Further commenting on motivation in the covenants he also says that covenantal "blessings and curses" were meant to "motivate loyalty" in ANE treaties.[202] These blessings and curses were interwoven into the Decalogue rather than being placed in another separate section at the end of the Decalogue.

Another researcher into relational-covenantal dynamics is Mike Breen.[203] Breen sees the themes of covenant and kingdom as the "double helix" spiritual DNA of the entire Bible.[204] He helpfully points out that in the relational-covenantal dynamics between the Triune God and his people, there is *a clear priority of vertical over horizontal relationship*. There is also a clear priority in the covenants God makes with his people that places a grasp of the people's *identity* (being) before their *obedience* (doing). Knowing one's vertical identity with God in covenant motivates obedience.[205] Also, Breen significantly stresses in the biblical covenants a firm grasp of one's vertical relational "identity" as sons of God, as people of God, etc., always precedes "obedience." Inverting the order is detrimental.

In Meredith Kline's[206] classic study on the ANE covenant structure of the book of Deuteronomy, he too points out some vitally important aspects of the relational dynamics of the covenant relationship. Regarding the purpose of the historic prologue section in an ANE covenant treaty document, he writes, "This element in the covenant document was clearly designed to inspire

---

[200] Block, 55.
[201] Block, 30.
[202] Block, 34.
[203] Michael J. Breen is originally from England and is a church leader, minister, and author.
[204] Mike Breen, *Covenant and Kingdom: The DNA of the Bible*, Google Books ed. (Pawleys Island, SC: 3D Ministries, 2010), 16.
[205] Breen, 178 101.
[206] Meredith G. Kline (1922-2002) was an American theologian and author. He was an ordained minister with the Orthodox Presbyterian Church. He served as professor in various evangelical seminaries, such as Westminster Theological Seminary, Gordon-Conwell Theological Seminary, the Claremont School of Theology, Reformed Theological Seminary, and Westminster Seminary California.

confidence and *gratitude* [italics ours] in the vassal and thereby to dispose him to attend to the covenant obligations, which constitute the third element in both Exodus 20 and the international treaties."[207] The historic prologue recounts the benevolent involvement of the suzerain towards the vassal. It communicates love from the sovereign to the vassal as well as the obligation of reciprocal love and gratitude from the vassal. So too in the Decalogue. Kline also finds that faithful loyal love of the vassal to the suzerain is the key ethic in ANE covenants. He says of the basic ethos in the covenant relationship, "the fundamental demand is always for thorough commitment to the suzerain to the exclusion of all alien alliances."[208] As with other authors considered above, Kline also writes of the fundamental motivation of the covenants which is *loving gratitude* to the gracious covenant Lord.[209]

In George Mendenhall's[210] early and influential work on the relationship of ANE treaty documents and biblical covenants, he pointed out some of the relational dynamics of those covenants. In the Israelite RCC, the Decalogue was not "law." Rather, it gave the covenant community the fundamental relational core or worldview principles of that culture regarding its relationship with God, first vertically and secondly horizontally with others in that community.[211] Later, specific "laws" were given by God through Moses that had their foundation in the Decalogue. For instance, the "Covenant Code" (i.e., Book of the Covenant) that comes after the first giving of the Decalogue in Exodus 21-23, is built on the foundational relational moral principles of the Decalogue. He writes, "We conclude that the morality and policy described in the Decalogue is certainly familiar and lies at the basis of the Covenant Code, but there is no slavish copying of the words of the Decalogue."[212] Many followed Mendenhall in rightly stating that *trust* and *obedience* were fundamental relational responses in the covenant relationship.[213] And, as many other authors confirmed after Mendenhall's work, "perpetual gratitude" to the gracious covenant Lord was the fundamental motivation for obedience in the covenant.[214]

---

[207] Meredith G. Kline, *Treaty of the Great King: The Covenant Structure of Deuteronomy: Studies and Commentary* (Grand Rapids, MI: William B. Eerdmans, 1963), 14.
[208] Kline, 14.
[209] Kline, 26.
[210] George E. Mendenhall (1916-2016) was a Bible scholar. He taught in the Department of Near Eastern Studies at the University of Michigan.
[211] George E. Mendenhall, *Law and Covenant in Israel and the Ancient near East* (Pittsburgh: The Biblical Colloquium, 1955), 5.
[212] Mendenhall, 16.
[213] Mendenhall, 30.
[214] Mendenhall, 32.

Max Stackhouse,[215] like Allen above, finds the framework for ethics in the biblical covenants. The author points out there are many cross-cultural references to covenants. This is significant for ethics, as it moves us toward the framework for universal ethical standards. He states, "in the very structure of human relationships we find traces of what God has graciously revealed to humanity in the fabric of creation."[216] He further underscores the essential covenantal nature of God's relationship to humankind when he writes, "[T]he primal relationship of God to humanity is covenantal, and the cosmic story of salvation is to be told in terms of the covenant of God with Adam, broken in the Fall, and the redemptive covenant of God with the second Adam, Christ, who points toward the promised covenant of a new heaven and new earth, a New Jerusalem, where all is perfected."[217]

Related to this theme of the covenants are two important relational frameworks. Each acknowledges the priority of the lordship of God in the relationship between God and his people. These two frameworks are Covenantal Triperspectivalism and the Relational Paradigm.

Covenantal Triperspectivalism

In each of the volumes in his impressive and important "Lordship Series," John Frame takes the time to describe a very important structural aspect found in every biblical covenantal relationship.[218] In each of God's sovereignly established covenants, he is the *Lord*. God exercises his covenantal lordship via the "lordship attributes" of *control*, *authority*, and *presence*. Frame primarily seeks to demonstrate this covenantal triad in a close study of the covenant name, *Yahweh*, and its usage. He then matches these "lordship attributes" to three ethical "perspectives," namely, *situational* (control), *normative* (authority), and *existential* (presence). Because this "triperspectival" scheme is based on the biblical covenants' concept of lordship, Frame has also called this framework "covenantal ethics."[219] Frame finds this triad clearly reflected in various passages. For instance, these attributes can be seen in Exodus 20:1-23:33, a very important passage for the

---

[215] Max L. Stackhouse (1935-2016) was an expert in biblical ethics and social life. He was the first director of Princeton Theological Seminary's Abraham Kuyper Center for Public Theology.

[216] Max L. Stackhouse, *Covenant and Commitments: Faith, Family, and Economic Life* (Louisville: Westminster John Knox Press, 1997), 144.

[217] Stackhouse, 150.

[218] Frame, *The Doctrine of the Knowledge of God*, 15-18; John M. Frame, *The Doctrine of God*, 4 vols., A Theology of Lordship, vol. 2 (Phillipsburg: P&R Publishing, 2002), 40-42; Frame, *The Doctrine of the Christian Life*, 21-24; John M. Frame, *The Doctrine of the Word of God*, 4 vols., A Theology of Lordship, vol. 4 (Phillipsburg: P&R Publishing, 2010), 10-11.

[219] John M. Frame, "Pastoral and Social Ethics," (Charlotte, NC: Reformed Theological Seminary-Virtual Campus, 2008), 9.

establishment of the Mosaic covenant which includes the Ten Commandments and the "Book of the Covenant."[220] Meredith Kline believes the Decalogue has the form of an ANE "suzerainty treaty."[221] If we include the Book of the Covenant, we can see the complete triad of covenantal lordship attributes.[222]

- **Control**. As Frame explains, God's covenant *control* means he makes all things happen in time and space. For instance, Exodus 20:2, the Lord summarizes his *covenant control* over all the redemptive-historical events that took places in his saving of his covenant people Israel out of Egypt. Frame abstracts this lordship attribute of control into the philosophical principle he calls the *situational perspective.*
- **Authority**. God's covenant *authority* means he has the right to be obeyed and thus stipulates the conditions of covenantal blessings and curses. For example, in Exodus 20:3-17, 20:22-26, 21:1-23:9, 23:10-19, the Lord exercises his *covenant authority* by giving them his basic moral, civil, and ceremonial law. The Lord shows his authority by his word. Frame abstracts this lordship attribute of authority into the philosophical principle he calls the *normative perspective.*
- **Presence**. God's covenant *presence* means God is personally with his covenant people to control history and to dispense his blessing and even curses. For instance, in Exodus 23:20-33, the Lord promises his *covenant presence* would be *experienced* by his people when his "Angel" would assure and strengthen them through the wilderness and into Canaan. Frame abstracts this lordship attribute of presence into the philosophical principle he calls the *existential perspective.*

As we proceed in this book, we will particularly focus on the covenantal attribute of God's *presence* with his people. As we will see, the Lord has always meant his presence to have an assuring and motivating power over his people.

Frame places *motives* under the *existential* category because motives often deal with internal subjective emotions, desires, and impulses that incite one to action.[223] He rightly concludes that in the Scriptures motives and Christian *virtues* are closely aligned. For instance, the key virtues of faith, hope, and love are all seen in the Scriptures as powerful motives for the Christian life. Faith was the motive that compelled Abraham to obey God (Gen. 12:1-4, 15:6; Rom. 4:3). Hope of being right with God now and in the future makes Paul bold in proclaiming the gospel (2 Cor. 3:12). Love should be the core motive for all our Christian good works according to Paul (1 Cor. 13:1-3).

---

[220] Exod. 20:22-23:33. Moses in Exod. 24:7 actually uses this phrase to describe this passage.
[221] Frame, *The Doctrine of God*, 31.
[222] Frame, *The Doctrine of God*, 94-95.
[223] Frame, *The Doctrine of the Christian Life*, 324.

However, Frame correctly qualifies his categorizing of motives under the *existential* heading by saying "the three perspectives overlap."[224] That is, in the Scriptures, factors that are *normative* like the commands of God or factors that are *situational* like God's works in providence can and do also serve as *motivational stimuli* for God's people. Additionally, it appears that the Triune God sometimes *simultaneously uses a mixture of motivational stimuli* to move his people to action. For instance, we can again look at Exodus 20-23 where Jehovah simultaneously uses a mixture of normative, situational, and existential motivational stimuli to arouse the right motivational responses and actions in his people.

Relational Paradigm

Enoch Wan's "relational paradigm" is an alternative ontological view (i.e., a fundamental theory of our being) and epistemological view (i.e., a fundamental theory of knowledge, or how humans can know things) that is based on the *vertical* and *horizontal* relationships between God and his created order.[225] It is offered as a better Christian alternative to "critical realism." [226] Ontologically, the relational paradigm underscores that God is triune, and therefore the inherent "key relational elements"[227] of the Godhead's nature have great ramification to the reality he created in his universe. He created creatures at various levels of his creation (i.e., angelic, human, animal world) that are capable of having personal relationships. As Wan puts it, "Ontologically, 'relational realism' is to be defined as 'the systematic understanding that "reality" is primarily based on the "vertical relationship" between God and the created order and secondarily "horizontal relationship" within the created order.'"[228] Epistemologically, the relational paradigm shows that knowledge of reality is also dependent relationally upon God. Humans need the ability to grasp reality as well as information about reality, and these too come from the Creator-creature relationship. The Relational Paradigm also stresses the primacy of the vertical relationship between God and humans before horizontal relationships between humans.

On this last point, other authors have observed from the Scriptures a similar notion about the primacy of the vertical relationship over the horizontal. For instance, above we have already mentioned the comments of Block and Breen. Additionally, Gentry and Wellum researched Genesis 1:26

---

[224] Frame, *The Doctrine of the Christian Life*, 324.
[225] Wan, "The Paradigm of 'Relational Realism,'" 1.
[226] Wan, "The Paradigm of 'Relational Realism,'" 2.
[227] Wan and Hedinger, 26-28. Some of those relational elements seen in the Trinity are personal, love, faithfulness, righteousness, perichorisis (i.e., the interaction and interpenetration of the Persons), polyphony (the Persons sharing of the spotlight without being totally diminished), equality yet diversity, hierarchy and submission, etc.
[228] Wan, "The Paradigm of 'Relational Realism'," 1.

regarding the meaning of humankind being in the "image" of God. Based on literary and cultural reasons, they understand this phrase as meaning faithful loyal relationship vertically to God, then horizontally to humankind. They believe it can be understood in a relational-covenantal way.[229] Gentry and Wellum are also convinced that Genesis 1:26 shows vertical and horizontal relationships are established, and they are both covenantal. The vertical relationship is "sonship," and the horizontal relationship is "servant kingship."[230]

A covenantal connection

We believe the Relational Paradigm is also covenantal in nature. We see at least two reasons for this assertion. First, *the Creator-creation distinction automatically puts all humankind in a basic covenantal relationship with the Trinity*. Sometimes this covenant has been called the "covenant of creation," the "covenant of works," as well as other labels. In Berkhof's *Systematic Theology,* he says that studying humankind "would not be complete without considering the mutual relationship between God and man, and especially the origin and nature of the religious life of man. That life was rooted in a covenant...variously known as the covenant of nature, the covenant of life, the Edenic covenant, and the covenant of works."[231] Frame also concurs with this when he writes:

> In a broad sense, all of God's dealings with creation are covenantal in character. Meredith Kline and others have observed that the creation narrative in Genesis 1 and 2 is parallel in important respects to other narratives that describe the establishment of covenants. During the creation week, all things, plants, animals, and persons are appointed to be covenant servants, to obey God's law, and to be instruments...of His gracious purpose. Thus everything and everybody is in covenant with God (cf. Isa. 24:5: all the "inhabitants of the earth" have broken the "everlasting covenant"). *The Creator-creature relation is a covenant relation, a Lord-servant relation* [italics ours].[232]

Therefore, the fundamental relational dynamics the Relational Paradigm identifies between God and man can also be said to be covenantal.

The second reason we believe the Relational Paradigm is a relational-covenantal model is because its principle of the primacy of the vertical relationship with God and secondary nature of horizontal relationships is related to the principle of the historical divine covenants of primarily loving

---

[229] Gentry and Wellum, Kindle locations 4565-4578.
[230] Gentry and Wellum, Kindle locations 4672-4690.
[231] Berkhof, 211.
[232] Frame, *The Doctrine of the Knowledge of God*, 12-13.

God and secondarily loving others. In the covenant-saturated content of Deuteronomy 6:4-6, the Shema states the fundamental ethic of the covenant – supreme love to the Lord, unrivaled loving commitment to the Lord in "allegiance, action, and affection" are primary.[233] Jesus in Matthew 22:36-40 answered the man in a way consistent with the divine covenants when he said the supreme ethical commands were love to God first and love to others next. Therefore, once again we are convinced that we can cast the Relational Paradigm in a covenantal light. This paradigm points out the primary relational importance of the vertical relationship between God and his covenant people. This is followed by the critical yet secondary relational importance of the horizontal relationships his people have with others. This is a significant RCC dynamic.

For the purposes of this book, to say that the Relational Paradigm is associated with relational-covenantal dynamics helps our assertion that we can integrate it with the other relational-covenantal model – Covenantal Triperspectivalism. This is an important integration for our study.

Another important RCC dynamic that the Relational Paradigm contains is, according to ANE treaty forms, the vertical relational stimuli like the covenant Lord's attitude and acts of abundant lovingkindness and mercy to the vassal will always affect the vassal's motives in his/her horizontal relationships. For instance, in the Decalogue, the historic prologue emphasizes the vertical blessings from the Lord to his people, and the first commandment underscores the vertical primary allegiance the vassal must have to the Lord. These vertical relational dynamics were meant to motivate the people's obedience in all the subsequent vertical and horizontal relational stipulations. According to Block and Mendenhall, the Decalogue is a crucially fundamental part of the biblical RCC worldview which requires firstly, vertical supreme gratitude and loving loyalty to God for his grace in redeeming us, and secondly, horizontal love to others. Other aspects of Israelite RCC (like law) grew up around this core worldview.[234] Another example of this RCC dynamic is seen in the NC in the structure of the Book of Ephesians.[235] In chapters 1-3, Paul lays out the tremendous vertical blessings God through Jesus gives to Christians. Then, in chapters 4-6 he describes the many ethical vertical and horizontal responsibilities of Christians. According to Paul, the vertical covenantal blessings will and should also motivate our vertical and horizontal motives and actions.

---

[233] Frame, *The Doctrine of the Christian Life*, 192-193.
[234] Daniel I. Block, "Reading the Decalogue Right to Left: The Ten Principles of Covenant Relationship in the Hebrew Bible," in *How I Love Your Torah, O LORD!: Studies in the Book of Deuteronomy* (Eugene, OR: Cascade Books, 2011), 46; Mendenhall, 5, 16.
[235] David Eckman, 神的接纳与我的感恩 *(Acceptance and Gratitude)*, Disc 1, BC101 Spiritual Life Formation (Pleasanton, CA: Becoming What God Intended Ministries), DVD.

Other Covenantal Truths

Structure of biblical covenants

The divine covenants of God not only structure redemptive history and the Scriptures, they also structure a believers' relationship with God and their Christian life.[236] Because "God entered into covenant commitments with men, and from beginning to end covenants encompassed and circumscribed the divine-relationships,"[237] and because the Christian life is to be seen as a relationship with God under the NC,[238] *therefore we can expect the covenant structure of a Christian's relationship with God to affect his assurance and motivation.*[239]

The *literary structure* of the ANE Hittite suzerain-vassal treaties have great similarity to the biblical covenants. Their structure is generally as follows:[240]

1. Name of the great Lord (preamble)
2. Historical prologue
3. Stipulations
4. Sanctions (blessings and curses)
5. Administration (use of the covenant and its continuity)

These covenants fundamentally establish a special relationship between the suzerain or Lord and the vassals or servants.

God used the ANE Hittite treaty forms and basic culture to fashion his specific RCC with his people.[241] There are several things in the RCC that are particularly relevant to our study. First, the "preamble" of an ANE covenant document *identifies* the suzerain/father figure and his greatness, and was "calculated to inspire awe and fear."[242] It also served to underscore the

---

[236] McKay, 9-10; Nichols, 1; Golding, 9; Robertson, vii.

[237] John R. Von Rohr, "Covenant and Assurance in Early English Puritanism," *Church History* 34, no. 2 (1965): 195.

[238] Luke 22:20; 2 Cor. 3:6; and Heb. 8:7-13

[239] Joel R. Beeke, *Puritan Reformed Spirituality* (Grand Rapids: Reformation Heritage Books, 2004), 296. English Puritan theologians as well as theologians of the Dutch Second Reformation, both believed "assurance is covenantally based...." In a subsequent section, we will explore more fully the important bearing covenants have upon assurance and motivation.

[240] Frame, *The Doctrine of the Christian Life*, 20-21, 401; Tremper Longman III and Raymond B. Dillard, *An Introduction to the Old Testament* (Grand Rapids, Mich.: Zondervan, 2006), 110; Nichols, 98-99; J. Ligon Duncan, "Systematic Theology III," (Charlotte, NC: Reformed Theological Seminary-Virtual Campus, 2003), 2-33.

[241] Allen, 15-81; Block, *How I Love Your Torah, O Lord!: Studies in the Book of Deuteronomy*, 21-55; Breen, 178-182; Gentry and Wellum, Kindle locations 13891-19022; Kline, 47-118; Meredith G. Kline, *The Structure of Biblical Authority*, 2nd; Google Books ed. (Eugene, OR: Wipf and Stock Publishers, 1997), 76-112; Mendenhall, 3-50.

[242] Kline, *Treaty of the Great King: The Covenant Structure of Deuteronomy: Studies and Commentary*, 14; Mendenhall, 32.

fundamental suzerain-vassal relationship, or in more familiar terms father-son relationship, that was established. These *identities* of the suzerain and vassal clearly imply the vassal's need to have ultimate allegiance and obedience to the covenant Lord.

Second, the covenant documents in the Bible (e.g., Mosaic in Exod. 19-23; the Decalogue of Exod. 20 and Deut. 5; all of Deuteronomy) also have "historic prologues" like other ANE treaties. The historic prologues recount the benevolent involvement of the suzerain towards the vassal. These prologues emphasize the critical importance of the *loyal covenant love* of the sovereign to the vassal as well as the obligation of *reciprocal love and gratitude* from the vassal. *This two-directional flow of covenant love between the Lord and servant is central to the relational dynamics in ANE covenants.* Significantly, Mendenhall considers the historic fact of the suzerain's grace towards the vassal as the *primary motivator for obedience in ANE covenants*. He writes, "We have seen that the historical prologue furnishes the foundation of obligation and the *motivation* [italics ours] for accepting the stipulations of the covenant as binding."[243]

Kline sums it up well:

> The comprehensiveness of Jesus' "first and great commandment" is evident from the preamble and historic prologue of the covenant document. Being introductory to the whole body of stipulations which follow, they are manifestly intended to inculcate the proper *motivation* [italics ours] for obedience not to three or four or five of the stipulations but to them all; and the *motivation* [italics ours] they inspirit is that of love to the Redeemer.[244]

Mendenhall writes:

> This section of the treaty is not mere embroidery, but a most important element, for, as Korosec says: "What the description amounts to is this, that the vassal is obligated to *perpetual gratitude* [italics ours] toward the great king because of the benevolence, consideration, and favor which he has already received. Immediately following this, the devotion of the vassal to the great king is expressed as a logical consequence."[245]

---

[243] Mendenhall, 32.
[244] Kline, *Treaty of the Great King: The Covenant Structure of Deuteronomy: Studies and Commentary*, 26.
[245] Mendenhall, 32.

Third, the "sanctions" section of the covenant document often contained "curses and blessings,"[246] or as in the case of the Decalogue (see Exod. 20:5, 6, 7, 11, and 12), they were "interspersed" in the document.[247] This section was meant to serve as both positive and negative *motivational stimuli* for the vassal.[248]

Another extremely important overarching "structure" (here we do *not* mean a "literary structure" but a fundamental aspect) in a biblical covenant is God's revealed covenant name, *Yahweh* (Exod. 3:13-14).[249] This name first of all shows the *personal* nature of the covenants he establishes.

These basic covenantal structures tell us that biblical covenants are about establishing and guiding a *personal relationship* between God and his people. *Our investigation of motivations for mission from a covenantal perspective is relational by nature. Therefore, in order to understand it biblically we must consider this phenomenon under the light of the covenants which give form to the relationship between God and his people.*

As an aside, the basic structure of *all* God-to-human (vertical) and human-to-human (horizontal) relationships is covenantal.[250] So the biblical covenants are fundamental in understanding vertical and horizontal relational dynamics, in general. Allen, having this covenant-oriented view of all relationships, believes it gives him a foundational framework for human ethics and Christian ethics in particular.[251]

Responses in biblical covenants

Another general feature of the biblical covenants we want to mention is that of the *proper human responses to the covenants.* Throughout redemptive history, we see the Lord blessing his covenant people if they have *two* very important responses. The first is dependent *faith*. The second is submissive *obedience*.[252] These are the expected responses the vassal/son is supposed to have towards the suzerain/father who himself has proven to have and

---

[246] Kline, *Treaty of the Great King: The Covenant Structure of Deuteronomy: Studies and Commentary*, 16; Mendenhall, 34.

[247] Kline, *Treaty of the Great King: The Covenant Structure of Deuteronomy: Studies and Commentary*, 16.

[248] Block, *How I Love Your Torah, O Lord!: Studies in the Book of Deuteronomy*, 34; Gentry and Wellum, Kindle locations 3592-3600; Kline, *Treaty of the Great King: The Covenant Structure of Deuteronomy: Studies and Commentary*, 16, 34, 78-79.

[249] Frame, *The Doctrine of the Christian Life*, 20, 402.

[250] Gentry and Wellum, Kindle locations 3826-3845.

[251] Joseph L. Allen, "A Covenantal Model of the Moral Life," in *Love and Conflict: A Covenantal Model of Christian Ethics* (Nashville: Abingdon Press, 1984), 46-48.

[252] William Ames was perhaps the first pioneering Reformed Puritan scholar that highlighted *faith* and *obedience* ("observance") as crucial covenantal responses that summed up Christian theology and life. See William Ames, *The Marrow of Theology*, ed. John D. Eusden (Grand Rapids, MI: Baker Books, 1997), 79-80; Beeke, 133-138.

demonstrated *"faithful loyal love"* towards the vassal/son.[253] Or as the hymn writer well said, "trust and obey."[254] Frame, consistent with his triperspectivalism, rightly adds a third – *worship.* He writes, "Three lordship attributes, three mandatory responses: faith, obedience, worship. These responses are the foundation of our ethical life."[255]

Faith

The response of *faith* to the Lord corresponds to his lordship attribute of *control.* At the very core of all God's covenants are his sovereign and *personal promises* to establish a covenant relationship with individuals, to bless compliance to his stipulations, and to curse non-compliance. Because *promise* is so central to the meaning of covenants,[256] thus *faith* is the proper counterpart to those gracious promises. Commenting on the importance of faith in the covenant life, Berkhof says the following, "It is only through faith that we can obtain a *conscious enjoyment* of the blessings of the covenant. Our experimental knowledge of the covenant life is entirely dependent on the exercise of *faith* [italics ours]. He who does not live a life of faith is, *as far as this consciousness is concerned*, practically outside of the covenant."[257] Mendenhall, in commenting upon the special relationship between the suzerain and the vassal in ANE covenants, said, "the vassal's obligation to trust in the benevolence of the sovereign" was a key response expected of the vassal.[258]

From Adam down to today, for humans to live in a happy covenant relationship with God requires *trust* in God and his promises as well as his warnings. In Genesis 3, when Adam and Eve disbelieved God's warning, they severely marred their covenant relationship with God. Contrariwise, Genesis 15:6 tells us that when Abraham believed, God "accounted it to him for righteousness." And so it is today, all who have faith in the gospel will experience the NC gospel blessings (Gal. 3:8-9). The requirement of faith/trust in the Lord is inextricably woven into the fabric of his covenants.

Obedience as love

The response of *obedience* to the Lord corresponds to his lordship attribute of *authority.* The Lord's covenants not only require dependent faith

---

[253] Gentry and Wellum, Kindle locations 3319-3419, 4705-4716, 5016-5027; Mendenhall, 30.
[254] *Trinity Hymnal*, (Philadelphia: Great Commission Publications, 1961; reprint, 1982), Hymn 700.
[255] Frame, *The Doctrine of the Christian Life*, 26.
[256] Nichols, 117; McKay, 11; Murray, *The Covenant of Grace*, 29.
[257] Berkhof, 280.
[258] Mendenhall, 30.

of the participants of the covenant, they also require *submissive obedience*.[259] As God is the suzerain in the covenant, so all those who enter into a covenant relationship with him must wholeheartedly obey him. In ANE covenants and in the biblical covenants like the OC, this covenant loyalty or allegiance is known as *love*.[260] The first stipulation in the ANE covenants often emphasized the need for the covenant servant to show supreme obedience or love to the suzerain. As we mentioned above, this reciprocal faithful loyal love is central to the RCC dynamics in the Bible. As we wrote earlier, the insight from Breen that our vertical relational "identity" with God must always come first and motivates our "obedience."[261] In the OC, this is exactly what we have in the first commandment in Exodus 20:3. After Moses' restatement of the Decalogue in Deuteronomy 5, he goes on in Deuteronomy 6:5 to summarize the essence of a proper response to God's law, "You shall love the LORD your God with all your heart and with all your soul and with all your might."

Gentry and Wellum do a study of an important Hebrew word pair that is at the heart of the covenant relational dynamics. The words are *hesed* and *emet*. From this study, they emphasize that a vassal's obedience in the covenant relationship should not be cold, perfunctory. Rather, it should be warm-hearted "faithful loyal love." In this phrase, Gentry and Wellum combine the meaning of the two Hebrew words. This lies at the heart of the covenant relationship.[262] We should note as well that in the covenant relationship, both the sovereign and the vassal are to be characterized by these words. In the RCC, there is expected a reciprocal relationship of the flow of faithful loyal love. The suzerain should show faithful loyal love to the vassal, and the vassal should do the same to the suzerain in return. Vine says this about *hesed*:

> In general, one may identify three basic meanings of the word, which always interact: "strength," "steadfastness," and "love." Any understanding of the word that fails to suggest all three inevitably loses some of its richness. "Love" by itself easily becomes sentimentalized or universalized

---

[259] By mentioning the importance of obedience in the divine covenants, we are *not* advocating a system of works salvation. Being Protestant and Reformed in our soteriology, we believe salvation, in OT and NT, has always been by God's grace through faith (see WCF 12.6). In this book, we discuss the importance of obedience in the covenants from the perspective of people *already in the covenant*. Whether in the OC or NC, the on-going obedience of God's covenant people was important to the existential enjoyment of covenant fellowship with their God. See also Mendenhall, 30.

[260] Frame, *The Doctrine of the Christian Life*, 192ff, 332ff.

[261] Breen, 178ff.

[262] Gentry and Wellum, Kindle locations 3307-3417. In this book, have already used this phrase several times. We have borrowed it from Gentry and Wellum.

apart from the covenant. Yet "strength" or "steadfastness" suggests only the fulfillment of a legal or other obligation.[263]

Genesis 24 is a specimen text to show the importance of faithful loyal love in the RCC. In that passage, Abraham makes a little covenant between him and his servant. It is highly significant to pay close attention to what motivated this servant who apparently knew well the things that ought to *motivate* him in this covenant he had with his master Abraham. The servant's overriding motivation was "covenant loyalty."[264] It is that combination of *hesed* and *emet* which Gentry and Wellum call "faithful loyal love" that motivated this servant.[265] By his actions, it is evident that the servant wanted to demonstrate faithful loyal love to his master Abraham. By his prayers to God, the servant desired the covenant God of Abraham to also show his master faithful loyal love.[266] By his request to Laban, the servant also desired this relative of Abraham to show his master faithful loyal love.[267]

Kline has demonstrated that the book of Deuteronomy has the structural form of an ANE covenant.[268] Moses in that book, *equates love with obedience.* That is, in the RCC love on the part of the vassal toward the suzerain displays itself as wholehearted obedience to him. Akin and co-authors have said:

> The command for God's people to love God with all their heart, soul, and mind begins with God's love for them. In this instance, God's love for his people surfaces from the *covenant context of his command* [italics ours]. By quoting from Deuteronomy, Jesus places his command in the context of God's *covenant with his people* [italics ours]. Deuteronomy is introduced as a *covenantal document* [italics ours] that recounts God's acts for and requirements of his people.[269]

A final point before we leave this important topic of obedience, is a point we have made before, yet it bears repeating. In the RCC, the covenant people's vertical *identity* should always precede and motivate their obedience.[270] They

---

[263] *Vine's Complete Expository Dictionary of Old and New Testament Words,* s.v. "Loving Kindness."

[264] See vv. 9, 12, 14, 27, 48, 49. John F. Walvoord and Roy B. Zuck, *The Bible Knowledge Commentary: An Exposition of the Scriptures,* Logos ed. (Wheaton, IL: Victor Books, 1985), 68.

[265] See above explanation of how Gentry and Wellum talk about this.

[266] See vv. 12-14, 27. The Hebrew important words *hesed* and *emet* are there in v. 27.

[267] See vv. 49. Again, the Hebrew important words *hesed* and *emet* are present

[268] Kline, *Treaty of the Great King: The Covenant Structure of Deuteronomy: Studies and Commentary,* 27-46.

[269] Daniel L. Akin, Benjamin L. Merkle, and George G. Robinson, *40 Questions About the Great Commission,* ed. Benjamin L. Merkle, 40 Questions Series (Grand Rapids, MI: Kregel Academic, 2020), 38.

[270] Breen, 178ff.

have a rich and multi-faceted identity. They are covenant servants of a sovereign. They are also covenant sons of a father.

As we will see, these covenant responses of *faith* and *obedience* are crucial elements of our covenant relationship with God in order to experience his assuring presence. And this presence, as we will see, is a biblical element in Christian spirituality that spontaneously stirs zeal for mission.

Worship

The response of *worship* to the Lord corresponds to his lordship attribute of *presence.* Throughout the Scriptures, when the Lord's presence was powerfully experienced, it resulted in his people bowing and worshipping him. In Exodus 3, Moses bowed down in worship before the Lord's presence in the burning bush. In Isaiah 6:1-5, Isaiah displays a worshipful attitude toward God who is "holy, holy, holy." And we can remember John's experience and worship when he wrote in Revelation 1:17, "And when I saw Him, I fell at His feet as though dead."[271]

Spirituality of biblical covenants

Another covenant-based truth we need for our analysis is in the various aspects of covenant *spirituality* found in the Bible. In particular, we limit our consideration to what the divine covenants show regarding *communion, motivation,* and *assurance.* As with the other truths we have considered thus far, we will use this truth in the next major section to analyze Paul's experience of missionary zeal. However first, we would like to briefly review some important literature regarding spirituality.

In studying literature on *spirituality,*[272] we consulted classic Reformed masters of the inner life such as John Calvin, John Owen, Thomas Brooks, Thomas Vincent, and Jonathan Edwards. Though we realize that in Church history Roman Catholics have a very developed concept of spirituality,[273] yet we deliberately focused on Evangelical and Reformed authors. Calvin's[274] *Institutes* was his *magnum opus*. It became one of the most influential books of the Reformation. Along with his clear systematic thinking on theological issues, Calvin wrote with a clear pastoral emphasis. His insights on the Holy

---

[271] Frame, *The Doctrine of the Christian Life*, 26.
[272] We earlier defined the term *spirituality* as a deep relationship with God.
[273] Richard F. Lovelace, *Dynamics of Spiritual Life: An Evangelical Theology of Renewal* (Downers Grove: InterVarsity Press, 1979), 11.
[274] John Calvin (1509-1564) was a French Protestant Reformer. Some believe next to Martin Luther, Calvin was the most influential Protestant Reformer. His book, *Institutes of the Christian Religion*, was highly influential. He is credited as beginning the second branch of the Protestant Reformation known as the "Reformed" tradition.

Spirit and the Christian spiritual life are very valuable.[275] Owen's[276] work is a classic Puritan treatment of Christian spiritual communion or fellowship with God.[277] Owen makes his launching-off text 1 John 1:3. Taking a major clue from the text, he uses a Trinitarian framework to understand this topic. Brooks'[278] work is one of the best examples of a strong stream in Puritan theology to see the legitimacy of an experiential sense of assurance in the Christian life.[279] Vincent gives a warm Puritan treatment of the blessed topic of communion with God.[280] In particular, in systematic theological terms, he analyzes the topic of a sensed assurance of salvation in the believer's life. In Edwards'[281] important sermon on the "divine light," he seeks to understand and describe the nature of religious experience.[282] He places a remarkably high value in the Christian life on sensible and biblical experiences of the soul given by God.

Additionally, we consulted more recent writings by Reformed and other evangelically conservative authors on the topic of spirituality. Arthur Pink's[283] work is a systematic look at the very important doctrine of union with Christ and the corresponding experience of communion with Christ.[284] Following in the footsteps of his Reformed-Puritan predecessors, Pink is thorough and experiential in his analysis. Francis Schaeffer's[285] classic work on spirituality was born out of his disillusionment with the failures of his past Reformed

---

[275] John Calvin, *Christianae Religionis Institutio (Institutes of the Christian Religion)*, ed. John T. McNeill, trans., Ford Lewis Battles, 2 vols., The Library of Christian Classics, vol. 1 (1559; reprint, Louisville, KY: Westminster John Knox Press, 2006), Book Three.

[276] John Owen (1616-1683) was an English Puritan and leading theologian of the Congregational Church. He was prolific and very influential in his writings.

[277] John Owen, *Communion with God: Abridged and Made Easy to Read by R.J.K. Law*, Puritan Paperbacks (Edinburgh: Banner of Truth, 2000), 1-209.

[278] Thomas Brooks (1608-1680) was an influential English Puritan pastor and writer.

[279] Thomas Brooks, *Heaven on Earth* (1654; reprint, Carlisle, PA: Banner of Truth Trust, 2008), 14-320.

[280] Thomas Vincent, *The True Christian's Love to the Unseen Christ* (reprint, Morgan, PA: Soli Deo Gloria Publications, 1994), 1-127.

[281] Jonathan Edwards (1703-1758) was an American colonial Congregational minister and theologian. He was also a missionary to the Indians of Massachusetts. He was the third president of the College of New Jersey (later Princeton University). He is often regarded as one of America's finest theologian philosophers.

[282] Jonathan Edwards, "A Divine and Supernatural Light Immediately Imparted to the Soul, by the Spirit of God, Shown to Be Both a Scriptural and Rational Doctrine," in *The Works of Jonathan Edwards, Ultimate Christian Library* [DVD] (Rio, WI: AGES Software, 2000), 585-603.

[283] Arthur W. Pink (1886-1952) was an English Bible teacher and writer who was influential in his writing to renew popular interest in Calvinism and Reformed theology.

[284] Arthur W. Pink, *Spiritual Union and Communion* (Lafayette, IN: Sovereign Grace Publishers, Inc., 2002), 7-160.

[285] Francis A. Schaeffer (1912–1984) was an American evangelical Presbyterian missionary to Europe, philosopher, author, and lecturer.

scholasticism.[286] This is Schaeffer's recording of the discoveries he made about a more biblical view of the Christian life. Frequently Schaeffer emphasizes that true Christian spirituality is primarily about entering into, maintaining, and cultivating a personal relationship with a personal God through the person and work of Christ, in the power of the Spirit, and by a "moment-by-moment" faith in Jesus. J. I. Packer's[287] work, coming from a historically Reformed and conservative viewpoint, takes a fresh biblical and historical look at the operations of the Holy Spirit in the Christian life. He charts a middle course finding truth and error (or imbalance?) in both Reformed and Charismatic/Pentecostal systems of sanctification and pneumatology.[288] Joel Beeke's[289] work on spirituality is a sweeping view of a topic that was very dear to the Reformed Puritans.[290] Beeke helps his readers to see the many biblical discoveries (e.g., assurance, covenants, meditation, etc.) the Puritans made in seeking to understand and enjoy a biblical relationship with God. Chan, as an expert in Puritan theology, sought in his work to do three things.[291] First, he wanted to show "spiritual theology" goes between "systematic theology" and "practical theology." Second, he developed a three-sided biblical spiritual theological framework (i.e., global-contextual, evangelical, and charismatic) that will give shape to "spirituality." And third, Chan then applied his "ascetical"[292] form of Christian spirituality.

Another more contemporary conservative evangelical work on spirituality that has become a standard is Richard Lovelace's[293] book.[294] It is a seminal evangelical work on "spiritual theology." With a clear eye to biblical and historical contours on spiritual renewal, Lovelace sees an "in Christ"-based or a gospel-based framework to understand a true Christian spirituality. Lovelace attempts to define something akin to a comprehensive "unified field

---

[286] Francis A. Schaeffer, *True Spirituality* (Wheaton: Tyndale House Publishers, 1971; reprint, Carol Stream: Tyndale House Publishers, 2001), 3-158.

[287] J. I. Packer is an English-born Canadian evangelical theologian and writer in the Reformed tradition. He is Professor of Theology at Regent College and author of numerous books such as *Knowing God*.

[288] Packer, 19-226.

[289] Joel R. Beeke is an American Reformed pastor and theologian. He is President of Puritan Reformed Theological Seminary where he also lectures in theology and homiletics. He is also an expert on the Puritans.

[290] Beeke, 1-443.

[291] Simon Chan, *Spiritual Theology: A Systematic Study of the Christian Life* (Downers Grove, IL: InterVarsity Press, 1998), 15-239.

[292] By *ascetical*, Chan means to stress the place of spiritual disciples or exercises for cultivating a Christian's relationship with God.

[293] Richard F. Lovelace was professor of church history at Gordon-Conwell Theological Seminary.

[294] Lovelace, 11-435.

theory of spirituality."[295] A large and ambitious undertaking indeed! This includes both "doctrinal and structural" reformation as well as "spiritual revitalization."[296] With a careful eye on the Scriptures as the final control or governing standard, Lovelace analyzes spiritual renewals or revivals since the Reformation, ever seeking to better understand the God-given "dynamics of the spiritual life." Then, he draws out principles for personal as well as church spiritual renewal.[297]

Using various arguments, Lovelace urges upon his readers an understanding that true, comprehensive, and lasting personal and church renewal must have two sides: doctrinal and structural, as well as Christian experience.[298] If there is one without the other, it leads only to partial revitalization. Then, Lovelace makes a striking application. He says, "A number of problems which have troubled the church in this century are only solvable if we return to the vital core of biblical teaching dealing with Christian experience...."[299] That is to say, simple one-sided doctrinal/structural reformation in the church does not solve these problems. What is needed is to include the cultivation of biblical Christian experience to solve these problems. We believe Lovelace is right and that this insight applies to the problem we research. As we stated earlier, we believe one of the problems the evangelical church continually faces is diminished or sometimes complete lack of motivation for mission. Following Lovelace, it is our speculation that *doctrinal/structural* reformation alone will not solve this problem. Rather, there must also be a revitalization of individual and corporate *Christian experience with the living Christ*. Then, and only then, will there be spontaneous zeal among God's people to carry Christ's gospel to the ends of the earth.

Covenantal communion

The first aspect of covenant spirituality we want to look at is *communion*.

God is personal

God is personal in his covenants because God is personal in his nature. And the fundamental reason God is personal in his nature is because at the heart of his nature is that he is one "substance" or "essence" in three "persons."[300] As Kelly has said, "God is eternally personal."[301] From all eternity

---

[295] Lovelace, 17.
[296] Lovelace, 16.
[297] Lovelace, 18-19.
[298] Lovelace, 16.
[299] Lovelace, 16.
[300] McKay, 39.
[301] Douglas Kelly, "Systematic Theology I," (Charlotte, NC: Reformed Theological Seminary-Virtual Campus, 2003), 40.

the three Persons of the Godhead have enjoyed communion. This is at the essence of God's personal nature. Athanasius, an early Church Father, was certainly correct when he observed that without this inward communion, then neither would God have been able to create or reveal himself outwardly.[302] The God of the Bible, the True and Living One, is not like the imagined Void or "impersonal force" of Eastern Religions. Rather, God is personal, and as a result he relates to his creation in a personal way.[303]

The Bible, especially its historical narratives, reveals God as personal. For instance, in the beginning of the Bible, the Pentateuch, we do not find God revealed to us in cold, abstract, impersonal categories as "omniscient" and "infinite." Rather, we read of God personally communicating with humans in the Garden of Eden. We read of him speaking with Moses at the burning bush and revealing his special name as "I am that I am." Thus, the covenants God establishes with humankind always reflect his personal nature.[304]

Humans are personal

If God establishes personal covenants, then it assumes that the parties with whom he establishes a covenant must be other persons. And indeed, the people God establishes a covenant relationship with are persons made in the "image of God" (Gen. 1:26). Humans, because we are made in the image of the personal God, also have personality. Thus, we are perfectly suited to enter into a personal covenant relationship with God.[305]

Understanding this fundamental identity of humans – image of God – helps us to appreciate the wonderful dignity God has bestowed upon us. God created humankind to enjoy personal and intimate covenant communion with him. There is no greater honor than this for a creature of God.[306]

Broken and restored communion with God

Seeing the wonderful intimacy of this "bond of love"[307] that Adam and Eve enjoyed with God before the Fall, it should shock us that our first parents chose to break this covenant relationship with their Creator. From Genesis 3:15 to the end of Revelation, covenant theology is correct in stating that the key biblical framework to understand God's redemptive activity in history is the covenant. It was this intimate personal covenant relationship that man

---

[302] Herman Bavinck, *Doctrine of God*, trans., William Hendriksen (Grand Rapids: Wm B. Eerdmans Publishing Company, 1951; reprint, Edinburgh, Scotland: The Banner of Truth Trust, 2003), 332.

[303] *The Compact Guide to World Religions*, ed. Dean C. Halverson (Minneapolis: Bethany House Publishers, 1996), 61, 221.

[304] McKay, 30.

[305] Kelly, 14.

[306] McKay, 69.

[307] McKay, 14.

lost with God in the Garden, and this is what God is working to restore to his covenant people all throughout human history.

Well did the Westminster divines summarize in the WSC the "misery of that estate whereinto man fell," namely, "All mankind by their fall lost communion with God...."[308] The greatest loss of humankind in the Garden of Eden was the loss of this personal covenant communion with their personal God.

On the other hand, the Westminster divines also did well to summarize the "benefits which in this life do accompany or flow from justification, adoption and sanctification." Namely, by faith in Christ and repentance of sin, one is restored in his covenant communion with God which includes the biblical experiences of "assurance of God's love, peace of conscience, joy in the Holy Spirit, increase of grace...."[309] These are those aspects the covenant life that the "first Adam" lost for humankind by his fall but the "second Adam," Christ, recovers by his saving work.

God in the Covenant of Grace,[310] and its various gracious phases, begins to restore this communion between himself and his covenant people. This relationship is at the heart of the covenant. David McKay wonderfully expresses this important point when he writes, "God relates to His people person-to-person. To be a child of God is not merely to hold certain intellectual convictions and perform certain religious rituals: it is to know God and be known by Him in a personal way.... *Covenant life entails personal relationships* [italics ours]."[311]

Covenant motto

There is a special phrase that God uses to describe the "heart" of the covenants of promise, *"I will be your God, and you will be my people."* The phrase occurs in the Abrahamic, the Mosaic, the Davidic, and the NC.[312] Below, we will briefly comment on the significance of this phrase in reference to these covenants of promise. It also occurs throughout the Prophets (e.g., Jer.

---

[308] *The Westminster Shorter Catechism*, (The Westminister Assembly, 1647). See Question 19.

[309] *The Westminster Shorter Catechism*. See Question 36.

[310] As Reformed believers we believe in much of what is taught in Reformed "covenant theology." Covenant theology believes that the "Covenant of Grace" is an overarching covenant. God's purpose in it is to bring salvific blessing to humankind through Christ. The explicit historic biblical covenants (e.g., Abraham, Moses, David, and the New Covenant) are "administrations" of the Covenant of Grace and carry forward the accomplishment of God's redemptive goals through Covenant of Grace. Berkhof, 272-283.

[311] McKay, 30.

[312] Robertson, 46.

11:4, 24:7, 30:22, 31:33, 32:38-40; Ezek. 11:20, 14:11, 34:23-25, 30-31, 36:25-28, 37:23, 26-27; Zech. 8:8; etc.) and in the NT (e.g., 2 Cor. 6:16; Rev. 21:3).[313]

Even before the theological fleshing out of "covenant theology" in the seventeenth century, Calvin profoundly noted the significance of the oft-repeated central "formula of the covenant" when he writes, "For the Lord always covenanted with his servants thus: '*I will be your God, and you shall be my people*' [italics ours] (Lev. 26:12). The prophets also commonly explained that life and salvation and the whole of blessedness are embraced in these words."[314] Further, Calvin reflects how the original audience perceived the saving significance of this central covenant promise:

And although nothing further was expressed, they had a clear enough promise of spiritual life in these words: "*I am ... your God*" [italics ours] (Exod. 6:7). For he did not declare that he would be a God to their bodies alone, but especially to their souls. Still, souls, unless they be joined to God through righteousness, remain estranged from him in death. On the other hand, such a union when present will bring everlasting salvation with it.[315]

Other theologians over the years have also commented on the central importance of this oft-repeated covenant promise. Kaiser rightly observes that starting in the Book of Exodus (e.g., Exod. 29:45), God adds a third part to this promise, God would dwell in the midst of his people. So the covenant motto is sometimes seen in the rest of Scripture in a "tripartite formula of promise: '*I will be your God, you shall be my people, and I will dwell in the midst of you*' [italics ours]."[316] Murray called this oft-repeated covenant promise the "central element of the blessing involved in covenant grace."[317] Berkhof called it the "main promise of God" into which all the other gracious promises of God could be subsumed.[318] Kelly has said this is the "central principle" of the Covenant of Grace.[319] McKay wrote that this promise is the "essence of God's covenant." It is the "central covenant promise."[320] Wenham calls it the "covenant formula," the "heart of the covenant."[321]

The phrase varies slightly throughout the Bible, yet the meaning is the same. The meaning of this covenant motto is *a promise to establish and*

---

[313] Berkhof, 277; G. L. Archer, "Covenant," in *Evangelical Dictionary of Theology*, ed. Walter A. Elwell (Grand Rapids: Baker Academic, 2001).
[314] Calvin, 434-435, 2.10.8.
[315] Calvin, 435.
[316] Walter C. Kaiser, *The Christian and the "Old" Testament* (Pasadena: William Carey Library, 1998), 56-57.
[317] Murray, *The Covenant of Grace*, 4.
[318] Berkhof, 277.
[319] Kelly, 146.
[320] McKay, 11, 30.
[321] Gordon J. Wenham, *Word Biblical Commentary : Genesis 16-50*, ed. David A. Hubbard et al., Word Biblical Commentary, vol. 2 (Dallas: Word, Incorporated, 2002), 22.

maintain a whole-hearted, intimate, loving communion between God and his people.[322] Robertson says this oft-used covenant formula communicates an "Immanuel principle"– God will be with his covenant people in an intimate way.[323] Robertson also says it is a fundamental promise for *deep personal union and communion* between God and his people.[324] In commenting on the new additional elements in the Abrahamic covenant compared to the Noahic covenant, Murray said this covenant formula indicated a promise for a covenant "spirituality." His meaning of "spirituality" intended an intimate covenant relationship or "union and communion with the Lord." [325] He says this is the central promise of the covenants. The salvation promised in the covenants had a higher goal, that of restored intimate communion between God and his people.[326]

There were several other related meanings to this oft-repeated covenant motto. God was indicating by this promise to give himself unreservedly to his covenant people, and his people were, out of gratitude, to give themselves back to their gracious covenant God.[327] The phrase indicates a "unique relationship" God would establish and maintain with his covenant people. He would not be the God of other people, rather the personal God of his covenant people. Likewise, his people were to exclusively have Jehovah as their God and not the false gods of the nations.[328]

It will be helpful to briefly trace through some of the major occurrences of this covenant formula as God established various administrations of the Covenant of Grace.[329] In Genesis 17:7, we have the first occurrence of this oft-repeated central promise of the divine covenants. God, in establishing the covenant with Abraham, promised him "to be God to you and your descendants after you." God promised this special relationship would transcend Abraham himself and also apply to all his posterity who entered into covenant with God.

In Exodus 6:3, God mentions to Moses the patriarchs of Israel: Abraham, Isaac, and Jacob. Centuries before, these men had heard this promise of God to establish with them and their posterity a special personal relationship. Now in Exodus 6:6-7 God commands Moses to say to the descendants of the patriarchs, to the people who had been in bondage in Egypt for over four hundred years, that he had not forgotten his promise to take them as his

---

[322] McKay, 11.
[323] Robertson, 46.
[324] Robertson, 293-294.
[325] Murray, *The Covenant of Grace*, 17, 18, 20.
[326] Kelly, 146.
[327] Archer.
[328] *New Bible Commentary: 21st Century Edition*, ed. D. A. Carson et al., 4th ed. (Downers Grove, IL: Inter-Varsity Press, 1994), Comments on Gen. 17:7; Wenham, 22.
[329] Murray, *The Covenant of Grace*, 3-4, 17, 18, 21, 28, 32; Robertson, 46-52.

special people and for him to be their God. In other parts of the Pentateuch, like Leviticus 11:45, 26:12, Deuteronomy 4:20, 29:13, God reiterates this central covenant promise to keep ever before ancient Israel that they were God's special people, and he and they were in a unique and special communion with each other.

In the Davidic covenant in 2 Samuel 7:24 we have another echo of the covenant formula. This time it is David praying to God acknowledging God's main covenant promise, "And you established for yourself your people Israel to be your people forever. And you, O Lord, became their God." An interesting intensification of this covenant communion in familial terms is seen in 7:14 where God says about David's "offspring" (v.12),[330] "I will be to him a father, and he shall be to me a son." God is addressing David here as Israel's representative.[331]

Finally, in the "group of prophesies"[332] in the OT that foretell God's establishment of a "new covenant," we have repeated mention of the covenant motto. Perhaps the most famous reiteration of that main covenant promise is found in Jeremiah 31:33 and its citation in Hebrews 8:10. Murray observes that this last of all the divine covenants also is the covenant *"par excellence"* to bring the full intended realization of the covenant relational promise, "I will be their God, and they shall be My people."[333]

Motivated by love

Another dimension of God's divine covenants that demonstrate their personal relational nature is the very motive of God to enter into covenant with a people. In Deuteronomy 7:7-8 Moses explained God's motives for choosing Israel to be his special covenant people. The motives Moses gives are his *sovereign love* and his *faithfulness* to the covenant given to the patriarchs. Also, in verse 9 we have an example of the oft-repeated association of two words - covenant (*berit*) and "covenant-love" (*hesed*, sometimes translated "lovingkindness" or "mercy").[334] God keeps his covenant out of love to his covenant people. The covenants of God are full of his love for his people.

In the NT, we again see that God's motive for choosing his NC people is also love. In Ephesians 1:4, 5 Paul writes, "even as he chose us in him before the foundation of the world, that we should be holy and blameless before him. In love he predestined us...." Also, in Romans 8:29, 30 Paul writes, "For those whom he foreknew he also predestined...." The word "foreknew" certainly

---

[330] Kaiser, 152. Kaiser says, "This 'seed' is a collective singular word implying both *all who believe* in Messiah and the *one who represents the whole body of believers*: Messiah himself."
[331] Kostenberger and O'Brien, 39.
[332] Robertson, 274.
[333] Murray, *The Covenant of Grace*, 28.
[334] Archer.

means that the omniscient God knew what was going to happen before hand. However, "foreknow" also has a relational meaning. It is synonymous with love.[335]

Covenantal motivational stimuli

The second aspect of covenant spirituality we want to consider is *motivation*. The Scriptures appear to tell us that there are three kinds of *motivational stimuli* to fuel our zeal to rightly respond to God – *redemption, command,* and *presence*.[336] It is very interesting how this three-part covenantal motivational model seems to match the triad of God's covenantal lordship attributes. So *redemption* maps to covenant control, *command* maps to covenant authority, and *presence* maps to covenant presence.[337] Furthermore, these three covenantal stimuli of *redemption, command,* and *presence* have a correspondence with the three key virtues of the Christian life of *hope, faith,* and *love,* respectively. Frame observes, "Faith trusts in God's revealed Word. Hope looks to God's controlling power, which will accomplish his purposes in the future, as in the past. And love treasures the presence of God in the intimate recesses of the heart and the new family into which God has adopted us."[338] Frame also rightly sees these virtues as motives.[339]

Redemption

First, in the covenantal motivational factor of historical *redemption*, God motivates his people to faith and obedience by persuading them to *think about what their covenant God has done and is doing*. That is, they think about what their covenant God has done and is doing in history to fulfill his covenant/gospel in their lives (e.g., redemptive acts, covenant blessings and curses on his people, etc.). They think about his ancient covenants and what he did to fulfill them. The question they answer here is, "What has our covenant God done or is doing in others' lives and in my life to fulfill his

---

[335] McKay, 55-56.

[336] Frame, *The Doctrine of the Christian Life*, 29-31. These three aspects of biblical motivation can be seen in both OC and NC. For instance, in the OC in Exod. 20:1-23:33, God at the end of the passage gives his people the mission to conquer the Promised Land. In the passage, the triad of motivational elements are all present. Also, in the NC in Matt. 28:18-20, Jesus gives his Church a new mission. The GC also interestingly includes this triplet of covenantal motivational factors.

[337] See the section above entitled, *Covenantal Triperspectivalism*. Viewed from Frame's triperspectival categories: *redemption* maps to the *situational perspective, command* maps to the *normative perspective,* and *presence* maps to the *existential perspective.* Viewed from philosophical traditions: *redemption* maps to the *teleological tradition, command* maps to the *deontological tradition,* and *presence* maps to the *existential tradition.*

[338] Frame, *The Doctrine of the Christian Life*, 27.

[339] Frame, *The Doctrine of the Christian Life*, 324-325.

covenant/gospel?" [340] The virtue of *hope* is associated with this factor; that virtue looks to the future and believes God to continue blessing his redemptive work.[341]

For instance, God's covenant *control* (situational perspective) shown in Israel's historical *redemption* from Egypt was meant to *motivate* them. In the prologue to the Decalogue in Exodus 20:1-2, God says, "I am the LORD your God, who brought you out of the land of Egypt, out of the house of slavery." The Lord's working in redemptive history to save Israel out of Egypt not only is the lead motivational factor for the Decalogue – the moral law (Exod. 20:3-20), it seems to also be a key motivation for the "Book of the Covenant" – the general civil and ceremonial laws (Exod. 20:22-23:33). And as we mentioned earlier, the very last stipulation God makes to his people at the very end of the Book of the Covenant is their mission - the conquest of Canaan (Exod. 23:20-33). *God's redemptive work was to motivate their loving and grateful obedience to God in carrying out their mission for his glory.*[342]

As we considered earlier, this is the <u>primary motivational stimuli</u> in the RCC. Mendenhall in his research found that it is *not* command as the primary motivational stimuli, but something "radically different which is the real motivation for obedience." In his description of the historic prologue of a covenant in Hittite treaty form, he points to loving gratitude to the suzerain for his *redemptive benevolence in history* to the vassal as the prime motivating stimuli.[343] Kline, in talking about motivational power of the historical prologue in an ANE covenant treaty document said, "This element in the covenant document was clearly designed to inspire confidence and *gratitude* [italics ours] in the vassal and thereby to dispose him to attend to the covenant obligations, which constitute the third element in both Exodus 20 and the international treaties."[344] He says further about the historical prologue:

Its purpose was to establish the historical justification for the lord's continuing reign. Benefits allegedly conferred by the lord upon the vassal were cited with a view *to grounding the vassal's allegiance in a sense of gratitude* [italics ours] complementary to the sense of fear which the

---

[340] We make this combination of "covenant/gospel" because the "gospel" has roots in the "covenant of grace" (see Gal. 3:8-9).

[341] Frame, *The Doctrine of the Christian Life*, 332.

[342] We believe the motivation of the *glory of God* is found here in this category. See Frame, *The Doctrine of the Christian Life*, chapter 17.

[343] Mendenhall, 32.

[344] Kline, *Treaty of the Great King: The Covenant Structure of Deuteronomy: Studies and Commentary*, 14.

preamble's grandiose identification of the suzerain had been calculated to inspire.[345]

The covenant Lord's historic redemptive benefits to his covenant people are what was to primarily stimulate or motive his people to loving obedience. Kline adds, "The past mercies of God rehearsed in the historical prologue prompt such love and the love reveals itself in reverent obedience to all God's particular commandments."[346]

Bancroft, in his helpful study on the key motive for global mission, approaches the topic not from a relational-covenantal framework as we have. Rather his relational framework comes from his analysis of Trinitarian and affective theologies. We believe our approaches are quite complementary to each other. In the end, Bancroft concludes the Scriptures teach that the *love of God*, shown in history, stimulates a response of *love to God* from us. This *love of* God then is the key *motive* that in turn results in obedience. It is this answering love that should be the "principal" motivator of the Church's engagement in mission. He writes:

> We are surrounded by the love of the triune God. God's love has so many amazing features, the depths of which we only begin to explore in this life and will experience even more in the life to come. As we have explored a theology of mission, a natural reality of our journey is the discovery that the motive for participating in God's mission is love. *Love of the triune God functions as the principal motive for participating in the Trinity's relational mission of redemption and reconciliation.*[347]

From a relational-covenantal perspective, we heartily agree with Bancroft's statement. Our triune God's display of redemptive love was always meant to be the prime motivating stimuli for God's covenant people's actions. However, in various places in his book,[348] Bancroft seems to be too dichotomistic as he appears to say that the love motive should be the sole motive for mission and that the motive of obeying the GC, because it is a command, is somehow inferior. For instance, he writes:

> In this book, I propose that the motives for participating in God's mission presented by the evangelical movement need to be reexamined and transformed. By fully engaging the doctrine of the Trinity, as well as the interaction of man's heart, and will, we come to grasp the love of the

---

[345] Kline, *Treaty of the Great King: The Covenant Structure of Deuteronomy: Studies and Commentary*, 53.

[346] Kline, *Treaty of the Great King: The Covenant Structure of Deuteronomy: Studies and Commentary*, 66.

[347] J. David Bancroft, *Overflowing: Love of the Triune God as the Motive for Global Missions* (Bloomington, IN: WestBow Press, 2015), 159-160.

[348] Bancroft, 27-28, 21-24, 65-72.

triune God as the principle motive for missions. We will discover that the motive for missions is rooted in God's overflowing love and in our *response* of love for him, *rather* [italics ours] than in fulfilling a spiritual *responsibility* [italics ours].[349]

In another place, this apparent dichotomy seems to come out again when he writes, "Have we in evangelical missiological circles been careful to guard the relational reality of Scripture, particularly when it comes to the Great Commission? How do we understand motivational features of Scripture in a relational manner *rather than solely as obedience to biblical mandates or principles* [italics ours]?"[350] If we are understanding him correctly, we are uncomfortable with this dichotomy Bancroft is making. A covenantal perspective on mission motivations, as we are advocating in this study, takes a more *holistic* approach for motivations for mission. There should be a mixture of motives. It affirms both the primary motivational stimuli of God's love and the motivational response of love, as well as an obedience-to-command motive. They are not mutually exclusive; they are *complementary* in the relational-covenantal way God motivates his people.

Command

Secondly, in the covenantal motivational factor of *command*, God motivates his people to faith and obedience by prompting them to *think about what their covenant God has said*. That is, they think about what God has said in the Scriptures about who he is as their covenant Lord. They also think about what God has said in the Scriptures about their covenant/gospel duties. The question they answer here is, "*What has our covenant God said are our covenant/gospel duties?*" The virtue of *faith* is associated with this factor. Faith focuses on the authority of God's Word.[351]

For instance, God's covenant *command* to conquer Canaan (normative perspective) in and of itself was a motivational stimulus for OC Israel to obey. As we saw in the covenant document as given by Yahweh at Mt. Sinai and recorded by Moses in Exodus 20:1-23:22, part of that document was God's command for the conquest of the land (Exod. 23:20-33).

Furthermore, we can see the importance of the command stimuli when we consider that in ANE covenants the "fundamental demand is always for thorough commitment to the suzerain to the exclusion of all alien alliances."[352] This commitment extends to the commands of the covenant Lord. The "ten

---

[349] Bancroft, xvi.
[350] Bancroft, 27-28.
[351] Frame, *The Doctrine of the Christian Life*, 332.
[352] Kline, *Treaty of the Great King: The Covenant Structure of Deuteronomy: Studies and Commentary*, 14.

words" or Decalogue of the OC were crucial in summing up the covenant life and thus extremely important;[353] therefore, they too were important motivational stimuli.

Presence

Thirdly, in the covenantal motivation factor of *presence*, God motivates his people to faith and obedience as they *experience their covenant God's presence*. That is, they experience their covenant God's covenant/gospel blessings and curses in their lives (positive and negative motivation stimuli). The questions they answer here are, "*How have we in the past experienced our covenant God's covenant/gospel blessings and curses? How can we now experience our covenant God's covenant/gospel blessings and avoid his curses?*"[354] The virtue of *love* is associated with this factor. Love focuses on the Triune God's intimate presence with us.[355]

God's *presence* (existential perspective) is another key type of motivational stimulus given in the Bible to encourage our obedience. *This is perhaps the most precious of all the motives*.[356] We say this because this motive seems to be closest to the heart of the covenants which our personal God establishes with his people. The oft-echoed covenant motto, "I will be your God, and you shall be my people" is the main promise of the biblical covenants. It speaks of God's supreme desire in his covenants, which is to establish an intimate "union and communion" between himself and his covenant people.[357] For instance, above all other motives, it was his precious presence with them that Yahweh repeatedly stressed to motivate Moses, Joshua, and all OC Israel to carry out his command to conquer Canaan (e.g., Exod. 23:20-23, 32:34, 33:1-23, 34:1-9; Deut. 7:21-26, 31:1-8; Josh. 1:1-9, 17-18). In the NC, it is the Holy Spirit who communicates the presence of the Lord to his people. As noted earlier, this is the "distinctive, constant, basic ministry of the Holy Spirit . . . " now in the NC.[358] His presence is also felt in his dispensing upon his people covenantal *curses* for disobedience and *blessings* for obedience.

---

[353] Kline, *Treaty of the Great King: The Covenant Structure of Deuteronomy: Studies and Commentary*, 16-17.

[354] As we mentioned before, the *sanctions* (i.e., blessings and curses) section of an ANE covenant was also powerful in motivational stimuli. See Block, *How I Love Your Torah, O Lord!: Studies in the Book of Deuteronomy*, 34; Gentry and Wellum, Kindle locations 3592-3600; Kline, *Treaty of the Great King: The Covenant Structure of Deuteronomy: Studies and Commentary*, 16, 78-79.

[355] Frame, *The Doctrine of the Christian Life*, 332.

[356] Frame, *The Doctrine of the Christian Life*, 23.

[357] Murray, *The Covenant of Grace*, 17, 21, 31.

[358] Packer, 43.

We further observe a difference in the motivating *presence* of God between the OC and NC. In the OC, his special presence with his people seemed to be tied to one location – Mt. Sinai, pillar of cloud/fire, tabernacle, and temple. It motivated God's OC people to huddle around it and to follow it. However, in the NC, God has given his Spirit to mediate his presence. And his Spirit resides in each person in the NC (Ezek. 36:27; Jer. 31:34; Rom. 8:9). In the NC, his presence by the Spirit still motivates us to huddle around him and to follow him. However, now in the NC his presence is not locked into one place as it was in the OC. This has significant motivational ramification for the Church's NC mission as we will see.

Besides the Covenantal Triperspectival aspects, there are other patterns of motivational stimuli in the covenantal relationship. For instance, we have noted before that the covenantal Relational Paradigm emphasizes how the *vertical relationship* is primary, and the *horizontal relationships* are secondary. As we pointed out before, *vertical relational identity* should always motivate *horizontal relational action/obedience.* So, the fact that God's identity in the covenant is as sovereign/father and his people are vassal/sons, should motivate them to faithful, loyal, loving obedience.

Covenantal assurance

The third aspect of covenant spirituality we want to consider is *assurance*. Christian writers have come up with many definitions of assurance. The WCF describes a Christian's experience of assurance as being "certainly assured that they are in the state of grace, and may rejoice in the hope of the glory of God, which hope shall never make them ashamed."[359] In his Puritan classic on assurance, Thomas Brooks defines it as follows, "Now assurance is a reflex act of a gracious soul, whereby he clearly and evidently sees himself in a gracious, blessed, and happy state; it is a sensible feeling, and an experimental discerning of a man's being in a state of grace, and of his having a right to a crown of glory . . ."[360]

Brooks often referred to assurance more concisely as "manifestations of his love."[361] Thomas Watson poetically described assurance as "the manna in the golden pot . . . the white stone . . . the wine of paradise . . . God's smile . . . the reflection of God's love upon the soul . . ."[362] Joel Beeke says, "assurance is

---

[359] *The Westminster Confession of Faith*, (The Westminister Assembly, 1647). Chapter 18, paragraph 1.
[360] Brooks, 14.
[361] Brooks, 53.
[362] Thomas Watson, *A Body of Divinity* (1890; reprint, Edinburgh: The Banner of Truth Trust, 1997), 253.

the conscious enjoyment of that justifying salvation."[363] Elsewhere, Beeke quotes Donald Whitney, defining assurance as follows:

Assurance of salvation is a God-given awareness that He has accepted the death of Christ on your behalf and forgiven you of your sins. It involves confidence that God loves you, that He has chosen you, and that you will go to heaven. Assurance includes a sense of freedom from the guilt of sin, relief from the fear of judgment, and joy in your relationship with God as your Father.[364]

J. I. Packer defines it thus when he writes, "The subjective realization of what it means to be one with Christ . . . an intensifying of the sense of acceptance, adoption, and fellowship with God, which the Spirit imparts to every Christian and sustains in him or her more or less clearly from conversion on . . ."[365]

In seeking to synthesize these definitions from a covenantal perspective, we believe assurance can be defined as a deep experiential sense of God's saving love and favor in Christ, which the Lord gives his covenant people, by his Spirit.

Assurance as covenantal presence

When we view the above definition for assurance from the covenantal triperspectival framework we described previously, it seems obvious that assurance matches remarkably well with the lordship attribute of *presence*.[366] God's presence with his covenant people has many aspects to it such as time, place, blessings and curses.[367] Another important aspect of this experienced covenantal presence is the powerful assurance it gives his people.

Throughout the Scriptures, God's *presence* with his people was a felt and sometimes visualized manifestation of his love and favor. God's presence assured them of that key covenant promise – the Lord was their God, and they were his people.[368] In Exodus 33, after the people of Israel sinned with the golden calf, the Lord commanded Moses to move ahead with bringing the people to the Promised Land. However, as consequence for their sin, the Lord said his presence would not be with them (v. 3). Moses knew the Lord's assuring presence was crucial for him and the people so he responds in vv.

---

[363] Beeke, 176.

[364] *Consolation in Discourses on Select Topics, Addressed to the Suffering People of God*, reprint ed. (Ligonier, PA: Soli Deo Gloria, 1992), 138; quoted in Joel R. Beeke, *The Quest for Full Assurance: The Legacy of Calvin and His Successors* (Carlisle, PA: Banner of Truth Trust, 1999; reprint, 2000), 6.

[365] Packer, 153.

[366] Edmund P. Clowney, *Christian Meditation*, 2002 ed. (Vancouver, BC: Regent College Publishing, 1979), 57-58.

[367] Frame, *The Doctrine of God*, 94-102.

[368] Frame, *The Doctrine of God*, 95.

15-16, "And he said to him, 'If your *presence* [italics ours] will not go with me, do not bring us up from here. For how shall it be known that I have found favor in your sight, I and your people? Is it not in your going with us, so that we are distinct, I and your people, from every other people on the face of the earth?'"

The pillar of cloud and fire, the tabernacle in the wilderness, the temple, and ultimately Jesus as Immanuel ("God with us") and his Spirit in Christians, all these manifestations of God's presence assured his people of his love and favor. Jesus himself in his GC in Matthew 28:20 promised his NC people that his presence would be with them to assure them on their NC mission to take the whole world for Christ.[369]

Promoted by covenantal elements

Of all the historical biblical covenants, Christians are particularly part of the NC.[370] The NC shares common features that are true for all the other divine covenants God established with his people. We have already mentioned some of those common features when we described the lordship attributes of covenant control, authority, and presence. Other common features that seem to be found in all covenants is that God blesses his people with an assuring sense of his presence when they respond to him with *faith* and *obedience*. Additionally, another common feature is that God made his assuring presence tangibly manifest by a special *cloud*[371] or by his *Spirit*. These important covenant features of faith, obedience, and the Spirit are key covenant "dynamics of the spiritual life."[372]

The classic Reformed statement on what promotes assurance is found in chapter 18 of the WCF. It alludes to this very triad of faith, obedience, and Spirit:

This certainty is not a bare conjectural and probable persuasion grounded upon a fallible hope; but an infallible assurance of faith founded upon the divine truth of the *promises of salvation, the inward evidence of those graces* [italics ours] unto which these promises are made, the *testimony of the Spirit*

---

[369] Frame, *The Doctrine of the Christian Life*, 211.

[370] Luke 22:20; 2 Cor. 3:6; and Heb. 8:7-13. In saying this, we yet acknowledge the truth that through all the divine covenants there is a measure of continuity. So, for instance the blessings Christians receive through the gospel can be seen as the fulfillment of the blessings promised in the Abrahamic covenant (see Gal. 3:8; and Eph. 2:11-13).

[371] In the OT, there was a pillar of cloud, a cloud was over the tabernacle, and a cloud filled the temple. This cloud gave his people a special sense of God's presence. See *Dictionary of Biblical Imagery*, Logos electronic ed. s.v. "Cloud."

[372] Lovelace, 73, 91, 115, 130ff, Chapter 6. We have borrowed this phrase from Richard Lovelace's book by this title. He too finds faith, obedience, and the Spirit as key dynamics in a healthy spirituality. We believe Lovelace's findings can be properly packaged as dynamics found in the covenant life.

[italics ours] of adoption witnessing with our spirits that we are the children of God, which Spirit is the earnest of our inheritance, whereby we are sealed to the day of redemption.[373]

According to the confession, when a Christian has *faith* in the "promises of salvation," "inward evidence of those graces" that manifest themselves by *obedience*, and the inward "testimony of the *Spirit* [italics ours]," this soul will likely experience the blessing of assurance.

Faith - In a covenant relationship with God, his word factors largely. It is by his word that he exercises his covenant authority over his people. His word is filled with promises of blessings as well as curses. Thus, the appropriate response to God's promises should be *faith*. In the NC, our faith is particularly focused on Jesus, the object of faith. When a Christian trusts and depends upon Jesus and his promises, the Lord will often bless with a sense of assurance. Jesus said in John 16:31-33, "Do you now believe? . . . I have said these things to you, that in me you may have peace." Paul knew the importance of on-going faith in Christ in the covenant life and said in Galatians 2:20, "And the life I now live in the flesh I live by faith in the Son of God, who loved me and gave himself for me."

Obedience - The words of the covenant Lord also include commands, principles, and precepts. Thus, the appropriate response to these in the covenant should be *obedience*. God always responds favorably when his people obey him. When a Christian obeys their Lord, he often blesses with a sense of assurance. Jesus spoke about this relationship between covenant obedience and feeling God's assuring presence in John 14:21, 23 when he says, "Whoever has my commandments and keeps them, he it is who loves me. And he who loves me will be loved by my Father, and I will love him and manifest myself to him. . . . If anyone loves me, he will keep my word, and my Father will love him, and we will come to him and make our home with him."

Holy Spirit - In the OC, a believer's experience of God's assuring presence was always a blessing that God sovereignly dispensed. It is the same in the NC. That is, a believer never can control or manipulate God to give this experience. As mentioned above, a Christian can cultivate faith and obedience in his or her covenant relationship with God. However, even these are no guarantee the Spirit will give this experience of assurance.

Paul seemed to recognize this truth in his two recorded prayers for the Christians in Ephesus in Ephesians 1:15-19, 3:14-19. We believe in both of the prayers he shared with the Ephesian believers he was praying that *God would be pleased* to give them the experience of his assuring presence.[374] Paul recognized God's sovereignty in dispensing this experience, so he prayed and

---

[373] *The Westminster Confession of Faith*. Chapter 18, paragraph 2.
[374] Carson, 167-203.

asked the Lord to give it to his friends in Ephesus for their growth and maturity.

The WCF also seems to acknowledge God's sovereign prerogative to dispense assurance when it uses tentative language (i.e., "may") as to the certainty of receiving assurance:

> But that a true believer may wait long, and conflict with many difficulties, before he be partaker of it: yet, being enabled by the Spirit to know the things which are freely given him of God, he *may* [italics ours], without extraordinary revelation in the right use of ordinary means, attain thereunto.[375]

That sincerity of heart, and conscience of duty, out of which, by the operation of the Spirit, this assurance *may* [italics ours], in due time, be revived . . .[376]

Connection between covenantal assurance and motivation

Among the things we previously considered in this major section of systematic theology were, covenantal *triperspectivalism, covenantal motivation stimuli,* and *covenantal assurance.* In this current brief section, we hope to show the apparent connection between assurance and motivation from a covenantal framework. *This we believe is one of the most important observations we will make in this book to understand the connection between spirituality and motivation for mission in Paul, and in us.*

If we are correct in those matters we previously covered in this major section of systematic theology, then it seems to us that the relationship between assurance and motivational stimulus for mission is as we diagram it below in Figure 2:

---

[375] *The Westminster Confession of Faith.* Chapter 18, paragraph 3.
[376] *The Westminster Confession of Faith.* Chapter 18, paragraph 4.

> *Covenantal Motivational Stimuli*
> a) Historical Redemption.
> Think about what our covenant God has done, is doing, and will do.
>
> b) Command.
> Think about what our covenant God has said.
>
> c) Presence (i.e., *covenantal assurance*).
> Experience our covenant God.
>
> Cultivate this *covenantal assurance* by:
> i. Strengthening *faith*
> ii. Strengthening *obedience*
> iii. Strengthening *experience of the Spirit*

Figure 2. Covenantal assurance and motivations for mission connection

This connection seems "hardwired" into God's covenant people. When believers experience his covenantal presence, they experience a subjective sense of assurance. This in turn will naturally lead to motivate his people. Many through the years have recognized that an assured believer is also a motivated believer.[377] This truth of understanding the relationship between covenantal assurance and motivation stimulus will be very important in our analysis of Paul's experience as typified in 2 Corinthians 5:14, 15 and Ephesians 3:14-21.[378]

Integration of a Relational-Covenantal Lens

In the previous sections of this chapter, we have gathered together pertinent relational and covenantal theological information. In this section, we integrate them into a RCL that we will use later for analysis. We believe we can integrate Covenantal Triperspectivalism and the Relational Paradigm

---

[377] J. I. Packer, *A Quest for Godliness: The Puritan Vision of the Christian Life* (Wheaton: Crossway Books, 1990), 183; Beeke, *Puritan Reformed Spirituality*, 296, 297; Beeke, *The Quest for Full Assurance: The Legacy of Calvin and His Successors*, 123; J. C. Ryle, *Holiness*, 1979 ed. (Hertfordshire: Evangelical Press, 1879; reprint, 1985), 109-110; *The Westminster Confession of Faith*, Chapter 18, paragraph 3; Watson, 253; Ben Johnson, *An Evangelism Primer: Practical Principles for Congregations* (Atlanta: John Knox Press, 1983), 35; Chapell, 107-109, 220; Carson, 192, 195; Richard F. Lovelace, *Renewal as a Way of Life: A Guidebook for Spiritual Growth* (Downers Grove: InterVarsity Press, 1985; reprint, Eugene, OR: Wipf and Stock Publishers, 2002), 143-144; John Murray, *Redemption Accomplished and Applied* (Grand Rapids: Wm. B. Eerdmans, 1955), 171; Frame, *The Doctrine of the Christian Life*, 276; Brooks, 58, 142, 145, 291; R. L. Dabney, *Systematic Theology* (Carlisle, PA: Banner of Truth, 1985; reprint, Simpsonville, SC: Christian Classics Foundation, 1996), Chapter 27, section 6.

[378] See the section below entitled, *Assurance in the New Covenant*.

because they both have common covenantal roots. We have explored their covenantal roots earlier in this chapter.

Parts of the Relational-Covenantal Lens

Figure 3 graphically depicts the three main parts that will make up our lens. The overlapping part is the composite lens.

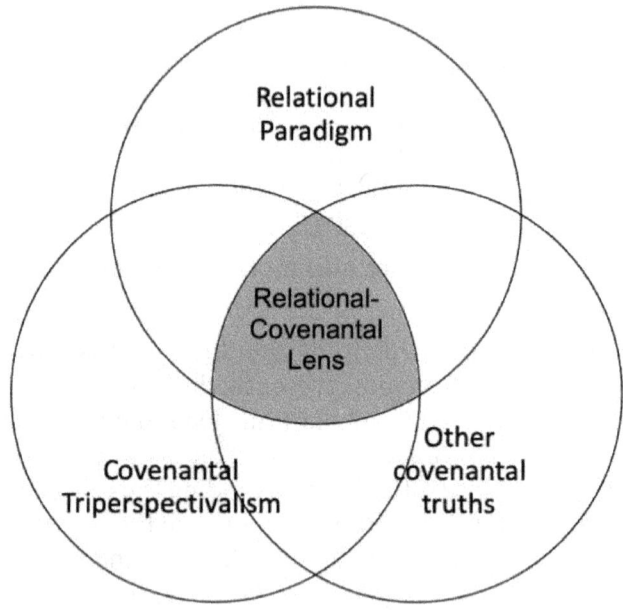

Figure 3. Parts of the Relational-Covenantal Lens

The Relational-Covenantal Lens

Figure 4 conceptually represents the *RCL*. We desire to depict through the figure the main personal beings that the lens focuses on, namely God and believers. We illustrate the types and flow of motivational stimuli as well as motivational responses to those stimuli. Additionally, we show the vertical and horizontal dimensions of relationships with the vertical having priority above the horizontal.

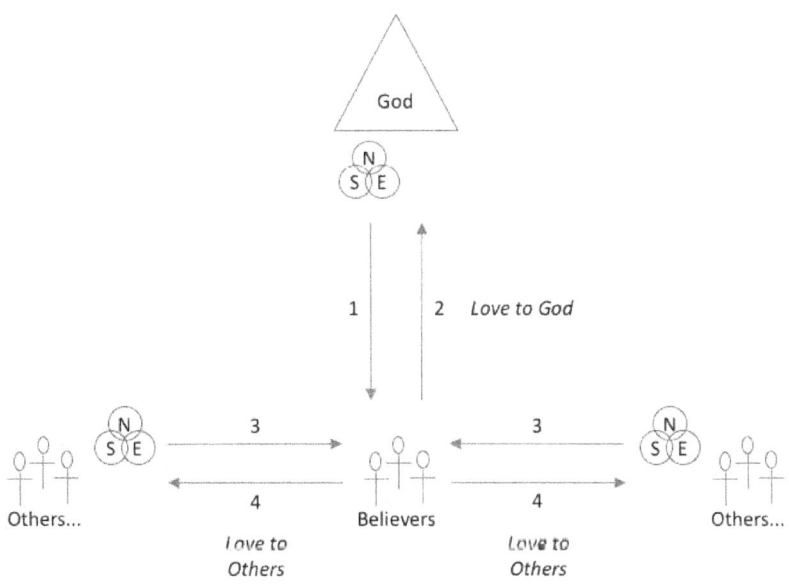

Figure 4. Relational-Covenantal Lens

Following is a more detailed description of the elements in the figure:
The "N, S, E" - This is our shorthand for *normative*, *situational*, and *existential* perspectives. To put them in more *relational* categories, we can say normative is *command*, situational is *redemption*, and existential is *presence*. According to Frame's research, as covenant Lord over his people, God reveals his lordship from three perspectives. From the "normative" perspective, the Lord uses his Word as his authoritative standard (e.g., *commands*, principles, precepts) in his lordship relationship with his people. From the "situational" perspective, the Lord uses his works in history (e.g., *redemption*, creation, providence) to demonstrate his lordship. From the "existential" perspective, the Lord uses his special *presence* (e.g., experienced assurance) to assure his people of his lordship.
Line numbers – We use numbers instead of descriptive text so as to keep the diagram from getting too cluttered. The numbers do not communicate sequence.

Vertical relationship:
1 – God using covenantal triperspectival motivational stimuli on believers
2 – Ideally, as a result of 1 stimuli, believers respond back to God. Ideally, this will be "love to God."

Horizontal relationship:
3 – Triperspectival motivational stimuli from other people on believers
4 – Ideally, as a result of 3 (and 1) stimuli, believers respond to others. Ideally, this will be "love to others."[379]

We have limited what we are depicting in this figure. First, though we believe in the three realms of personal beings (i.e., God, spirits, humans), we are not considering the spirit world so as to narrow our focus on the relational dynamics between God and his people. Second, we are not studying the God-others link, so we do not draw those relational links between God and others in the figure.

Applied to motivations for mission

In Table 1, we apply the relational-covenantal insights from Covenantal Triperspectivalism to our focus on motivations for mission.

---

[379] Vertical relational motivational stimuli can incite vertical *and* horizontal relational motivational responses.

Table 1. Covenantal Triperspectivalism and motivational stimuli

			Covenantal Triperspectivalism Categories of *Motivational Stimuli (Motivators)*	
Cov. Triperspec. Category[380]	Relational Category	Virtue/ Mnemonic Categories	Correspondence to ANE Treaty/Covenant Structure	Implications for Motivations for Mission
1. Normative	Command	Faith/ "Head"	Located in the "stipulations" section. The vassal knows it is ethically right to obey the suzerain. So, the suzerain's powerful *commands* have motivational force	1.1 The Christian ought to obey Jesus' (Lord of the NC) "Great Commission" found in various forms in the Gospels and Book of Acts.
2. Situational	Redemption	Hope/ "Hands"[381]	Located in the "historic prologue." The suzerain summarizes all his love and grace demonstrated to the vassal in history. This is the *primary* motivational stimulus in ANE covenants.	2.1 The Christian ought to be deeply moved to engage in mission as he/she meditates upon the love of Jesus for him/her at the cross. He/she responds out of reciprocal *"faithful loyal love" to the Lord.* 2.2 The Christian ought to engage in mission so as to move toward the goal of all peoples *glorifying the Lord.* 2.3 The Christian ought, in the covenantal sacraments of Baptism and the Lord's Supper, to find incitement to engage in mission. 2.4 The Christian ought, from the multi-faceted ways God displays his on-going covenantal love to the Christian, to find inducement to engage in mission.

---

[380] Interestingly, John Frame's covenantal triperspectivalism categories of normative, situational, and existential seem to correspond rather well with Benjamin Bloom's well-respected educational taxonomy of cognitive, behavioral, and affective. Also, they seem to match well with Kohl's categories for cross-cultural training of knowledge, skills, and attitudes. See Wan and Hedinger, 173; L. Robert Kohls and Herbert L. Brussow, *Training Know-How for Cross-Cultural and Diversity Trainers* (Duncaville, TX: Adult Learning Systems, Inc., 1996), 45.

[381] These are the gracious works the "hands" of the suzerain/father has done on behalf of the vassal/son. In the Christian context, these would be the great gracious displays of God's redemptive works for his covenant people in OT and NT.

Cov. Triperspec. Category[380]	Relational Category	Virtue/ Mnemonic Categories	Correspondence to ANE Treaty/Covenant Structure	Implications for Motivations for Mission
Covenantal Triperspectivalism *Categories of Motivational Stimuli (Motivators)*				
3. Existential	Presence	Love/ "Heart"	Located in the "curses and blessings" (i.e., "sanctions") section.	3.1 The Christian ought to *seek the biblical experience of assurance of God's love and acceptance in Christ,* and this should compel him/her to engage in mission. 3.2 The Christian's contemplation and/or experience of the Lord's displeasure and discipline for not engaging in mission ought to incite him/her to engage in mission.

In Table 2, we apply the insights from the covenantal Relational Paradigm to motivations for mission

Table 2. Covenantal Relational Paradigm and motivational dimensions

Covenantal Relational Paradigm *Motivational Dimensions*		
Dimension	Order of Importance	Implications for Motivations for Mission
1. Vertical	*Primary*	1.1 The Christian ought to engage in mission *first and foremost* out of "love to God" as his/her supreme allegiance to the Lord. 1.2 A Christian's problem with weak or lack of motivation to engage in mission could be because he/she *does not have supreme allegiance to the Lord* but to someone or something else. The Christian must be more self-aware and repentant.
2. Horizontal	Secondary	2.1 The Christian ought to engage in mission *secondly* out of "love to others" who are also in a covenant relationship with God,[382] but who are in rebellion against him and his rule and thus under his wrath and curse.

---

[382] All unbelievers are still under the covenant of works with God. See Berkhof, 218; Grudem, 517-518; Robertson, 67-81.

In Table 3, we integrate the main axis of Table 1 (motivational stimuli) and Table 2 (motivational dimensions) to come up with a grid of *basic RCC motivational responses for mission. In other words, these are the basic RCM for mission.* We have seen the "gratitude to God" motivation is *primary*, though not an exclusive motivational response, in the RCC. Therefore, we have placed a bold frame around that cell. Additionally, these motivational responses can work in concert with each other. For instance, as a response to the motivational stimuli of God's gracious redemptive work, there can be an initial response of "gratitude to God" which in turn leads to the motivational response of "obedience to God."[383]

Table 3. Basic Relational-Covenantal Culture motivational responses for mission

Integration of Covenantal Motivational Stimuli and Dimensions *Motivational Responses*		
Dimensions[384] / Stimuli[385]	"Love to God" Vertical (Primary)	"Love to Others" Horizontal[386] (Secondary)
Command (Normative/Faith/"Head")	Obedience to God (C-V)	Obedience to others[387] (C-H)
Redemption (Situational/Hope/"Hands")	**Gratitude to God[388] (R-V)**	Mercy to others[389] (R-H)
Presence (Existential/Love/"Heart")	Enjoying God (P-V)	Enjoying others (P-H)

---

[383] See the previous sections of *Structure of biblical covenants* and *Covenantal motivational stimuli* where we explore this.

[384] See Table 1 for a summary description of covenantal motivational *stimuli*.

[385] See Table 2 for a summary description of covenantal motivational *dimensions*.

[386] As we mentioned in the section entitled, *Relational Paradigm* in this chapter, in RCC dynamics the *vertical relational* stimuli also affect *horizontal relational* motives. We did not visually build this element into the table lest we clutter the main meaning of the table. Furthermore, in this book, we are primarily researching the *vertical* motivational stimuli and responses. It is beyond the scope of this book to research the *horizontal* motivational stimuli and motivational responses.

[387] These "others" are earthly authority figures. Their lawful commands to us (horizontally), should motivate us to obey them (e.g., Exod. 20:12).

[388] This is the *prime motive* in the RCC. We believe the teleological motive of *glorifying God* is an outflow of the primary motive of loving gratitude to God for his gracious redemption. See Frame, *The Doctrine of the Christian Life*, 298-313.

[389] Because of the Lord's love and mercy to his people (vertically), his people should want to display love and mercy to others (horizontally) in their needy conditions. Additionally, when others show great kindness in helping us (horizontally), there is a motivation to reciprocate and help them in their need (e.g., For Saul's lovingkindness to them, the men of Jabesh-gilead showed lovingkindness to Saul. See 1 Sam. 11 and 2 Sam. 2.).

This brings us to the end of the important section on *Considering Relational-Covenantal Truths* in our systematic theology analysis. In the next section, we use what we have learned about RCC motivations for mission to *analyze* the specimen passages from our biblical theology analysis section.

Analysis using the Relational-Covenantal Lens

In an earlier section in this chapter, we did a *biblical theology* analysis of several of Paul's statements that stated or implied his motivations for mission. In this section, we now use different facets of the *RCL* that we constructed in the previous section to *analyze* these passages.

Relational Paradigm perspective

As we have seen, one of the key relational principles this model emphasizes is the *vertical* relationship between God and his people takes precedence over the *horizontal* relationship with others. These relational dimensions of vertical and horizontal are not necessarily in diametric opposition to each other, though sometimes they can be. Rather, it is a matter of giving first covenant loyalty to the Lord in the vertical relationship. This vertical-first-before-horizontal covenantal principle also gives us a *motif to understand the flow of covenantal motivation stimulus and motivational response.*

Additionally, as we saw earlier in this chapter, *vertical relational truths about identity motivate horizontal relational actions*. There is a pattern in the Bible of this. In literature analysis of the Scriptures, this is sometimes called the "indicative and the imperative" pattern. In a relational analysis of the Bible, this may be termed the "being before doing" pattern.[390]

Use this RCL aspect to analyze Paul's experience

Paul in 2 Corinthians 5:14, 15 first calls our attention to *a vertical motivation stimulus from the Lord* – "the love of Christ."[391] It motivates Paul and his missionary band ("compels us") to both a *horizontal motivational response* (i.e., "live no longer for themselves") and a *vertical motivational response* (i.e., "live...for Him who died for them and rose again."). Given the literary context of Paul talking about what motivated him in his missionary ministry, we believe there is another *horizontal motivational response* and that of missionary activity among people.[392] We could visually mark up the

---

[390] Chamblin, *Paul and the Self: Apostolic Teaching for Personal Wholeness*, 155-156; Greidanus, 326; Ridderbos, 253-258.

[391] In the section below entitled, *Motivation in the New Covenant*, we use a triperspectival view to classify the motivation Paul is experiencing.

[392] In our biblical theology analysis of this passage, we demonstrated Paul and his missionary band are talking in context about their missionary ministry motivations.

text with arrows to show the relational directional flow. A legend for the marks is as follows:

⬇ - A blue vertical downward facing arrow means *a motivation stimulus from God*.
➡ - A blue horizontal rightward facing arrow means motivation stimulus from others or the environment.
⬆ - A gold vertical upward facing arrow means a believer's *motivational response to God*.
➡ - A gold horizontal rightward facing arrow means a believer's motivational response to others.

The marked passage is as follows:
For the love of Christ (⬇) controls us (➡)[393], because we have concluded this: that one has died for all, therefore all have died; and he died for all, that those who live might no longer live for themselves (➡), but for him (⬆) who for their sake died and was raised.

It is interesting to note how motivationally powerful this vertical experience of the "love of Christ" is on Paul and his friends. It results in two horizontal responses and one vertical response.

A New-Covenant spirituality

Paul, as with all Christians, is part of the NC. Jesus in Luke 22:20 said at the first Lord's Supper that he was inaugurating the NC. Paul in 2 Corinthians 3:6 tells us that the NC shaped his own ministry. The author of Hebrews, in Hebrews 8:7-13, clearly saw all Christians in the NC. As we saw earlier, the divine covenants mold and guide the relationship between God and his people. Spirituality is all about cultivating a deeper relationship with God. Therefore, the NC is fundamental in structuring or giving shape to Christian spirituality.[394] *Paul's experience in the passages we considered in the biblical theology section can be understood by seeing it in light of the features of NC spirituality.*

In the remaining sections of this chapter, we do two things. First, building upon our previous analysis of general covenant truths, we specifically focus in

---

[393] This arrow designates Paul and his co-workers' horizontal response to engage in mission. Again, this is drawn out in our biblical theology analysis of this passage that we did earlier in this chapter.

[394] As we mentioned earlier in the book, there are other biblical structures scholars have observed that should affect our spirituality, and we acknowledge them. We do not believe the covenants are the only biblical structure that can help us to understand what a biblical spirituality is. However, as we also mentioned before, we find a surprising lack of material on how the covenants affect the shape of Christian spirituality.

on NC spirituality's *structure, communion, motivation,* and *assurance*.[395] Second, in each of these aspects of NC spirituality, we analyze Paul's experience in the passages we previously considered.

We need to make an important qualification at this point. When we analyze Paul's experiences using these aspects of NC spirituality, we are only asserting it will help *us* to understand it in this way so we can draw missiological implications later from it. However, we are *not* asserting that Paul *himself* was necessarily and consciously analyzing and understanding his experience in light of these covenantal dynamics.

Structure of the New Covenant

In the OT, a group of texts contain prophecies about the NC.[396] Perhaps the most important prophecy about the NC in the OT is Jeremiah 31:31-34. We say this is the preeminent prophecy because it is the only prophecy that uses the terminology "new covenant," and it is the term Jesus used himself in Luke 22:20 to refer to this last historic biblical covenant. Another reason the NC prophecy should be considered the main text on the NC is the exclusive prominence the inspired author of the Book of Hebrews gave to it as the definitive prophecy for the NC (Heb. 8). For this reason, our survey of the NC will be mainly focused on Jeremiah 31:31-34.

Similar to other biblical covenants

As we mentioned earlier, the general structure of ANE treaties can be seen in many of the historic covenants of the Bible. This is generally true with the NC as well. Again, those key structures are as follows: name of the great Lord, historic prologue, stipulations, sanctions, and administration. In the NC, there appears to be the presence of several of these typical elements.

---

[395] Exploring spirituality from the NC angle is of tremendous interest to us. However, to do a thorough job of it is beyond the scope of this book. There are many other aspects of a NC spirituality we could explore. Suffice it to say, we believe it would be of great help to pursue an understanding of NC spirituality using the covenantal triperspectival framework of the Situational perspective, Normative perspective, and Existential perspective. John Frame has already laid a solid groundwork in Part Three of his triperspectival work on the Christian life. See Frame, *The Doctrine of the Christian Life*, 131-360. Yet we chose to only focus on these four Existential perspective elements (i.e., structure, communion, motivation, and assurance) because we judged them to be most pertinent to our study. Lord willing in the future, in another academic context, if he grants an opportunity, we will have a chance to explore NC spirituality more fully.

[396] Robertson, 274; Nichols, 257. Please consider the following: Isaiah 42:1-7, 49:5-13, 54:9-10, 55:1-5, 59:20-21, 61:1-9; Jeremiah 31:31-34, 32:36-42; Ezekiel 16:60-63, 34:23-31, 36:24-28, 33-36, 37:21-28

Name of the Lord

In the broader context of Jeremiah 31:31-34, God repeatedly used his special covenant name, Yahweh (e.g., Jer. 31:23, 28, 31). It is none other than Israel's covenant God who will establish this NC with them.

Historic prologue

Several authors correctly observe the importance of the historical context of this prophecy in order to properly understand the NC.[397] Additionally, it appears that from Jeremiah 30:1 to the actual prophecy of the NC in Jeremiah 31:31-34, Yahweh is having his prophet record the historic prologue for the NC. That is, Yahweh promises to work a "new exodus," a "second exodus"[398] for his people out of captivity in Babylon back into the Promised Land. This future historic redemptive event that Yahweh will accomplish is to provide a covenantal basis for their on-going covenant loyalty to him in the NC.

Stipulations

In the NC, God promises that *he will* "give you a new heart, and a new spirit I will put within you. . . . put my Spirit within you, and cause you to walk in my statutes and be careful to obey my rules." (Ezek. 36:26-27). God promises *he will* "put *my law within them, and I will write it on their hearts*" [italics ours] (Jer. 31:33). This implies that the moral law is still a part of the stipulations in the NC. In contrast to the other covenants, however, God in the NC takes the gracious initiative to ensure his NC people will have the internal power and ability to keep the stipulations.[399]

Sanctions

We will discuss the sanctions of the NC in the next section.

Promised blessings

We mentioned earlier that the OT has a group of texts that contain prophecies about the NC.[400] From these texts, we collate at least eight significant blessings of the NC. They are as follows:
1. God puts the law in our hearts
2. Universal faith and relationship with God
3. Real forgiveness of sins
4. Regenerated heart and Spirit in the heart
5. Emphasis of Spirit and Word
6. New heavens and earth to dwell where there is peace

---

[397] Nichols, 258; Robertson, 273-275.
[398] *Dictionary of Biblical Imagery*, Logos electronic ed. s.v. "Exodus, Second Exodus."
[399] Golding, 161-162.
[400] We mentioned them at the head of this section in a footnote.

7. Israel's Messiah as King of the NC community
8. God forever dwelling in the midst of the NC community

In our main passage for the NC, Jeremiah 31:31-34, we can clearly identify the first three blessings: law written on the heart, relationship with God, and forgiveness of sins. These three promised NC blessings can also be helpfully labeled *moral blessing, experiential blessing,* and *legal blessing.*[401] These interestingly correspond to triperspectivalism's perspectives of the *normative, existential,* and *situational,* respectively.[402]

It is significant to note that according to Jeremiah 31:34, the *experiential blessing* rests on the necessary foundation of the *legal blessing*. Because a believer is forgiven of his/her sins through Christ, therefore he/she can experience this intimate communion with God. Note also that both the forgiveness of sin and the knowing of God are *experienced* or *existential* blessings.

As we study the promises of the NC, another highly significant truth emerges. When we study these promises in the prophecies about the NC, we see the *organic unity between the NC with other covenants.*[403] For instance, in the Jeremiah 32:39-41 prophecy of the NC God said he would "plant them in this land in faithfulness . . ." which is a clear echo of the Abrahamic covenant's land promise. Another passage like Ezekiel 37:24-26, links several key promises in the Abrahamic, Mosaic, and Davidic covenants and incorporates them into the NC to find their ultimate fulfillment. Additionally, when we turn to NT passages like Luke 1:68-75, Acts 3:25-26, Galatians 3:6-9, 13-14, 29, we see ever more clearly as Nichols says, "the Abraham covenant is foundational to the new covenant."[404] In a subsequent section, we will further explore this important organic link between the Abrahamic covenant and the Church's NC mission.

Use this RCL aspect to analyze Paul's experience

How do these observations about the *structure of the NC* relate to Paul's experience found in 2 Corinthians 5:14, 15 and Ephesians 3:14-21? Paul as a Christian is a member of the NC. Therefore, the spiritual dynamics of these truths affected him. Paul experienced the NC *legal blessings* that came from Christ's reconciling work on the cross for him. This in turn laid the foundation for Paul's enjoyment of the NC *experiential blessings* of knowing God in a personal relationship. The NC blessing of the Spirit in his heart allowed Paul to deeply feel the "love of Christ" for him.

---

[401] Nichols, 265.
[402] Frame, *The Doctrine of the Christian Life*, 33-34.
[403] Robertson, 41-44, 280-286; Golding, 161-163; Murray, *The Covenant of Grace*, 25-29.
[404] Nichols, 258.

Furthermore, we can use this part of the lens to consider Paul's experience in Galatians 2:20. Paul as a NC believer has a new regenerated heart. As such, Paul's new heart's response was to place *faith* in Christ when he heard the gospel. And now as a believer, his new heart causes him to "live by *faith* [italics ours] in the Son of God" as a life principle.[405] Though the passage does not mention the virtue of *hope*, yet because hope is the future-looking aspect of faith, it is reasonable to assume it is there in Paul's heart too.

Communion in the New Covenant

Earlier, we undertook a general survey of the covenantal communion between the Lord and his people.[406] Here, we want to more specifically consider communion in the NC.

Personal aspects of the New Covenant

By looking closely at Jeremiah 31:33-34, we can discern at least three promises in the NC. First, there is the promise, "I will put my law within them, and I will write it on their hearts. And I will be their God, and they shall be my people." Second, God promises that those in the NC shall "all know me, from the least of them to the greatest, declares the Lord." The third promise is in these words, "For I will forgive their iniquity, and I will remember their sin no more." Notice that each of these promises have a *personal relationship* dimension to them. In the NC, all the promises for "spiritual relationship" found in the covenant with Noah, Abraham, Moses, and David find their "ripest fruition ... highest level of achievement."[407] In all these personal blessings of the NC, "we have the covenant as a sovereign administration of grace and promise, constituting the relations of communion with God, coming to its richest and fullest expression."[408]

Another amazingly gracious promise of the NC is the internalized presence of the Holy Spirit in every member of the NC (Ezek. 36:27). It is this promise of the Spirit that also serves as the promised "how" of making these intimate, personal, relational, covenantal blessings a *reality in the experience of a believer's life*. We mentioned earlier that Packer makes this point very well. His quote is worth repeating:

> The distinctive, constant, *basic ministry of the Holy Spirit under the new covenant is so to mediate Christ's presence* [italics ours] to believers-that is, to give them such knowledge of his presence with them as their Savior, Lord, and God – that three things keep happening. First, *personal*

---

[405] Frame talks about "two phases of faith...the initial saving faith and faith as a mentality that pervades the Christian life." See Frame, *The Doctrine of the Christian Life*, 328.
[406] See the section in this book entitled, *Covenantal Communion*.
[407] Murray, *The Covenant of Grace*, 28-29.
[408] Murray, *The Covenant of Grace*, 29.

fellowship with Jesus [italics ours], . . . Second, personal transformation of character into Jesus' likeness, . . . Third, the *Spirit-given certainty of being loved, redeemed, and adopted* [italics ours].[409]

We should note that none of these promises are "new" in the sense that they have never occurred in previous divine covenants. Nor are they considered "better promises" (Heb. 8:6) because they are completely different from the promises of the previous covenants.[410] So where does the "newness" or "better-ness" of the NC lie? There are several things to consider.

It is a "new" covenant that has "better" promises because there will be a "*heightened individualism* [italics ours]" over and above the previous covenants.[411] Jeremiah 31:29-31 brings this out clearly. God will hold guilty and will forgive more on an individual basis rather than on a genealogical basis. Each member of the NC will have the "law on the heart." Each will "know God." Each will have their sins forgiven.

Another reason is the *heightened universality of an inward work of grace*. That is, *all* the participants of the NC will individually "know God." The law of God will be written on the hearts of *all* the covenant members. In Hebrews 8:8, the author said God found "fault" not with the previous covenants themselves but with "them," the people. So, in the NC, God will correct this main fault by transforming each and every person who enters the covenant. In other prophetic passages that foretell the blessings of the NC, there is this consistent testimony of a heightened internalized work of God in *all* members of the covenant by giving them a "new heart" and the Holy Spirit (Jer. 32:38-39; Ezek. 36:25-28; 37:14).[412]

We should also note from a Christian standpoint the Bible tells us that the enjoyment of this personal covenant communion with God has two eras of fulfillment – the Present Age (time before Christ's Return) and the Age to Come (time after Christ's Return). John Owen recognized the eschatological duality of this covenant communion with God. He spoke of what we can experience *now*, before the Second Coming, of that real spiritual fellowship with God as "first-fruits and dawnings of that future perfection."[413]

The eschatological dualism of the "already" and "not yet"[414] also applies to this covenant communion with God. Christ at the Last Supper formally inaugurated the NC (see Luke 22:20). All who have entered the NC by faith in Christ have also been given access to this personal covenant communion with

---

[409] Packer, *Keep in Step with the Spirit: Finding Fullness in Our Walk with God*, 42-43.
[410] Waldron and Barcellos, 70-71; Robertson, 275; Kaiser, 217.
[411] Malone, 74-78.
[412] Waldron and Barcellos, 71; Malone, 85; Kaiser, 218; Robertson, 276.
[413] Owen, 3.
[414] Ridderbos, 29.

God *now* (the "already") in this life. Jesus in John 15:1-8 and John 17:3, 21, makes amazing statements about the incredibly intimate fellowship believers can enjoy *now* with the Triune God. This is the NC communion the Prophets had foreseen and wrote about.

Yet, the Bible also tells us that there is a greater dimension of this covenant communion that is for the future after Christ returns (the "not yet"). For instance, Paul in 1 Corinthians 13:12-13 and 2 Corinthians 5:1-8 indicates there is *now* in this life an experience of fellowship with God that is inferior to a greater reality that will happen when we personally meet our Lord. In Revelation 21:3 at Christ's Return, the NC's promised experience of personal union and communion with God will reach its ultimate climax. Here we have the last echo of the essence of the covenant that's been reverberating throughout all of the Scriptures: "Behold, the tabernacle of God is with men, and He will dwell with them, and they shall be His people. God Himself will be with them and be their God."

Foundation is union with Christ

As we noted above, the prophecy of the NC in Jeremiah 31:31-34 promised an intimate relationship between God and his people – "And I will be their God, and they shall be my people. . . . all know me, from the least of them to the greatest, declares the Lord." The Lord goes on in the passage to describe in clear terms the *foundation* of this communion, "For I will forgive their iniquity, and I will remember their sin no more." It took Christ's life, cross, and resurrection, and Apostle Paul's inspired writings, to explain the meaning of this NC forgiveness that would be the grounds for NC fellowship with God.

Paul's oft used phrase, "in Christ," can be best understood as a covenantal term.[415] Paul in 1 Corinthians 15 and Romans 5 clearly uses this phrase to indicate that just as Adam exercised a covenantal *federal headship* of all humanity, so Christ exercises a like federal headship with those in *union* with him. Golding believes that this *union* is implied in the very nature of the NC when he writes, "The covenant *form* varies, depending on the type of covenant, but the *essence* of the covenant, *union* between the parties concerned, of one sort or another, is invariable."[416]

The blessings from this union affect all aspects of a Christian's salvation.[417] And one of those amazing blessings is that this union with Christ provides the

---

[415] George Eldon Ladd, *A Theology of the New Testament*, ed. Donald A. Hagner, Revised ed. (Grand Rapids: Eerdmans, 1974; reprint, 1993), 314, 524ff; Duncan, 58; Berkhof, 448; Maurice Roberts, *Union and Communion with Christ* (Grand Rapids, MI: Reformation Heritage Books, 2008), 5.

[416] Golding, 71.

[417] Murray, *Redemption Accomplished and Applied*, 162-165.

foundation for a Christian's NC communion with the Triune God – Father, Son, and Spirit. Beeke said it well in the Foreword to Robert's book when he wrote, "This *union* [italics ours] in turn produces through Spirit-worked faith *communion* [italics ours] with Christ, by which believers participate in Christ's benefits."[418] Other theologians would agree with this.[419]

Use this RCL aspect to analyze Paul's experience

How do these observations about *communion with God in the NC* relate to Paul's experience found in 2 Corinthians 5:14, 15 and Ephesians 3:14-21? Paul as a NC saint was in union with Christ by faith.[420] The cross of Christ and all its saving benefits flowed to him as a result of that union. This union also brought Paul to an enjoyment of NC communion with his God. Part of that communion included the NC Spirit communicating to Paul an understanding and felt sense of the "love of Christ." As we will see in the next two sections, this experience motivated him.

Additionally, in the Galatians 2:20 passage we considered, we read Paul using language that clearly suggests his understanding of *communion with Christ*. He writes about being "crucified with Christ" and "Christ who lives in me." His union with Christ was initiated by faith (Gal. 1:16), and the union strengthens Paul's *faith* in Christ. We will see in the following section how *faith*, and its future-looking sister virtue of *hope*, also motivated Paul on mission.

Motivation in the New Covenant

Earlier, we commenced a general survey of covenantal motivation.[421] Now, we want to look more specifically at motivation within the NC.

Similar to other biblical covenants

Earlier, we looked at a triad of motivational stimuli in biblical covenants. We believe these are also present in the NC. For review, they are *redemption, command,* and *presence.* We also observed in that earlier section that these three have a correspondence with the three key virtues of *hope, faith,* and *love*, respectively.

---

[418] Roberts, vii.
[419] Pink, 9, 10; Murray, *Redemption Accomplished and Applied*, 169-172.
[420] Of course, Paul *is* still in union with Christ in heaven as are all the saints who have gone home to be with Christ.
[421] See the section earlier entitled, *Covenantal motivational stimuli*.

Redemption

As mentioned above, in the *historic prologue* of the NC, God promises a "second exodus,"[422] that is, a deliverance Yahweh would perform for Israel out from Babylon. This is a *type* of Christ's ultimate deliverance of his people from the bondage of sin through his cross and resurrection.[423] As is true in covenants, the prologue captures significant *historical redemptive events* that are meant to motivate the servant participants of the covenant. God's deliverance of Hebrew Israel from Babylonian slavery is pointed to as a deliverance to incite their covenant gratitude and love to God in the NC. In the ultimate fulfillment of the NC, Christian Israel, the Church, should look to Jesus' historic deliverance of them from sin, death, and Satan as tremendous covenantal incentive to love the Lord of the NC. Furthermore, the virtue of *hope* is related here as a motivating stimulus. The promise of a "second exodus" gave hope to Israel at that time and was meant to motivate them. So too now, the Church's eschatological hope of Christ achieving his gospel mission through his Church and the hope of Christ's Return have always motivated Christians.

Command

A striking feature of the NC in contrast to the OC is the *internalizing* of the "law" into the heart.[424] What law? It is the moral law of the Decalogue because God wrote it before on tablets of stone, but in Jeremiah 31:33 he said he would write it again on hearts. As a result, NC believers will have strong motivational force to love and obey their covenant God flowing from their hearts.[425] One of the qualities of the NC that makes it distinctly "new" compared to the previous historical biblical covenants is that God internalized the law in his NC thus facilitating their obedience. Williamson writes, "More significantly, as is highlighted by the following verse (Jer. 31:34), such radical transformation involving the internalizing of Yahweh's law would affect the *entire* covenant community. It is perhaps this, more than anything else, that constitutes the most radical distinctive of the new covenant."[426] Therefore, the motive of obedience to the command for the Church corporately and Christians individually to engage in mission should be a natural part of living out the NC reality in our hearts. Additionally, the virtue of *faith* in Christ and his promises is related to our discussion here. The Church experiences motivational force for mission when it by faith lays hold of Christ and his promises.

---

[422] *Dictionary of Biblical Imagery.*
[423] Nichols, 258.
[424] Golding, 161.
[425] Nichols, 265, 275; Robertson, 276; Waldron and Barcellos, 33-41.
[426] Williamson, 154.

Presence

As we saw previously, covenant participants are also motivated by the covenant *presence* of their God. In the OC, important manifestations of his presence included the pillar of fire and cloud, the tabernacle, and the temple. However, in the NC, the prophecies in Isaiah 59:21; Ezekiel 36:25-27, 37:14 tell us that a key NC characteristic will be the *internalizing* of the Spirit of God in the hearts of the participants. Thus, in a superior way, the NC believers will more personally experience the main covenant promise of his presence, "I will be your God, and you shall be my people." The Lord's presence in the heart of NC people by the Spirit would incite them to love and obedience. And this is certainly what we see Paul discussing in passages like Romans 8, 2 Corinthians 3:6ff, and Galatians 5:16-26. We point out, as we did previously, that the covenant presence had another important difference in the OC and NC. In the OC, it was locked primarily to one geographic location. However in the NC, it is in the heart of every single NC believer by the Spirit. This has significant motivational ramifications for the NC's GC as we will see soon. Moreover, the virtue of *love* is related to this factor of God's presence. The Christian's love is an answering love. It answers or reflects the love that first comes from God. This reflective love motivates the Christian toward mission.

Great Commission

As an apostle, Paul likely knew Christ's GC as we know it in Matthew 28:18-20. That is not to say anachronistically that he had that very text in hand. However, it is very probable through oral tradition and through special revelation[427] he knew of Christ's words in the GC. If that is so, it is also possible that he felt the covenantal motivational stimulus built into the GC itself. And this made up part of the motivational mixture in Paul's heart to be zealous in his mission ministry. We will use the covenantal framework discussed earlier to describe the covenantal ethical motivations found in the GC.

The apparent covenantal structure of the GC in Matthew 28 can be seen in two ways. First, it appears to contain a *literary structure* similar to other biblical covenants and other ANE covenants. Second, it appears to contain content that is *parallel to the conquest stipulation* in the OC.

First, as we mentioned earlier, there is a similarity between ANE Hittite suzerain-vassal treaties and biblical covenants. They often have the structure of name of the Lord, a historical prologue, stipulations, sanctions, and administration. It is striking that when we consider our Lord's GC in Matthew 28, there is a rough match between this commission of our Lord and covenantal literary structure. We do not mean to imply that Jesus is

---

[427] Acts 9:16, 22:21, 23:11, 26:14-18; 2 Cor. 12:1-10; and Gal. 1:6,7

establishing a new "GC covenant" for his Church in lieu of the NC. Rather, we believe the GC is a further detailing of the content of the NC which he said he had inaugurated by his blood (Matt. 26:28). The GC appears to have the covenant structure of *historic prologue* (v. 18), *stipulations* (vv. 19-20), *sanctions* (v. 20). Later we will briefly explore these three elements.

Secondly, the GC appears to have a covenantal structure because it also appears to parallel the OC covenant stipulation for the conquest of the land of Canaan. In passages such as Exodus 23:20-33, 33:1-6; Deuteronomy 7:17-26, and 11:8-12, God's command to his OC people to conquer Canaan was clearly in the context of the stipulations of that covenant. For instance, Exodus 23:20-33 comes at the very end of what the Scripture itself calls the "Book of the Covenant" (Exod. 24:7).[428] The OC's "Book of the Covenant" is found in Exodus 20:22-23:33. It is significant that the command for conquest is clearly within the stipulations section of the OC as given in Exodus. Furthermore, the command to conquer Canaan in Deuteronomy 7:17-26 and 11:8-12 are within the covenant stipulation section of Deuteronomy's covenant structure as borne out by Kline's and Kitchen's research.[429] So the OC command for Israel to engage in the conquest of Canaan is clearly a covenant stipulation. If his people obey the command, God promises blessings, but if they disobey, their God promises curses.

As we turn to the GC in Matthew 28, we can hear echoes of the OC conquest command. Frame quotes Poythress who confirms our observation that the NC GC is an anti-type of the OC mandate to conquer the land of Canaan.[430] In the GC, Jesus as Lord commands his Church to spiritually conquer the world by making disciples of the nations. In the OC, their special covenant mission was the conquest of Canaan. In the NC, the Church's "new mission" is none other than the conquest of the whole world through the gospel!

Prologue

"All authority in heaven and on earth has been given to me." Matthew 28:18, if we are right, would be similar to a covenant's *historic prologue.* The Lord's words here are an echo of Daniel 7:13-14 about the "Son of Man" receiving universal and eternal kingdom authority.[431] It also appears to echo Psalm 2:8 about Messiah as the "Son of God" receiving kingdom authority over all the nations. And it seems also an echo of Psalm 72 about Messiah's "sea to

---

[428] Richard L. Pratt, "Genesis through Joshua," (Charlotte, NC: Reformed Theological Seminary-Virtual Campus, 2003), 122-127.
[429] Longman III and Dillard, 110.
[430] Frame, *The Doctrine of the Christian Life*, 210-212.
[431] J. Knox Chamblin, "A Commentary on the Gospel According to Matthew," (Charlotte, NC: Reformed Theological Seminary-Virtual Campus, 2003), 311.

sea" dominion. Jesus as the Lord conquered sin, death, and Satan at the cross and by his resurrection.[432] He achieved a great *redemptive-historical* deliverance for his people. As a result, God the Father blesses his Servant, Jesus Messiah, with authority over all things.[433]

This prologue contains the covenantal motivational factor of *historic redemption* for the GC. The historical prologue of Exodus 20:2 regarding God's deliverance of them from Egypt was meant to motivate Israel to OC obedience. So too in the NC's GC, the Lord Jesus' accomplished deliverance of his people through his historic death and resurrection and reign is meant to motivate his Church with gratitude to obey their Lord. Being part of our Lord's great redemptive plan in history must motivate the Church to be part of God's great covenant gospel plan!

Additionally, his lordship *control* over all things is meant to encourage our obedience in the GC.[434] Jesus our risen and victorious King is in the driver's seat of history. He is arranging the flow of history so that his Church can fulfill his mission mandate.[435]

Furthermore, Matthew 28:18 seems to support an Amillennial eschatological position. Christ here is echoing Daniel 7:13-14 about the Son of Man establishing his rule and reign, his kingdom. King Jesus, by the fact that he has established his kingdom rule and reign, intends to motivate his Church to carry out the mission of the GC.

As there is an apparent parallel between the OC and NC mission, so there seems to be a *parallel of motives* between the mission of the OC and NC. From a *situational* perspective, in the OC God's deliverance of Israel from Egypt motivated the people for their mission to conquer Canaan. Correspondingly in the NC, Christ's deliverance of his people and kingdom is to motivate Christians to conquer the world through his gospel.

Stipulations

"Go therefore and make disciples of all nations . . ." Matthew 28:19-20a would be equivalent to a covenant's *stipulations* section. The Lord commands his Church to "make disciples of all the nations." And he says she needs to do so by "going . . . baptizing . . . teaching. . . ."[436] These stipulations contain the covenantal motivational factor of *command* for the GC.

---

[432] Col. 2:11-15

[433] Nichols, 258. It is significant that the prophecies about the NC in Isaiah, Jeremiah, and Ezekiel all foretell that with the coming of Messiah he will establish the NC. If we see Matt. 28:18 as another declaration of his Messiahship, then this further confirms our understanding that the GC is part of the NC.

[434] Frame, *The Doctrine of the Christian Life*, 276-282.

[435] R. T. France, *Matthew: An Introduction and Commentary*, ed. Leon Morris, Tyndale New Testament Commentaries, vol. 1 (Downers Grove: InterVarsity Press, 1985), 419.

[436] Hesselgrave, 19-22.

Jesus' command for his disciples to "go ... make disciples of all the nations" should have sounded like an echo from the Abrahamic Covenant's promise that "In your seed all the nations of the earth shall be blessed ..." (Gen. 22:18; cf. Gal. 3:8).[437] Wright points out that the call to Abraham in Genesis 12:1-3 could be structured as "'Go,' and, 'Be a blessing'."[438] It is interesting that a key *sanction* (a blessing) in the Abrahamic Covenant, of being a blessing to all the nations, has become a key *stipulation* in the NC's GC. This shift, this movement, this overlap gives motivational force to the Christian to obey this stipulation. Jesus is "the Seed of Abraham" and we are also "seed of Abraham" (Gal. 3:16, 29); our covenant God is behind us to be a blessing to all the nations! God's covenant love always moves him to faithfully keep his covenant sanctions. Thus, the Church's mission to bring gospel blessing in Christ to all the nations will never be in vain. God's promise in the Abrahamic Covenant is carried forward and ultimately fulfilled by Christ and his Church in the NC's GC. This connection to that ancient promise to Abraham is an important motivational engine to propel the Church out into the nations in obedience to her Lord.

Furthermore, as we have seen, the Church's NC mission corresponds to OC Israel's mission to conquer Canaan. From a *normative* perspective, in the OC God's plain *command* to conquer Canaan motivated Israel. Likewise, in the NC, our Lord's plain *command* to make disciples of all the nations is to motivate the Church.

In this sub-section on the *stipulations* of the GC, we want to make a final observation on the Lord's command to "make disciples of all the nations." The observation is that this command, as important as it is, is but one of many other passages in the NT that should inform the Church about her mission. For instance, in Acts 1:8, Jesus gives us a more *relational* understanding of the Church's mission as "witnesses" in the world to his gracious person and redemptive works. That passage and others must also shape a definition of the Church's mission in the world.[439]

We believe that imbalance in our mission theology and theory can come when we so focus on this command to the exclusion of other important biblical passages. It is crucial to see the GC of Matthew 28:18-20 in its greater narrative structure in the Gospel of Matthew. In so doing, we see that Jesus "relationally trained" his disciples in "kingdom-orientation (vertically)." As a result, the GC at the end of Matthew is the expected obedient response of the

---

[437] Nichols, 298.
[438] Christopher J. H. Wright, *The Mission of God: Unlocking the Bible's Grand Narrative* (Downers Grove: InterVarsity Press, 2006), 201.
[439] Other examples of passages that must shape a *relational* understanding of the Church's mission include Luke 24:44-48 and John 20:21-23. It is beyond the scope of this book to engage in a fuller justification of this idea.

disciples *motivated by the gracious loving being of God and his redemptive acts.*[440] Wan writes, "God's own should be witnesses to God's abundant grace and unmerited favor to serve and glorify Him."[441] The mission of the Church is broader than merely the "doing" of the GC. The popular and primarily GC doing-orientation of mission is an unhealthy truncated view of biblical mission that needs correction by the *relational* elements of mission. Wan says, "The popular view of Christian 'mission' is usually narrow in focus - doing (making disciples) without the sequential base of 'being.'"[442]

In this regard we imagine mission as a great tree. If mission could be likened to such a tree, then the activities of mission in the "doing" of the GC are like the branches and leaves. The branches and leaves of mission, are absolutely dependent upon the root of mission which is all the relational "being" elements of the Triune God himself and his abundant grace in redeeming and reconciling his people to himself. Because of this root of mission, the branches and leaves can properly flourish. In this way, the "doing" of mission flows out of the "being" of mission. Wan writes, "The popular action-oriented and programmatic approach of Christian mission has a misguided emphasis on the secondary – DOING; instead of BEING. The correct way is sequential: BEING precedes DOING; nevertheless with both."[443]

Wan's insights here also very powerfully corroborate an important finding in this chapter on RCM for mission. We have seen that in the RCC the gracious loving heart and acts of the lord/father of the covenant toward the vassal/son should incite the vassal/son to heartfelt acts of loving gratitude to the lord/father. The vassal/son shows gratitude to the lord/father in faithful, loyal loving obedience to all the lord/father desires. This is an important RCC pattern, and this is the sequence.[444] So it should be with the Christian and the Church in mission. The abundance of grace in God's "being," and even the Christian's new "being" in Christ, should motivate the Christian's and the Church's "doing" in mission, in that sequence.

Sanctions

"And behold, I am with you always, to the end of the age." Matthew 28:20 seems to be similar to a covenant's *sanction* section wherein the Lord promises blessing to his people. Here Jesus the Lord is promising the greatest blessing that is found in all the biblical covenants – his special *personal*

---

[440] Enoch Wan, "Diaspora Missiology and International Student Ministry (ISM)," in *Diaspora Mission to International Students*, ed. Enoch Wan, Diaspora Studies (Portland, OR: Center of Diaspora and Relational Research-Western Seminary Press, 2019), 15.

[441] Wan, "Diaspora Missiology and International Student Ministry (ISM)," 15.

[442] Wan, "Diaspora Missiology and International Student Ministry (ISM)," 17.

[443] Wan, "Diaspora Missiology and International Student Ministry (ISM)," 16.

[444] Additionally, the truth of vassal/son "being" loved of the lord/father and "being" a vassal/son, is also fundamental to the vassal/son's motivation in "doing."

presence with his people. This sanction contains the covenantal motivational stimulus of *presence* for the GC.

He promises his covenant *presence* to be with his people as they obey his GC. Jesus commands his Church to go to all nations and make disciples. Then he promises his *presence* to be with them. When one thinks carefully about this, Jesus is in effect saying *anywhere the Church goes in the world to "make disciples of all the nations" his presence will be there.* This is a staggering promise! Thus, in terms of guidance for mission, anywhere is good for obeying the GC because Jesus promised to be there! As we mentioned in earlier sections, the special covenant presence in the OC and NC have similarities and differences. As in the OC, God's presence motivates his people to huddle around the presence and to follow it. It motivates them with courage to obey. However, a significant difference is that the covenant presence in the OC was typically only in *one geographic location* (e.g., Sinai, pillar of cloud/fire, tabernacle, temple). However now in the NC, by virtue of the Spirit being in every NC member's heart, the special presence of God *is in many geographical locations at once. Wherever his people are, Christ's special presence is there too. That is what our Lord is saying.*

The NT tells us that it is by the Spirit that Christ makes his presence known to his people (John 14-15). At the heart of all the biblical covenants was the main covenant promise, "I will be your God, and you shall be my people." It promised God's fellowship. It promised God's presence. The NC prophecy in Jeremiah 31:33 also contained this promise. Jesus' words in Matthew 28:20 echo this promise. As Moses, Joshua, and OC Israel had as a *crucial motivation the presence of God* to accomplish their mission (e.g., Exod. 33:1-34:9; Josh. 1), so a *crucial motivation* for the Church to carry out her mission in the GC[445] is the *personal experiential presence of Christ himself by his Spirit.* From this *existential* perspective, in the OC God's presence of pillar of cloud/fire and the Angel of the Lord motivated his people, and in the NC the presence of Christ by the Holy Spirit motivates the Church to engage in its mission. Our Lord himself will be with us wherever we go to make disciples of the nations! France said it well when he wrote, "The promise of God's presence often accompanied his call to service in the Old Testament (e.g. Exod. 3:12; Josh. 1:5); it is not so much a cozy reassurance as a necessary equipment for mission."[446]

---

[445] We want to qualify this statement by underscoring what we said in the previous *Great Commission* section that the Church's mission includes the Matthew 28:19 GC command to "make disciples," but it includes more relational elements as well.

[446] France, 422.

Use this RCL aspect to analyze Paul's experience

How do these observations about *motivation in the NC* relate to Paul's experience found in 2 Corinthians 5:14, 15? The *redemption* event of the NC, the cross of Christ, was clearly on Paul's mind when he said, "the love of Christ controls us. . . ." And in true covenant-motivational fashion, Paul's appreciation of this event compelled Paul to go on mission for his Lord. Though the *commands* of the NC's GC are not mentioned in 2 Corinthians 5:14, 15, yet a survey of Paul's missionary ministry reveal they had a compelling force upon him as well. Paul likewise was motivated in ways consistent with God's covenants by sensing Christ's *presence* when he not only considered but also felt the "love of Christ" for him. It is this assuring presence that we will now look at more closely in the next section. *So, in terms of the RCC motivational responses I summarized in Table 3, in 2 Corinthians 5:14, 15 it was both a "gratitude to God" and an "enjoying God" that were Paul's motivations.*

Similarly, these observations about *motivation in the NC* shed light in understanding Ephesians 3:14-21. Paul prayed and encouraged the Ephesian Christians to experience the motivating power of "the love of Christ that surpasses knowledge" in their lives. *In terms of RCC motivational responses as organized in Table 3, Paul wanted the Ephesian believers to also have the motivational responses of both a "gratitude to God" and an "enjoying God."*

In light of these factors regarding *motivation in the NC,* we can analyze Romans 15:14-24 that we considered earlier. Paul had *faith* in the *commands* of Christ who had called and commissioned him as a missionary to the Gentiles. Paul had *hope* in Christ's future blessing on his *redemptive* gospel plans to the western part of the Mediterranean. These virtues motivated him. *So, in terms of the RCC motivational responses I summarized in Table 3, in Romans 15:14-24 it was both an "obedience to God" and a "gratitude to God" that were Paul's motivations.*

Assurance in the New Covenant

Experienced as presence of Christ and his love

We saw in an earlier section that in God's covenants *covenantal presence is assurance.*[447] And in another section we saw that in the covenants there is a *connection between covenantal assurance and motivation.*[448] In the NC these spiritual dynamics hold true. In Matthew 28:20, Christ, the Lord of the NC, promised his perpetual presence with his people. In Romans 5:5, Paul tells us it is the Spirit who pours out a powerful sense of Christ's love upon his NC people.

---

[447] See the section entitled, *Assurance as Covenantal Presence.*
[448] See the section entitled, *Connection between Covenantal Assurance and Motivation.*

Experienced by faith

Precisely as in the other divine covenants God graciously responds to his people's faith and obedience by blessing them with his assuring presence, so too in the NC. In John 14:21 and 23, Jesus promised the faith-filled obedience of his people would be met by a powerful assuring sense of his and the Father's presence with them. And in John 14:15-18, Jesus promised that the Spirit in the NC would communicate a sense of his assuring presence to his disciples.

Use this RCL aspect to analyze Paul's experience

How do these observations about *assurance in the NC* relate to Paul's experience found in 2 Corinthians 5:14, 15? It was the Spirit doing his NC work of communicating a felt sense of the assuring "love of Christ" to his faith-filled and obedient servant Paul. As is true in the other historic covenants, a powerful sense of the assuring presence of God spontaneously "controlled" or "compelled" Paul to further zealous mission service. *Again, in terms of the summarized RCC motivational responses in Table 3, it was both a "gratitude to God" and an "enjoying God" that were his motivations for mission.*

Similarly, in Ephesians 3:14-21 that we looked at earlier, Paul was praying and encouraging in the Ephesian Christians an experience of the *felt assuring love of Christ* for them. This was so they would be *motivated* to live in obedience to their loving gracious God's will as Paul makes clear in Ephesians 4-6. *So, in terms of the summarized RCC motivational responses in Table 3, it was both a "gratitude to God" and an "enjoying God" that Paul wanted for the Ephesian believers to share in.*

Summary of Systematic Theology Analysis

In this section, we used the tools of systematic theology to explore various aspects of covenantal truths that relate to motivations for mission. First, we looked at such truths as Covenantal Triperspectivalism, the Relational Paradigm, and other relational-covenantal truths, and we integrated them into a "lens," the RCL. *Crucial visual summaries of what we learned in that portion are found in Figures 2, 3, and 4, as well as Tables 1, 2, and 3.* Second, we took the RCL and analyzed Paul's motivations for mission in the various passages we considered earlier in the biblical theology section of this study. An important finding was that Paul's motivations for mission were consistent with relational-covenantal dynamics.

Analysis Based on Historical Theology

In this section, we again use the RCL we built in the systematic theology analysis to focus our historical investigation on one particular category of motivation for mission. We consider a select sample of former theologians, foreign missionaries, and contemporary theologians in Church history. However first, we would like to broadly review some relevant literature in recent Church history regarding motivations for mission.

As we mentioned earlier, the Church has had many different motives to engage in mission. When we look at the motives for the Christian life in general or the motives for engaging in mission in particular, the Apostle Paul had various motivations for both. Brooks, in his study of Paul's motives for the Christian life, finds that "[m]otivation in the Pauline epistles is diverse and variegated."[449] He groups Paul's motivations into three main categories – historical motivation, eschatological motivation, and exemplary motivation.[450] Cummings, in his study in particular on Paul's motivations for mission, groups Paul's varied motives into five categories – Paul's conversion, call, and commission, the lordship of Christ, the gospel of Christ, the love of Christ, and the return of Christ.[451]

Green's important study about the evangelism of the Early Church included an investigation about the Church's motivations for evangelism. Green discovered three primary motivations in the Early Church. First, there was *gratitude* for God's love expressed through Christ. The second was a sense of *responsibility* to the Lord to whom they were accountable as servants. And the third motive was a sense of *concern* for the unevangelized.[452]

Verkuyl believes he can identify various "pure motives" for mission from the NT itself. And he recognizes these motives are also present in mission history.[453] The first pure motive he sees is that of *obedience*. Paul showed a duty to the will of God to preach the gospel and a sense of obligation to the unsaved to evangelize them.[454] Verkuyl also sees evidence of motives of *love, mercy,* and *pity* for lost souls. He also identifies the motive of *doxology* as is found in various Pauline texts where glory to the Father for Jesus is seen as an end of mission.[455] There is also an *eschatological motive* as seen in Jesus' desire that his disciples would often pray to the Father that his "kingdom come." He also sees a good motive of *haste.* That is, there appeared in Jesus and Paul and missionaries in history an urgent desire to get the message of the gospel out quickly. And then, Verkuyl finds in the NT a *personal* motive of the missionary deriving gospel blessing as he/she engages in mission. For

---

[449] Brent T. Brooks, "A Biblical Theology of Motivation in the Pauline Epistles" (Th.M. thesis, Dallas Theological Seminary, 1984), 29, Theological Research Exchange Network, 001-0187, http://www.tren.com/e-docs/search.cfm?001-0187.
[450] Brooks, 29.
[451] Cummings, 15-216.
[452] Green, Kindle locations 3068-3384.
[453] Verkuyl, 164-168.
[454] See for instance 1 Cor. 1:17, 1 Cor. 9:16, and Rom. 1:14.
[455] See for instance 2 Thess. 3:1, Phil. 2:11.

instance, in 1 Corinthians 9:23, Paul says, "I do it all for the sake of the gospel, that I may share with them in its blessings." Verkuyl also finds in mission history many "impure motives."[456] He includes in this list an imperialist motive, a cultural motive, the commercial motive, and the ecclesiastical colonialism motive.

Other researchers have looked at different segments of Church history to discover trends in the Church's mission motivations. For instance, Koschade[457] sees Luther as recognizing the gospel's good news as containing inherent motivational power.[458] Creasman[459] believes that saving people from hell was the primary motivation for Wesley's mission activity.[460] In Van Den Berg's classic study of the evangelical missionary motives[461] between the years 1698 to 1815 in Great Britain, he identifies ten significant motives: political motive, humanitarian-cultural motive, ascetic motive, motive of debt, romantic motives, theocentric motive, motive of love and compassion, ecclesiological motive, eschatological motive, and the command of Christ motive.[462] Beaver sees the glory of God as being the leading motive in early American Protestant mission.[463] Calhoun catalogs various motives for mission like the GC, Christian compassion, duty to be co-workers with God, love to others, millennialism, and even nationalism.[464] Varg in his paper takes a sweeping look at the progression of American Protestant mission motivation between 1890 to 1917. The motivations evolved from the purely religious (e.g., salvation from hell and enjoying God) to an amalgamation of humanitarian and nationalistic views.[465] Pieratt,[466] in a recent

---

[456] Verkuyl, 168-175.

[457] Alfred Koschade was a former missionary in Papua, New Guinea and a pastor of several Lutheran churches in America.

[458] Alfred Koschade, "Luther on Missionary Motivation," *Lutheran Quarterly* 17, no. 3 (1965): 224-239.

[459] Ron Creasman is Adjunct Professor of Theology at Asbury Theological Seminary.

[460] Ron Creasman, "Why Do Missions? A Probe of Wesley's Life and Ministry in Search of Motivational Resources for Missions in the Twenty-First Century," *Wesleyan Theological Journal* 38, no. 1 (2003): 210-225.

[461] Timothy George, Professor of Divinity and Dean at Beeson Divinity School at Samford University, called it a "classic work." David Calhoun, Professor of Church History at Covenant Theological Seminary, has called it "the most complete work of this topic…" See Timothy George, "Evangelical Revival and the Missionary Awakening," in *The Great Commission: Evangelicals and the History of World Missions*, ed. Martin Klauber and Scott M. Manetsch (Nashville, TN: B&H Academic, 2008), 58. See David B. Calhoun, "The Last Command: Princeton Theological Seminary and Missions (1812-1862)" (Ph.D. dissertation, Princeton Theological Seminary, 1983), 235.

[462] Van Den Berg, 59-165.

[463] Beaver, 216-226.

[464] Calhoun, Chapters 4 and 5.

[465] Varg, 68-81.

[466] Jason Pieratt is Executive Vice President of Children's Relief International.

phenomenological study of motivations of ten Children's Relief International missionaries, compared their motivations with nineteen missionaries in Church history. He found five significant similarities: "a sense of obedience to God; a sense of responsibility to a specific people group or place; a progressive experience of calling; the importance of prayer and meditation; and the encouragement of others to join the vocation."[467]

Christopher Little[468] wrote an article reviewing Ralph Winter's article[469] on the future of evangelicals in mission. In his article, Christopher Little rightly points out the great aim of the Triune God to glorify himself (i.e., *"gloria Dei"*) and how this purpose in the *missio Dei* ought also to be the great motive of the Church in mission.[470]

Wan wrote a critique of Van Engen's article[471] about the definition of "mission." Wan in his article seeks to show the relational interaction of the Triune God in his Persons and with humankind as he works out the *missio Dei*. Significant for our study is Wan's observation that the Triune God interacts with both individual Christians and the institutional Church. We extend this insight to observe that the Trinity motivates both Christians personally and the Church corporately to engage in mission.

J. David Bancroft's[472] important book departs from the typical historical study of mission motivations. Instead, Bancroft seeks to engage the topic with "deep *theological reflection* [italics ours]."[473] His theological reflections on the topic come from two main angles. The first is from relational aspects of Trinitarian theology. The second is from "affective theology."[474] Bancroft is critical of the traditional evangelical obedience-oriented and responsibility-oriented motives for mission. Using a two-fold ontological theological framework (i.e., one, an ontology of God found in Trinitarian theology, and

---

[467] Jason Pieratt, "Calling to the Missionary Vocation: A Study of the Lived Experience of American and Majority World Missionaries of Children's Relief International" (D.Int.St. dissertation, Western Seminary, 2018), 122, Theological Research Exchange Network, 002-0949.

[468] Christopher Little is professor of Intercultural Studies at Columbia International University.

[469] Ralph D. Winter, "The Future of Evangelicals in Mission," in *Missionshift: Global Mission Issues in the Third Millennium*, ed. David Hesselgrave and Ed Stetzer (Nashville, TN: B&H Academic, 2010).

[470] Christopher R. Little, "In Response to 'the Future of Evangelicals in Missions,'" in *Missionshift: Global Mission Issues in the Third Millennium*, ed. David Hesselgrave and Ed Stetzer (Nashville, TN: B&H Academic, 2010).

[471] Charles Van Engen, "'Mission' Defined and Described," in *Missionshift: Global Mission Issues in the Third Millennium*, ed. David Hesselgrave and Ed Stetzer (Nashville, TN: B&H Academic, 2010).

[472] J. David Bancroft master's thesis became the basis of his book. Since 2007, he and his family live in the Balkans and engage in cross-cultural church planting. Bancroft, viii, xii.

[473] Bancroft, vii.

[474] Bancroft, vii-viii, xvi.

two, an ontology of humankind found in "affective theology"), he tries to demonstrate the only real motive for mission should be a responsive motive of love back to God for all his love to us.

Of particular interest to us was a book by former missionary and devotional literature author Andrew Murray.[475] In his work, Murray traces the problem of low missionary zeal to a personal spiritual problem. He locates the solution to this problem in the revitalization of Christians and churches in *experiencing God's love*.

Analysis Using the Relational-Covenantal Lens Focusing on the Existential Motivation of Assurance

In the systematic theology analysis section of this chapter, we summarized in Table 1[476] and Table 3 a mixture of RCC-related motivational stimuli and responses, respectively. We saw in our analysis of Paul's motivations for mission from various passages he wrote, *the fact of Christ's love at the cross and the experience of Christ love were some of Paul's most powerful motivational stimuli. These stimuli appear to arouse him to both "gratitude to God"*[477] *and "enjoying God" motivations for mission.*

As we have seen, Paul in 2 Corinthians 5:14, 15 and in Ephesian 3:14-21 was describing an experience that is a spiritual dynamic of NC life. His vibrant spirituality, in particular a strong sense of the assurance of Christ's love, fanned the flames of his mission zeal. *This connection of spirituality and mission zeal is what we want to focus on in this section*. And this is the same experience of many others throughout Church history. As Gregg Allison well said:

> Believers throughout history who have possessed a strong *sense of assurance* [italics ours] have stood fearlessly in giving testimony for Christ. . . . The history of Protestant mission during the last two hundred years is filled with the stories of thousands of cross-cultural missionaries *whose assurance of salvation enabled them to give their lives, literally, for gospel proclamation* [italics ours].[478]

---

[475] Andrew Murray, *The Key to the Missionary Problem* (Fort Washington, PA: CLC Publications, 2001), 33-64.

[476] See also Figure 4 for a graphical depiction of the flow of the motivational stimuli.

[477] In Michael Green's important study on evangelism/mission in the Early Church, he identifies three main motives: *gratitude, responsibility,* and *concern*. They seem to correspond well with Covenantal Triperspectivalism's taxonomy of existential, normative, and situational, respectively. See Green, Kindle locations 3068-3384.

[478] Gregg R. Allison, "Assurance of Salvation," in *Evangelical Dictionary of World Missions*, ed. A. Scott Moreau, Harold Netland, and Charles Van Engen (Grand Rapids: Baker Reference Library, 2000).

In this historical section, we consider a small number of Christians who wrote about and/or shared this experience. It is beyond the scope of this book to reflect on more than this sampling from history of individuals and movements that demonstrate this connection. We consider briefly three groups of Christians: *former theologians and movements, foreign missionaries,* and *contemporary theologians and authors.*

Former Theologians

We have selected theologians and movements who were Protestants. It would have been fascinating to delve into Roman Catholic history to see if they experienced and wrote about this connection, but that is beyond the scope of our study.

John Calvin

Chan helpfully summarizes that the Protestant doctrine of assurance was not fully developed by the Reformers.[479] It was the generation after the Reformation that gave more rigor to understanding this biblical doctrine and reality in the Christian life. The Puritans were especially diligent in understanding assurance. They took their cue from Calvin who pointed to the work of the Spirit as being crucial in understanding a Christian's experience of assurance.

Calvin believed that biblical assurance of salvation had both objective and subjective elements to it. He gave a definition of faith that included assurance in it when he wrote, "Now we shall possess a right definition of faith if we call it a firm and certain knowledge of God's benevolence towards us, founded upon the truth of the freely given promise in Christ, both revealed to our minds and sealed upon our hearts through the Holy Spirit."[480]

We are aware such a definition that makes assurance part of the essence of faith is controversial. However, it is beyond the scope of this book to dive into that issue here. Beeke in his work on Reformed spirituality has a done an excellent job of opening up this issue and explaining Calvin's thoughts more fully.[481] We simply want to point out that Calvin recognized in biblical assurance there were both objective and subjective elements. Regarding the former, Calvin stated that Christ alone is the "mirror" of our election.[482] That is, we are to look at Christ alone - his person, his promises, us being "in him" - to find our ultimate assurance of our election. Calvin cautioned that to

---

[479] Chan, 85-88.
[480] Calvin, 3.2.7.
[481] Beeke, *Puritan Reformed Spirituality*, 34-49.
[482] John Calvin, *Christianae Religionis Institutio (Institutes of the Christian Religion)*, ed. John T. McNeill, trans., Ford Lewis Battles, 2 vols., The Library of Christian Classics, vol. 2 (1559; reprint, Louisville, KY: Westminster John Knox Press, 2006), 3.24.4, 5.

principally seek our assurance "outside the way," that is, by things exterior to God's Word of promise, we are sure to sink into despair.[483] Regarding the latter, Calvin said this commenting on Romans 8:16, "The Spirit of God gives us such a testimony, that when he is our guide and teacher, our spirit is made assured of the adoption of God: for our mind of its own self, without the preceding testimony of the Spirit, could not convey to us this assurance."[484]

Calvin significantly observes the *connection between spirituality and motivation for the service of God.* His observations here touch more closely to the main point of this section. A central purpose in Calvin's *Institutes* was to provide Christians with a *theological and practical handbook for piety.* As one has said, it is Calvin's "piety described at length."[485] Or as another author put it, his *Institutes* "can be interpreted as an effort to formulate an authentic spirituality. . . ."[486]

In his *Institutes,* Calvin's doctrine of the knowledge of God followed the Scriptures. Calvin said the Bible taught that knowing God was not simply *comprehending content* about God, but it was *experiencing effects* on one's life as a result. One of the most important effects was that it should lead to "piety." He defined piety the following way:

I call "piety" that reverence joined with love of God which the knowledge of his benefits induces. For until men recognize that they owe everything to God, that they are nourished by his fatherly care, that he is the Author of their every good, that they should seek nothing beyond him-they will never yield him *willing service* [italics ours]. Nay, unless they establish their complete happiness in him, they will never give themselves truly and sincerely to him.[487]

Calvin commented on Jesus' words in John 17:3 that "the final goal of the blessed life, moreover, rests in the knowledge of God. . . ."[488] And the *effects* of a true intellectual and experiential knowledge of God is piety or in other words "willing service" of believers giving "themselves truly and sincerely to him."[489] For Calvin, the result of the knowledge of God was not stuffy head knowledge but a life of piety.

Further buttressing his point of the connection between an experience of knowing God and service Calvin said, "Indeed, no one gives himself freely and

---

[483] Kelly, 89.
[484] John Calvin, *Commentary on the Epistle to the Romans*, trans., John Owen, *Ultimate Christian Library* [DVD] (Rio, WI: AGES Software, 2000), 231.
[485] Beeke, *Puritan Reformed Spirituality*, 1. Beeke quotes John T. McNeill.
[486] Timothy George, *Theology of the Reformers* (Nashville, TN: Broadman & Holman Publishers, 1988), 224.
[487] Calvin, *Christianae Religionis Institutio (Institutes of the Christian Religion)*, 1.2.1.
[488] Calvin, *Christianae Religionis Institutio (Institutes of the Christian Religion)*, 1.5.1.
[489] Calvin, *Christianae Religionis Institutio (Institutes of the Christian Religion)*, 1.2.1.

willingly to God's service unless, having tasted of his fatherly love, he is drawn to love and worship him in return."[490]

Puritans

J. I. Packer once wrote of the Puritans, "The covenant of grace has been called the characteristic Puritan doctrine, as justification by faith was the characteristic doctrine of Luther. And to the minds of the Puritans the direct end and purpose of the covenant of grace was to bring men into union and communion with God."[491]

The Puritans understood and promoted a covenant-oriented "union and communion" with God (or in terms we have used in this book, a covenantal spirituality). Regarding John Owen, who is regarded as the "prince of the Puritans," and the one who expresses the epitome of Puritan spirituality, Packer writes, "For him, as for all the Puritans, sanctification was just one facet and cross-section of the more comprehensive reality that is central to Christian existence – namely, *communion with God*."[492] In Owen's famous work on communion with God, he explained that he saw it covenantally when he wrote, "It is, then, I say, of that mutual communication in giving and receiving, after a most holy and spiritual manner, which is between God and the saints while they walk together in a covenant of peace, ratified in the blood of Jesus, whereof we are to treat."[493]

One of the dynamics in that covenant spirituality of which the Puritans wrote was how experienced assurance, which we traced earlier back to covenantal presence, motivated action in the Christian life. Brooks said in his classic work on assurance:

> The manifestations of divine love put heat and life into the soul, it makes the soul very serious and studious how to act for God, and live to God, and walk with God.[494]
>
> It gives vigour in Christian service. . . .In a word, assurance will have a powerful influence upon thy heart. In all the duties and services of religion, nothing will make a man love like this and live like this. . .[495]

Watson noted the practical effects of assurance when he wrote:

---

[490] Calvin, *Christianae Religionis Institutio (Institutes of the Christian Religion)*, 1.5.3.
[491] Packer, *A Quest for Godliness: The Puritan Vision of the Christian Life*, 202.
[492] Packer, *A Quest for Godliness: The Puritan Vision of the Christian Life*, 201.
[493] John Owen, *The Works of John Owen*, ed. William H. Goold, 23 vols., vol. 2, *Ultimate Christian Library* [DVD] (Rio, WI: AGES Software, 2000), 17.
[494] Brooks, 56.
[495] Brooks, 145, 146.

Assurance will make us active and lively in God's service; it will excite prayer, and quicken obedience.... Assurance makes us mount up to heaven, as eagles, in holy duties ... Faith will make us walk, but assurance will make us run: we shall never think we can do enough for God. Assurance will be as wings to the bird, as weights to the clock, to set all the wheels of obedience running.[496]

Anthony Burgess wrote, "[Assurance] keeps up excellent Fellowship and Acquaintance with God....It will work a Filial and an Evangelical frame of heart...."[497] Thomas Goodwin said about assurance, "when once ... the love of God is shed abroad in a man's heart, it makes a man work for God ten times more than before...."[498] Thomas Brooks said, "assurance will strongly put men upon the winning of others.... A soul under assurance is unwilling to go to heaven without company."[499] The WCF, very much a Puritan document, clearly makes this connection between assurance and motivation to serve Christ when it says, "That thereby his heart may be enlarged in peace and joy in the Holy Ghost, in love and thankfulness to God, and in strength and cheerfulness in the duties of obedience..."[500]

Additionally, J. C. Ryle, not a Puritan *per se*, but one greatly influenced by them has said, "Assurance is to be desired, because it tends to make a Christian an active working Christian."[501] Joel Beeke who is also greatly influenced by the Puritans says, "When assurance is vibrant, a concern for God's honor and the progress of His kingdom is present."[502]

Pietists

In the providence of God, the Protestant Reformation spawned many interconnected movements. Mark Noll credits historian W. R. Ward for tracing the connections of several significant Protestant movements of renewal "that linked pietists on the Continent, evangelicals in Britain, and revivalists on the American frontier."[503] Two of those interlinked movements were Puritanism and Pietism. Noll correctly observes that the devotional theology of the Dutch

---

[496] Watson, 253.
[497] Anthony Burgess, *Spiritual Refining: Or a Treatise of Grace and Assurance* (London: A. Miller for Thomas Underhil, 1652; reprint, Ames IA: International Outreach, 1990), 26, 681-683; quoted in Beeke, *The Quest for Full Assurance: The Legacy of Calvin and His Successors*, 155.
[498] Thomas Goodwin, *Works*, ed. J. Miller, vol. I (London: James Nichol, 1861), 250; quoted in Packer, *A Quest for Godliness: The Puritan Vision of the Christian Life*, 183.
[499] Thomas Brooks, *Works*, vol. II (Edinburgh: James Nichol, 1867), 515; quoted in Packer, *A Quest for Godliness: The Puritan Vision of the Christian Life*, 183.
[500] *The Westminster Confession of Faith*, 18.3.
[501] Ryle, 109.
[502] Beeke, *Puritan Reformed Spirituality*, 170.
[503] Mark A. Noll, *Turning Points: Decisive Moments in the History of Christianity*, Second ed. (Grand Rapids: Baker Academic, 1997; reprint, 2005), 229.

Nadre Reformation and English Puritanism poured over the border into Germany and was influential in igniting German Pietism.[504]

These two movements had two important emphases: first, the Bible is the standard for the Christian life and practice, and secondly Christians needed to cultivate and enjoy an experiential relationship with God. Noll calls this dual emphasis "experiential Biblicism."[505] In turn, this powerful biblical combination of foundational truths, blessed by God's Spirit, provided a powerful spiritual motivation engine that launched and propelled the early Protestant mission movement. Richard Lovelace, another Christian historian and researcher of renewal movements, confirms this understanding when he wrote, "Pietism and Puritanism, the two theological siblings which energized Protestant development in evangelistic mission and social action in the seventeenth and eighteenth century."[506] The deep gospel renewal (what Lovelace calls "Primary elements of renewal")[507] that happened in the Protestant Reformation led to the "evangelical movement."[508] This widespread gospel renewal led in turn to the blooming of zeal for foreign mission, first among the German Pietists, then among evangelical Christians in England and America.[509]

Once more we see the pattern. When there is a healthy increase in Christian spirituality (with assurance being a prime ingredient), it often leads to a spontaneous zeal for mission.

Moravians

The Moravian Brethren[510] have their origins in the 15th century with John Hus in Bohemia (modern day Czech Republic). They were persecuted and hunted in the 1700s. In God's providence they found refuge on the estate of a Christian nobleman, Count Ludwig von Zinzendorf. They had then as they do now as one of their chief characteristic a deep "devotion to the Lord Jesus."[511] Proportionately, the Moravians have sent out more Protestant missionaries than any denomination; some were even willing to be sold into slavery in order to make it out to some mission fields and to preach the gospel.[512] At the

---

[504] Noll, 229.
[505] Noll, 241.
[506] Lovelace, *Dynamics of Spiritual Life: An Evangelical Theology of Renewal*, 13.
[507] Lovelace, *Dynamics of Spiritual Life: An Evangelical Theology of Renewal*, 75.
[508] Lovelace, *Dynamics of Spiritual Life: An Evangelical Theology of Renewal*, 149.
[509] Justo L. Gonzalez, *The Story of Christianity Volume II: The Reformation to the Present Day*, Second ed., vol. 2 (New York: HarperCollins Publishers, 2010), 262-264.
[510] Murray, *The Key to the Missionary Problem*, 34ff; Colin A. Grant, "Europe's Moravians: A Pioneer Missionary Church," in *Perspectives on the World Christian Movement: A Reader*, ed. Ralph D. Winter and Steven C. Hawthorne (Pasadena: William Carey Library, 1999).
[511] Murray, *The Key to the Missionary Problem*, 44.
[512] Murray, *The Key to the Missionary Problem*, 45.

famous 1900 Missions Conference in New York, the General Secretary for the Board of Missions of the Moravian Church, addressed the assembly and shared the key motivation for the Moravians to engage in mission:

> While acknowledging the supreme authority of the Great Commission, the Moravian Brethren have always emphasized as their chief incentive the inspiring truth from Isaiah 52:10-12: making our Lord's suffering the spur to all their activity. From the prophecy they drew their missionary battle cry: "To win for the Lamb that was slain, the reward of His sufferings." We feel that we must compensate Him in some way for the awful suffering which He endured in working out our salvation. The only way we can reward Him is by bringing souls to Him. That is compensation for the travail of His soul. In no other way can we so effectively bring the suffering Saviour the reward of His passion as by missionary labor, whether we go ourselves or enable others to go. Get this burning thought of *"personal love for the Saviour who redeemed me" into the hearts of all Christians, and you have the most powerful incentive for missionary effort* [italics ours]. Oh if we could make this missionary problem a personal one! If we could fill the hearts of the people with a personal love for this Saviour who died for them, the indifference of Christendom would disappear, and the kingdom of Christ would appear.[513]

By the testimony of their lips and lives, the Moravian Brethren also confirm this link between deep spirituality and mission zeal.

First and Second Great Awakenings

The recovery of the biblical gospel during the Protestant Reformation spread. The First and Second Great Awakenings[514] in England and America, led to a passion for mission.[515] There is an undeniable tie between the First and Second Great Awakenings and the incredible zeal for mission among Protestants that has become known by missiologists as the "Great Century for Missions."[516] During the First Great Awakening, the "theological tool" that was used of the Spirit to bring about renewal in people and churches was the *experientializing of Reformation theology*.[517] This experientializing

---

[513] Murray, *The Key to the Missionary Problem*, 34.

[514] The First Great Awakening was roughly between 1720-1740, and Second Great Awakening was approximately between 1790 to 1820. See Kenneth Scott Latourette, *A History of Christianity Volume II: A. D. 1500 - A. D. 1975*, 2 vols., vol. 2 (New York: Harper & Row, 1975), 958, 1036-1037.

[515] Lovelace, *Dynamics of Spiritual Life: An Evangelical Theology of Renewal*, 149.

[516] This refers to the time between 1792 and 1910. See Paul E. Pierson, "Great Century of Missions," in *Evangelical Dictionary of World Missions*, ed. A. Scott Moreau, Harold Netland, and Charles Van Engen (Grand Rapids: Baker Reference Library, 2000).

[517] Lovelace, *Dynamics of Spiritual Life: An Evangelical Theology of Renewal*, 44.

emphasized a personal conversion to faith in Christ and on-going trust and dependence upon Christ.

Jonathan Edwards was a participant in the First Great Awakening. Edwards in his 1734 sermon entitled, *A Divine and Supernatural Light*, used the metaphor of "divine light" to describe the Spirit's *immediate* work on the faculty of the heart (inclination/will) to produce deep emotional experiences. Here too, Edwards is unequivocal of the vital importance of such religious affections given by the penetrating rays of divine light:

This light is such as effectually influences the inclination, and changes the nature of the soul [italics ours]. *It assimilates our nature to the divine nature, and changes the soul into an image of the same glory that is beheld. . . . This knowledge will wean from the world, and raise the inclination to heavenly things* [italics ours]. *It will turn the heart to God as the fountain of good, and to choose him for the only portion. This light, and this only, will bring the soul to a saving close with Christ* [italics ours]. *It conforms the heart to the gospel, mortifies its enmity and opposition against the scheme of salvation therein revealed: it causes the heart to embrace the joyful tidings, and entirely to adhere to, and acquiesce in the revelation of Christ as our Saviour: it causes the whole soul to accord and symphonize with it, admitting it with entire credit and respect, cleaving to it with full inclination and affection; and it effectually disposes the soul to give up itself entirely to Christ. . . . This light, and this only, has its fruit in an universal holiness of life. No merely notional or speculative understanding of the doctrines of religion will ever bring to this. But this light, as it reaches the bottom of the heart, and changes the nature, so it will effectually dispose to an universal obedience* [italics ours].[518]

What Edwards calls "divine light" we believe is that operation of Spirit in the NC where he assures his people of Christ's love and acceptance of them. Notice Edwards also sees this assurance, this covenantal presence, as motivating "universal obedience." Certainly one area of such obedience would be to take the gospel to the unsaved.

During the Second Great Awakening, "Old Princeton"[519] had already been started in 1812. Her original godly professors wanted to forge a *"via media"* in the theology they taught the students.[520] They wanted to steer a balanced path between objective biblical theological knowledge and biblical subjective religious experience. A wonderful example of this was in the Sabbath

---

[518] Edwards, in *The Works of Jonathan Edwards* 603.

[519] We have heard this term refers to Princeton Seminary before the 1929 decision of the General Assembly to move the seminary in a more liberal direction. See David B. Calhoun, *Princeton Seminary. Vol. 2, the Majestic Testimony 1869-1929* (Edinburgh: Banner of Truth Trust, 1996), 395.

[520] Andrew Hoffecker, *Piety and the Princeton Theologians* (Phillipsburg, NJ: Presbyterian and Reformed Publishing Co., 1981), vii.

Afternoon Conference that was held in the seminary's Oratory room. It was designed to be a "serious conference with the students on subjects relating more immediately to experimental religion."[521] These conferences were "directed solely to the cultivation of the heart...."[522] This cultivation of the spirituality of the students was blessed of the Spirit. According to many graduates of the seminary, it was one of the most memorable and life transforming exercises of their whole seminary career.[523] This increase in a healthy spirituality resulted in many committing to serve their Lord on the foreign mission field. Graduate of Princeton Seminary and missionary Walter Lowrie wrote, "There are brethren in China and India, and I believe in heaven too, who will long remember room No. 29 [the Oratory], in Princeton Seminary, hallowed as it has been by conference, by tears and prayers."[524]

Calhoun quotes Princeton missionary to China, Caleb Baldwin, as having written "that room where love for the Saviour and love for souls have so glowed in my heart."[525]

Pentecostals and Charismatics

One of the positive things we can learn from the Pentecostal and Charismatic movements is this very dynamic we have been writing about, of how a deepening spirituality with Christ often translates to zeal for evangelism and mission. Pentecostals and Charismatics see their emphasis on the experience of the Holy Spirit and their emphasis on mission as almost synonymous.[526] Bruner makes this very irenic and balanced statement about Pentecostalism:

> In terms of the church's theology and mission Pentecostalism's significance may be that it incarnates a neglected reality of the New Testament church: the Holy Spirit in the experience of the believer. What to some may seem an overemphasis of the Spirit and especially of the Spirit's more noticeable operations may, perhaps, be intended to startle the church into an awareness of its little emphasis of the same Spirit. Perhaps in the divine perspective a

---

[521] David B. Calhoun, *Princeton Seminary. Vol. 1, Faith and Learning 1812-1868* (Edinburgh: Banner of Truth Trust, 1994), 132.

[522] James W. Alexander, *The Life of Archibald Alexander, D.D. First Professor in the Theological Seminary, at Princeton* (New York: Charles Scribner, 1854), 420; quoted in Calhoun, "The Last Command: Princeton Theological Seminary and Missions (1812-1862)," 164.

[523] Calhoun, *Princeton Seminary. Vol. 1, Faith and Learning 1812-1868*, 132, 136, 159.

[524] Walter M. Lowrie, *Memoirs of the Rev. Walter M. Lowrie*, ed. Walter Lowrie (New York: Board of Foreign Missions of the Presbyterian Church, 1851), 451; quoted in Calhoun, *Princeton Seminary. Vol. 1, Faith and Learning 1812-1868*, 136.

[525] Calhoun, *Princeton Seminary. Vol. 1, Faith and Learning 1812-1868*, 159.

[526] Frederick Dale Bruner, *A Theology of the Holy Spirit: The Pentacostal Experience and the New Testament Witness* (Grand Rapids: William B. Eerdmans, 1970), 32.

> church that gives too much attention to the Spirit is no more culpable – perhaps less – than a church that gives him too little. Perhaps the Pentecostal movement is a voice – albeit an ecstatic and at times a harsh voice – calling the people to hear what the Spirit is capable of saying to and doing with a church that listens.[527]

For these movements, the Spirit-worked experience of God's love in their souls fuels their evangelistic and mission zeal.

Foreign Missionaries

We have selected missionaries who were Reformed and some who were not. We did this to demonstrate that this connection between spirituality and mission zeal is a dynamic that has affected different parts of the Church.

Hudson Taylor

Hudson Taylor is one of the most famous Protestant foreign missionaries to China. Yet early in his career he wrestled profoundly in his Christian walk. He found a "spiritual secret" - a deep abiding in Christ that led to a soul-stirring assurance of Christ's sufficiency for him. By his own admission, this empowered him in all of his mission endeavors in China. Writing to his sister, Mrs. Broomhall, Taylor poured out his heart on his deep experience of assurance that made him a "new man."[528]

In that letter, the marks of a deep biblical assurance are there in his description. First, there is a strengthened faith. He said he knew that Christ was the source and "fatness" his soul needed. However, he did not know how to get it. Then he realized it was by faith that was "the hand to lay hold on His fullness. . . ." Then, he agonized on how to strengthen faith in Christ. Later, through a sentence his friend "dear McCarthy" used in a letter to him, he realized that he must not strive for faith itself but to simply rest in Christ, the object of faith, who already said he would never leave his people and always provide for them.[529] Taylor wrote:

> When my agony of soul was at its height, a sentence in a letter from dear McCarthy was used to remove the scales from my eyes, and the Spirit of God revealed to me the truth of our oneness with Jesus as I had never known in before. McCarthy, who had been much exercised by the same

---

[527] Bruner, 33.
[528] Howard Taylor and Mrs. Howard Taylor, *Hudson Taylor's Spiritual Secret*, PDF ed. (OMF International, 2002), 74. http://www.missionstomilitary.org/discipleship/lessons/Hudson Taylors Spiritual Secret.pdf (accessed 14 August, 2011).
[529] Taylor and Taylor, 76.

sense of failure but saw the light before I did, wrote (I quote from memory):

"But how to get faith strengthened? Not by striving after faith, but by resting on the Faithful One."

As I read, I saw it all! "If we believe not, he abideth faithful." I looked to Jesus and saw (and when I saw, oh, how joy flowed!) that He had said, "I will never leave thee."

"Ah, there is rest!" I thought. "I have striven in vain to rest in Him. I'll strive no more. For has not He promised to abide with me - never to leave me, never to fail me?" And, dearie, He never will. . . .[530]

After this experience of assurance, his zeal for mission never waned. He is reported to have said, "If I had a thousand pounds, China should have it. If I had a thousand lives, China should have them. No! not China, but Christ. Can we do too much for him?"[531]

John G. Paton

One cannot read the autobiography of John G. Paton and not make the connection between his deep experiential devotion to Christ and his zeal as a missionary to the New Hebrides (now Vanuatu). His autobiography from start to finish talks about an experiential piety he learned from his father that fueled his love and resultant service to his Lord.

In his earlier years, the experiential religion he learned from his father already moved him to engage in mission service. He wrote:

How much my father's prayers at this time impressed me I can never explain, nor could any stranger understand. When, on his knees and all of us kneeling around him in Family Worship, he poured out his whole soul with tears for the conversion of the Heathen World to the service of Jesus, and for every personal and domestic need, *we all felt as if in the presence of the living Saviour* [italics ours], and learned to know and love Him as our Divine Friend. As we rose from our knees, I used to look at the light on my father's face, and wish I were like him in spirit, - hoping that, in answer to his prayers, I might

---

[530] Taylor and Taylor, 76.
[531] "National Director Commissioning Celebration | Omf," http://www.omf.org/omf/us/about_omf_international/news/national_director_commissioning_celebration (14 August 2011).

be privileged and prepared to carry the blessed Gospel to some portion of the Heathen World.[532]

Having served for a time on the island of Tanna and experienced great suffering, Paton wrote of how the experience of Christ's assuring love kept him on the field:

The ever-merciful Lord sustained me, to lay the precious dust of my beloved Ones in the same quiet grave, dug for them close by at the end of the house; in all of which last offices my own hands, despite breaking heart, had to take the principal share! I built the grave round and round with coral blocks, and covered the top with beautiful white coral, broken small as gravel; and that spot became my sacred and much-frequented shrine, during all the following months and years when I laboured on for the salvation of these savage Islanders amidst difficulties, dangers, and deaths. Whensoever Tanna turns to the Lord, and is won for Christ, men in after-days will find the memory of that spot still green, - where with ceaseless prayers and tears I claimed that land for God in which I had "buried my dead" with faith and hope. *But for Jesus, and the fellowship He vouchsafed me there* [italics ours], I must have gone mad and died beside that lonely grave![533]

Still later in his time on Tanna, he reflected back on his harrowing escape from the cannibals he had come to serve. Again the experience of a real sense of covenant assurance from Christ compelled him. He wrote:

I climbed into the tree, and was left there alone in the bush. The hours I spent there live all before me as if it were but of yesterday. I heard the frequent discharging of muskets, and the yells of the Savages. Yet I sat there among the branches, as safe in the arms of Jesus. *Never, in all my sorrows, did my Lord draw nearer to me, and speak more soothingly in my soul* [italics ours], than when the moonlight flicked among the chestnut leaves, and the night air played on my throbbing brow, as I told all my heart to Jesus. Alone, yet not alone! If it be to glorify my God, I will not grudge to spend many nights alone in such a tree, *to feel again my Saviour's spiritual presence, to enjoy His consoling fellowship* [italics ours]. If thus thrown back upon your own soul, alone, all, all alone, in the midnight, in the bush, in the very embrace of death itself, have you a Friend that will not fail you then?[534]

---

[532] John G. Paton, *John G. Paton: Missionary to the New Hebrides*, ed. James Paton (1891; reprint, Edinburgh, Scotland: The Banner of Truth Trust, 1994), 20.
[533] Paton, 80.
[534] Paton, 200.

Roland Allen

Roland Allen was an Anglican minister and missionary strategist in the late 1800s and early 1900s. A missionary to China from 1895-1903,[535] he once wrote:

> The rapid and wide expansion of the Church in the early centuries was due in the first place mainly to the spontaneous activity of individuals.... a natural instinct to share with others a new-found joy, strengthened and enlightened by the divine Grace of Christ, the Saviour, inevitably tends to impel men to propagate the Gospel. The early Church recognized this natural instinct and this divine Grace, and gave free scope to it.[536]

Allen's writings were often more interested in reforming the methodological or structural way the Church did mission than talking about the connection of spirituality and mission zeal. However, here he recognized the general shape of that spiritual dynamic. Namely, the spiritual experience of divine grace in the heart often naturally leads to spontaneous zeal for mission.

Andrew Murray

Andrew Murray, a minister of the gospel best known for his many devotional books, was a Scottish Presbyterian serving as a missionary in South Africa.[537] He is one of the clearest Christian writers we have found who articulates this link between spirituality and missionary zeal. He wrote, "Closely connected to missionary motivation is the deepening of spiritual life."[538] And writing about the findings of the Anglican Church's evangelical mission organization, Church Missionary Society (CMS), he wrote, "The principle lesson the C.M.S. history teaches is that its great forward movement was intimately connected with a deep revival of spiritual life, and the teaching of a higher standard of devotion to the Lord Jesus."[539]

Additionally he said, "The movement for the deepening of spiritual life at Keswick was indeed very closely allied to the quickening of the missionary spirit in the Society."[540] Murray also quotes a powerful statement by the CMS summarizing its own experience of sending and maintaining missionaries.

---

[535] J. D. Douglas, Philip Wesley Comfort, and Donald Mitchell, *Who's Who in Church History* (Wheaton, IL: Tyndale House, 1992), 20.
[536] Roland Allen, *The Spontaneous Expansion of the Church* (Grand Rapids: Wm. B. Eerdmans, 1962; reprint, Eugene, OR: Wipf and Stock Publishers, 1997), 143.
[537] Douglas, Comfort, and Mitchell, 495, 496.
[538] Murray, *The Key to the Missionary Problem*, 53.
[539] Murray, *The Key to the Missionary Problem*, 55.
[540] Murray, *The Key to the Missionary Problem*, 57.

The CMS discovered this same positive correlation between a healthy spirituality and missionary zeal. He quoted:

We have learned in our long survey that *missionary advance depends upon spiritual life.* Evangelical orthodoxy is powerless in itself to spread the gospel. Unimpeachable Protestant teaching in the pulpit, and the plainest of gospel declaration in the church services, may be seen in combination with entire neglect of the Lord's Great Commission. Yet if the Holy Spirit Himself stirs the hearts and enlightens the eyes, then the conversion of the unconverted becomes a matter of anxious concern.[541]

Finally, Murray reflected back to the missionary zeal of the first disciples and wrote, "What was it that enabled poor fishermen and common men so simply to accept, and so loyally to carry out, such a divine commission? Two things. The one was: *Their hearts had been prepared for it by their intense devotion to* Jesus. . . . The other: *It was Jesus Himself who spoke the words.*"[542]

J. O. Fraser

In the early 1900s, J. O. Fraser was an evangelical Protestant missionary to the Lisu tribe in the remote western mountains of China's Yunnan province. Mrs. Howard Taylor, Fraser's biographer, wrote of his spiritual condition and how it affected his mission zeal:

Unless a close walk with God is maintained, discouragement replaces early zeal and consecration, and the decline begins that means loss of joy and power. Realizing the danger, Fraser set himself to watch and pray. . . . And most of all he is depending upon the *personal presence* [italics ours] of the One Who said, "Lo, I am with you alway." "What is Christian experience," wrote an eminent theologian who humbly walked with God, "what is Christian experience but the secret history of the affection of the soul for an ever-present Saviour?" Secret, steadfast, ever-growing "affection of the soul," let that have the first place, in practical reality, and there will be no drifting of decline.[543]

Roger Greenway

Roger Greenway was a Reformed missionary to Sri Lanka. He wrote of his call to become a missionary and said that feeling Christ's suffering for him and wanting to serve Christ out of love and gratitude was the driving force behind his call and his ministry.[544]

---

[541] Murray, *The Key to the Missionary Problem*, 57.
[542] Murray, *The Key to the Missionary Problem*, 121.
[543] Mrs. Howard Taylor, *Behind the Ranges: Fraser of Lisuland Southwest China* (London: China Inland Mission, Lutterworth Press, 1944; reprint, 1956), 30, 31.
[544] Roger S. Greenway, "My Pilgrimage in Mission," *International Bulletin of Missionary Research* 30, no. 3 (2006): 144.

Greenway also tells a personal story about his time on the mission field in Sri Lanka. The church he and others planted called the "Fellowship Center" exhibited a phenomenon that was apparent in the Early Church. Namely, among the locals they saw a positive correlation between the dynamic of *spontaneous zeal in evangelism and mission* and *experience of a vital fellowship with God through the Spirit*.[545]

Contemporary Theologians

Having looked at former theologians and missionaries, we now want to consider the testimony of a few more recent theologians and authors regarding this apparent connection between spirituality and missionary zeal.

J. I. Packer

J. I. Packer defines knowing God as not only knowing things *about* God but also knowing God personally and experientially through Christ.[546] We submit part of a biblical knowing of God includes experiencing his love for us by a healthy spirituality that senses his covenantal assuring love. Packer, like Daniel 11:32, said that this experiential knowledge in turn would prompt "the people that know their God shall stand firm and take action."[547] The experience of communion with God motivates action for God and his kingdom.

Tom Wells

In Wells' book on mission, his primary focus is to promote a higher motivation for individual Christians and the corporate Church to engage in mission. He identifies two motivations: First, "God is worthy to be known and proclaimed for who He is, and that fact is an important part of the missionary motive and message," second, "Those who know the most about God are the most responsible and best equipped to tell of Him."[548]

We agree with these higher motives. As we said earlier, we believe there are many biblical motives that move the Church to engage in mission. However, we think Wells does not go far enough in his book about what it is for God to be made "known" and to "know" God. He seems confined in his understanding to the *intellectual* aspect of this knowledge. We believe biblically the "knowledge" of God that will spontaneously fuel zeal for mission encompasses the *whole heart* and not simply the intellect. That is, it is a knowledge of God that *intellectually* knows he is the best of all beings and should be known by others, that *emotionally* has experienced God's covenant

---

[545] Roger S. Greenway and Timothy M. Monsma, *Cities: Missions' New Frontier*, Second ed. (Grand Rapids, MI: Baker Books, 2000), 50-52.
[546] J. I. Packer, *Knowing God* (Downers Grove: InterVarsity Press, 1973), 21.
[547] Packer, *Knowing God*, 23, 24.
[548] Tom Wells, *A Vision for Missions* (Carlisle, PA: The Banner of Truth, 1985), 9, 10.

love in Christ, and that *volitionally* wants this God to be loved and appreciated by others in the world.

Michael Haykin

The title Haykin gives to chapter 9 in his book on spirituality clearly captures the main argument in this section: "Mission-the Inevitable Fruit of True Spirituality." He goes on to say, "Historically, where there has been spiritual vitality and life in evangelical circles, there has been a concern for mission, prayerful and active concern for the salvation of the lost." [549]

Douglas Kelly

In one of my, Chris', seminary courses, D. Kelly was speaking about the amazing privilege afforded to all those saved by Christ to enjoy communion with the Trinity. God opens the door for weak mortals to enter into the sacred communion of love that the Trinity has enjoyed for eternity. Then he said:

> Real joy is going to be in this sense of leaning upon the bosom of the Father, of how wonderful the Father is, and Jesus brings us right to him in the Holy Spirit. That is the source of the Church's power, and joy, and love, and willingness to sacrifice everything [italics ours]. When a church or an individual Christian starts getting stingy, and resentful of any call to sacrifice, and sort of protective of self-interest above all else, it makes you wonder if they haven't lost sight of how wonderful the care and love of their Heavenly Father is and how near he is to them, or they wouldn't be stingy and self-protecting in that way.[550]

Kelly is here also recognizing the correlation between spirituality and zeal for service.

David McKay

McKay identified "love for God" as the supreme motive for the Church to engage in mission. He said, "The deepest missionary motivation must come from love for God, from which true love for neighbours springs."[551] How are we to understand this love for God to which he is referring? In the overall context of his book that explores the wonders of the Christian's covenant relationship with God, this love for God is a *reciprocal* love from the Christian back to God because of who he is, what he has said, and what he has done. Thus, to stoke the flames of this love for God which should be the supreme

---

[549] Michael A. G. Haykin, *The God Who Draws Near: An Introduction to Biblical Spirituality* (Webster, NY: Evangelical Press, 2007), 85.

[550] Douglas Kelly, *Systematic Theology I* (Charlotte, NC: Reformed Theological Seminary-Virtual Campus), 12 Sys I - Lesson 7.mp3, MP3. This occurred about one minute into the lecture.

[551] McKay, 235.

motive for mission, the Christian must intellectually and experientially know God's covenant love for him.

Richard F. Lovelace

Lovelace observed that in the Bible and Church history, individual or corporate renewal was often due to dual factors – reformation in "doctrine and structure" and/or "spiritual revitalization."[552] Applying the covenantal triperspectival framework we have been using in this book, Lovelace's dual factors actually fit the familiar categories of covenant life of *doctrine*, *structure*, and *experience*.[553] He argues that the "primary elements of renewal" include all three of these factors.[554]

In particular, when the Church more biblically teaches and preaches a full "in Christ" gospel that applies to justification as well as sanctification, the Church reforms in the covenantal elements of *doctrine* and *structure*. As a result, the Spirit often will bless people under this reform with revitalization in the covenantal element of *experience*. That is, if they are unbelievers they are saved, and if they are already believers they will experience a sense of assurance. Lovelace then observed that this Spirit-generated experience of assurance will engender as one of the "secondary elements" of renewal *an orientation towards mission*.[555]

In another one of his works, Lovelace drew out the spiritual cause-and-effect connection between warmly experiencing Christ's redemptive work and zeal for mission. He spoke of the appropriating by faith Christ's gospel in justification, sanctification, Spirit indwelling, and authority over spiritual forces as "primary elements" in *personal renewal*. According to Lovelace, these "primary elements" cause "secondary elements" of *corporate renewal* to take place. One of those elements is zeal for *mission*. He writes:

As secondary colors are derived from primary colors, these secondary elements of renewal draw out the larger, corporate implications of the primary elements. Primary responses of faith are centered in individual Christians, as they appropriate the fruits of his redemptive work. Secondary responses of faith move beyond individual growth to encompass the world, the church and the whole of life and thought . . .[556]

---

[552] Lovelace, *Dynamics of Spiritual Life: An Evangelical Theology of Renewal*, 16.
[553] The combination of Richard Lovelace's insights into the "dual factors" for spiritual renewal and John Frame's insights into covenantal triperspectivalism has profoundly helped us in our studies on the connection between spirituality and mission zeal.
[554] Lovelace, *Dynamics of Spiritual Life: An Evangelical Theology of Renewal*, 73-75.
[555] Lovelace, *Dynamics of Spiritual Life: An Evangelical Theology of Renewal*, 78, 145ff.
[556] Lovelace, *Renewal as a Way of Life: A Guidebook for Spiritual Growth*, 161-163.

Summary of Historical Theology Analysis

In summary, in this section we have surveyed Church history. We have found in a sampling of theologians, missionaries, Christian movements, and mission organizations, examples of a parallel belief and experience similar to Paul's in 2 Corinthians 5:14, 15 and in Ephesians 3:14-21. That is, a powerful motivation for Christians to engage in mission occurs when they experience by the Spirit a deep sense of God's assuring love for them in Christ.

Summary

In this chapter we have sought to answer the key question, "*How do the biblical covenants motivate God's people to engage in mission?*" We used a three-fold biblical, systematic, and historical theological analysis method. In the biblical theology section, we analyzed several biblical texts from the Apostle Paul's writings that contained evidence of his mission motivations. In the systematic theology section, we explored relevant elements that make up a RCC and a RCL. Figures 2 through 4 and Tables 1 through 3 provide an important summary of our findings. We used the RCL to analyze Paul's motives in the various Pauline texts we considered in the biblical theology section. Paul knew and experienced Christ's *love*. This provided powerful motivational stimuli in his heart. As a result, he responded with motives of "gratitude to God" and "enjoying God" by going on mission. Paul also knew a *faith* and *hope* in Christ and in Christ's call upon his life as a missionary to the Gentiles. Paul responded with motives of "obedience to God" and "gratitude to God." Finally, in the historical theology section, we explored the writings of various missionaries and theologians throughout Church history. They, like Paul, experienced (or wrote of others who experienced) similar motivational stimuli of the love of Christ and similar responses for their engagement in mission.

CHAPTER 3

EXAMINE MOTIVATIONS FOR MISSION WITH MOTIVATIONAL THEORIES

Introduction

Our second key question is, "What are some aspects of motivational theories that correspond with covenantal motivations for mission?" In this chapter we answer this question.

In chapter 1, we defined motivations for mission as internal drives in a Christian individually and the Church institutionally to continue on and carry out the missio Dei of the Triune God.[557] We also went on to say that we distinguish between "motivational stimuli" and "motivational responses." We recognize that there can be both extrinsic and intrinsic stimuli that foster responses in a believer to engage in mission.[558] In this chapter, we look at motivations theoretically from the perspective of motivational theories from the behavioral sciences. In particular, we will survey several theories, evaluate them, integrate acceptable aspects into the RCL, examine motivations for mission with the augmented RCL, and summarize our findings. However before we undertake these tasks, we want to summarize four fundamental aspects of the study of motivations from the behavioral sciences. Those four characteristics are as follows: a definition, categorization of the theories, hedonism as an assumed principle, and individual and organizational perspectives.

Martin Bolt[559] generally *defines* motivation as "factors that energize and direct behavior. It addresses why behavior is initiated, continues, and stops, as well as what choices are made."[560] Similarly, Steers and Porter[561] state that the study of motivations is "primarily concerned with (1) what energizes human behavior, (2) what directs or channels such behavior, (3) how this

---

[557] We want to qualify this statement by underscoring things we said in chapter 2 under the section the *Great Commission*. We said there that we believed the Church's mission includes the Matthew 28:19 GC command "make disciples", but it includes more relational elements as well.

[558] The cognitive perspective to understanding motivation is commonly where one will see this extrinsic-intrinsic distinction. M. Bolt, "Motivation," in *Baker Encyclopedia of Psychology & Counseling*, ed. David G. Brenner and Peter C. Hill, Baker Reference Library (Grand Rapids, MI: Baker Books, 1999), 767.

[559] Martin Bolt was Professor of Psychology at Calvin College.

[560] Bolt, 766.

[561] Richard M. Steers is the Kazumitsu Shiomi Professor of Management and International Studies in the Graduate School of Management at the University of Oregon. Lyman W. Porter was the dean of the Graduate School of Management at the University of California, Irvine.

behavior is maintained or sustained."[562] These parts are often found in the psychological study of motivation. The first part looks at what drives behavior. The second part investigates the goal towards which the person directs behavior. And, the final part looks at the influences that give feedback to the person to continue or desist in such motivations and behavior.

A second preliminary item to point out is that there are typically three *categories of theories* for motivation. Following Steers' and Porter's taxonomy, they are *instinct, cognitive,* and *drive and reinforcement* theories for motivation.[563] These are loosely aligned with another taxonomy of the theories under *biological, psychologically-oriented*, and *learned* theories.[564] The first category sees human motivation arising primarily not from rational but a physical desire to meet the needs of food, shelter, safety, sex and the like. The first few lower levels of Maslow's hierarchy of needs deal with such physical needs. The second category of theories view motivations as primarily arising from the rational aspect of humans. For instance, Vroom's expectancy theory, that humans are motivated by a combination of expectancy of attaining a goal and the goal's value, fits here in this classification. The third category of theories believes that motivations are learned from past experiences. Those motivations that led to favorable outcomes are retained and perpetuated. A good example of that is McClelland's achievement theory as it is a "learned needs theory."[565]

The third matter to mention is that the *principle of hedonism* is a fundamental assumption in the study of motivation in the behavioral sciences.[566] Hedonism was written about by the ancient Greeks. The principle states that humans in their decision-making behavior will typically make choices that *maximize pleasure and minimize pain.*

A final preliminary feature we want to mention is that researchers have *studied motivation in the individual as well as in organizations.* Steers and Porter look at motivation within an organization and say, "Motivation as a concept represents a highly complex phenomenon that affects, and is affected by, a multitude of factors in the organizational milieu."[567] Their words here are relevant to our research as we see motivations for mission not only has an

---

[562] Richard M. Steers and Lyman W. Porter, *Motivation and Work Behavior*, Fifth, International ed., Mcgraw-Hill Series in Management (Singapore: McGraw-Hill, 1991), 6.

[563] Steers and Porter, 9-14.

[564] "Motivation," in *The Gale Encyclopedia of Psychology* 778-779.

[565] David J. Cherrington, "Need Theories of Motivation," in *Motivation and Work Behavior*, ed. Richard M. Steers and Lyman W. Porter, Mcgraw-Hill Series in Management (Singapore: McGraw-Hill, 1991), 39.

[566] Victor H. Vroom, *Work and Motivation*, Jossey-Bass Management Series (San Francisco, CA: Jossey-Bass Publishers, 1995), 11; Cherrington, 31-32; Steers and Porter, 8.

[567] Steers and Porter, 3.

individual dimension, it also has an organizational dimension in the Church universal and in local churches.

Survey of Motivational Theories

We have chosen to investigate three popular and influential theories which are as follows: *Maslow's Hierarchy of Needs, McClelland's Need for Achievement*, and *Vroom's Expectancy Theory*. We have already stated that one reason we chose these three theories is because they are popular motivational theories. Another reason we implied in the previous section is that they represent the three major categories of motivational theories. Also, we will investigate some relevant research in *prosocial motivational research*.[568]

Abraham Maslow's Hierarchy of Needs

Abraham Harold Maslow (1908-1970) was a humanistic psychologist who earned his PhD at the University of Wisconsin. His 1943 article, "A Theory of Human Motivation," was so well received that it was soon reprinted in twenty-two works by other authors. With this article, his hierarchy of motivational needs became public.[569] In the final 1970 revision of his famous book, *Motivation and Personality*, Maslow said that his motivational theory was an integration of functionalism, holism, and dynamism.[570] His theory's fundamental outlook upon human nature is "humanistic and holistic."[571] By humanistic, he means an optimistic presupposition that man is fundamentally good, honest, kind, generous, and full of good affections. His theory's holistic framework seeks to view humans as being motivated as a whole as opposed to a Newtonian atomistic view of humans being motivated by merely one or another part of their being.[572] His theory came from his clinical experiences and his desire to integrate the thinking of various schools of thought on motivation.[573]

It is common to say that Maslow's theory contained five levels of hierarchy of needs, or motives.[574] Those levels of needs being *biological* (e.g., food, water, sex), *safety*, *belongingness* (e.g., emotional and physical love, belonging to a group), *esteem* (e.g., being respected by self and others), and

---

[568] For convenience, when we use the term *"motivational theories,"* we also include prosocial behavioral research that relates to motivations.

[569] J. A. Hammes, "Maslow, Abraham Harold," in *Baker Encyclopedia of Psychology & Counseling*, ed. David G. Brenner and Peter C. Hill, Baker Reference Library (Grand Rapids, MI: Baker Books, 1999), 724.

[570] Abraham H. Maslow, *Motivation and Personality*, 2nd ed. (New York, NY: Harper & Row, 1970), 35.

[571] Maslow, xi.

[572] Maslow, 19.

[573] Cherrington, 34-35; Hammes, 724.

[574] "Motivation," in *The Gale Encyclopedia of Psychology* 779; Cherrington, 35.

self-actualization (e.g., realizing one's potential). However, Maslow in his last revision of his theory mentioned that he believed there to be a higher need which is *aesthetic* (e.g., enjoying beauty and being beautiful).[575] He believed there were universal needs, yet they were ordered between basic lower-level needs (i.e., biological and safety) and higher-level needs (i.e., esteem, belonging, self-actualization, aesthetic). He believed people addressed first in priority the lower-level needs before attempting to satisfy higher-level needs.[576]

David McClelland's Need for Achievement

David C. McClelland (1917-1998) received his PhD in experimental psychology from Yale. He then chaired the psychology department at Wesleyan University. Later he was part of the psychology department at Harvard, then Boston University. The theory found its genesis in research he was doing on the connection between hunger needs and the degree to which food dominated the thought processes of a subject the longer he/she was without food. McClelland later extended similar research to other needs.[577] McClelland and his associate John Atkinson, and others, studied three other needs in this way: achievement, affiliation, and power. They gave these needs short-hand names, "nAch," "nAff," and "nPow." McClelland and Atkinson more fully researched nAch.[578] McClelland and his associates published their findings in 1953 in their book *The Achievement Motive*.

McClelland and his associates defined motive as "the redintegration by a cue of a change in an affective situation."[579] This definition is consistent with his theory as we will soon see. McClelland believed a need that motivates action in humans was *learned* behavior.[580] As the person matures and faces achievement situations, his/her experienced outcome causes either a positive or a negative association with achievement. The person who has associated positive pleasure to achievement situations will in the future find that "cues" for new achievement stimulates in him/her a desire to engage in the situation. The longer this person is without satisfying this need for achievement, the

---

[575] Maslow, 51.
[576] Cherrington, 34.
[577] David C. McClelland and others, *The Achievement Motive*, WorldCat.org (East Norwalk, Conn.: Appleton-Century-Crofts, 1953), 319. https://search-proquest-com.dtl.idm.oclc.org/publication/177429 (accessed 10 June 2019); John B. Miner, *Organizational Behavior 1 : Essential Theories of Motivation and Leadership* (Armonk, NY: M.E. Sharpe, 2005), 47-48. http://ebookcentral.proquest.com/lib/westernseminary-ebooks/detail.action?docID=302474 (accessed 17 August 2018).
[578] Cherrington, 39.
[579] McClelland and others, 28.
[580] McClelland and others, 67-68; Miner, 48; Cherrington, 39.

more the potential pleasure of achieving will dominate his/her thought processes.[581]

Victor Vroom's Expectancy Theory

Victor H. Vroom earned various degrees in psychology including a PhD in industrial psychology from the University of Michigan. Later he joined the psychology faculty at the University of Pennsylvania. There he wrote his book entitled, *Work and Motivation*, publishing it in 1964. In it, Vroom formally and publicly made known his version of the expectancy theory of motivation. Later still, he was professor of organization and management at Yale University.[582] Vroom's expectancy theory is a cognitive approach to motivation.[583] Because Vroom in his theory for motivation emphasizes the importance of interaction of the variables of *valence, instrumentality,* and *expectancy,* therefore, this theory is sometimes called "VIE Theory."[584] We will simplify and call it expectancy theory.

Vroom defined motivation as "a process governing choices made by persons or lower organisms among alternative forms of voluntary activity."[585] His theory is consistently related to that definition. His theory seeks to describe *how* people are motivated.[586] Generally speaking, Vroom's expectancy theory states that behavior is motivated by a joint working of three psychological factors or variables. First, there is the perceived emotional value one attaches to a choice (*valence*) that the choice will give pleasure. Second, there is the perceived likeliness that choice will help in achieving other related and subsequent goals (*instrumentality*). And finally, there is the expectation of achieving a desired goal (*expectancy*).[587] These three psychological factors of valence, instrumentality, and expectancy work within the person to cause a motivational force to likely determine behavior either to bring pleasure or avoid pain.[588]

---

[581] Miner, 48.
[582] Miner, 95; Vroom, xxix.
[583] Bolt, 767.
[584] Craig C. Pinder, "Valence-Instrumentality-Expectancy Theory," in *Motivation and Work Behavior*, ed. Richard M. Steers and Lyman W. Porter, Mcgraw-Hill Series in Management (Singapore: McGraw-Hill, 1991), 144.
[585] Vroom, 7.
[586] Sultan Kermally, *Gurus on People Management* (London: Thorogood Publishing, 1999), 51. http://ebookcentral.proquest.com/lib/westernseminary-ebooks/detail.action?docID=308965 (accessed 17 August 2018).
[587] Miner, 97-98.
[588] Pinder, 148.

Prosocial Motivational Research

The final group of theoretical literature we investigated has to do with *altruistic* or *prosocial motivation.* Because we can classify mission as a type of prosocial behavior and we can describe motives for mission as a form of altruism, therefore, we believe literature in this area is relevant to our study. In this subfield of social psychology, the terms altruism and prosocial are often used interchangeably. Altruism means "a motivational state with the goal of increasing another's welfare...," and prosocial means "any behavior that benefits someone other than oneself, regardless of the motivation involved."[589] However, according to C. Daniel Batson,[590] the terms should not be used synonymously because strictly speaking "altruism" is a motivational concept while "prosocial" refers to behavior and action.[591]

According to Batson, prosocial behavior "covers the broad range of actions intended to benefit one or more people other than oneself..."[592] Batson and associates define *religious prosocial motivation* as "motivation to benefit one or more others – evoked by religion."[593]

In prosocial behavioral research, researchers have sought to understand why people engage (or not engage) in prosocial behavior. They have found three ways to answer that question. First, is by pointing to "instincts and/or socialization" factors. These include things such as personality traits and learning. Second, is by looking at "situational factors." These include pressure and information overload. And third, is by considering "psychological processes, both cognitive and affective" factors. These include such things as, to what one attributes the causes of another person's need (and thus making a judgment to help or not) and the feeling of empathy for a person in need.[594]

We can place the research into three broad categories to help predict who and when prosocial behavior will likely occur. Those three are as follows:

---

[589] "Altruism and Prosocial Behavior," in *International Encyclopedia of the Social Sciences*, ed. William A. Darity, Jr., Macmillan Reference USA, *Gale Virtual Reference Library* (Gale, 2016), 88. https://go-gale-com.westernseminary.idm.oclc.org/ps/retrieve.d...E%7CCX3045300068&searchId=R4&userGroupName=s4556763&inPS=true (accessed 30 September 2019).

[590] C. Daniel Batson is an American social psychologist and expert in prosocial motivation. He has a doctorate in psychology from Princeton University and a doctorate in theology from Princeton Theological Seminary. He is emeritus professor of psychology at the University of Tennessee.

[591] C. Daniel Batson, "A History of Prosocial Behavior," in *Handbook of the History of Social Psychology*, ed. Arie W. Kruglanski and Wolfgang Stroebe (New York: Psychology Press, 2012), 243.

[592] Batson, 243.

[593] C. Daniel Batson, Stephanie L. Anderson, and Elizabeth Collins, "Personal Religion and Prosocial Motivation," in *Motivation and Religion*, ed. Stuart A. Karabenick and Martin L. Maehr (Bingley, United Kingdom: Emerald Publishing Limited, 2005), 154.

[594] Batson, 243-255.

dispositional factors (e.g., personal characteristics), situational factors (e.g., prosocial norms), and evolutionary factors (e.g., natural-selection instinct to promote survival of one's genes).[595]

Evaluate the Motivational Theories

As an evangelical Christian who believes in the standard of God's special revelation in the Scriptures as the ultimate standard for faith and practice, we must evaluate these three motivational theories from the perspective of God's Word. The Apostle Paul tells us in Romans 12:1, 2 that we are to submit to the lordship of Christ such that we seek to conform even our thinking to Christ's will. Paul also tells us in 2 Corinthians 10:4-5 that we are to evaluate all ideas and bring them under the lordship of Christ.

Hesselgrave echoes these concerns when he advises "strictures" upon the Christian who is selecting findings for use from non-Christian psychological motivational theories. He writes:

> The Christian persuader, however, has three strictures that apply in his selection and use of the insights of psychologists. First, those insights must not be in conflict with the teaching of the Word of God. Second, they must be used in accordance with divine purposes and ends. Third, they must be used in subjection to biblical principles and the direction of the Spirit of God.[596]

An example of a Christian researcher seeking to evaluate motivational research from a Christian perspective is Ronald Koteskey.[597] Koteskey sought as a Christian psychologist to be careful about his approach in evaluating secular psychological motivational theories. His main point is that "biological motivation is an aspect of humans which has its analogue in animals while cognitive motivation is an aspect of humans which has its analogue in God."[598] He acknowledges that humans are "unified beings" with biological and cognitive elements such that our motivations are affected by both. Koteskey believes that, "as we develop and become more godlike, our motivation would be expected to be increasingly dominated by cognitive factors."[599] As already stated, a fundamental Christian assumption is that we are made in the image of God. Therefore, our motivations are not merely biological and mechanistic. They also have a cognitive origin because we think, feel, and will like our

---

[595] "Altruism and Prosocial Behavior," in *International Encyclopedia of the Social Sciences* 00.
[596] David J. Hesselgrave, *Communicating Christ Cross-Culturally*, 2nd ed. (Grand Rapids: Zondervan, 1991), 588.
[597] Ronald L. Koteskey was a professor of psychology at Asbury College.
[598] Ronald L. Koteskey, "Toward the Development of a Christian Psychology: Motivation," *Journal of Psychology & Theology* 7, no. 1 (1979): 3.
[599] Koteskey, 3.

Creator. Importantly implied in this fundamental assumption is that we have a *moral and ethical responsibility* associated with the motives that energize our actions. As image bearers of God we cannot excuse our motives and actions to automatic biological and mechanistic dynamics at work in us.

Evaluate using the Relational-Critical Contextualization Model

In order to evaluate these theories and to decide if we should integrate their elements into our research, we need an evangelical contextualization method. The method we use to analyze these motivational theories is what we are calling the Relational-Critical Contextualization Model. It is our own synthesis of Hiebert's Critical Contextualization Model,[600] summarized in Table 4 below, with Wan's Relational Paradigm. This synthesis provides a framework for our evaluation process.

Table 4. Hiebert's Critical Contextualization Model[601]

Step	Description
1. Exegesis of the Culture	To exegete some cultural item (e.g., physical artifact, behavior, value, belief) so as to ascertain its meaning in that culture context
2. Exegesis of Scripture and the Hermeneutical Bridge	To exegete the Scripture to gain insight on God's view of that cultural item
3. Critical Response	To discuss with local Christians how to understand this cultural item scripturally
4. New Contextualized Practices	To guide local Christians and allow them to decide on new attitudes and practices that honor the Scriptures and yet are sensitive to the culture. Note: At times the scriptural response is to shun a cultural item because it clearly violates God's Word.

According to Scott Moreau,[602] Paul Hiebert's "Critical Contextualization" model "is perhaps the most widely used evangelical mode for contextualization in academic settings."[603] Hiebert's model is very good from a horizontal relational dimension (i.e., on the human relational plane) and from

---

[600] We believe it is necessary to have an evangelical "contextualization" method as we evaluate the "artifacts" of motivational theories that come from a non-Christian secular behavioral science "culture."

[601] Paul G. Hiebert, *Anthropological Reflections on Missiological Issues* (Grand Rapids, MI: Baker Books, 1994), 88-91.

[602] A. Scott Moreau is the Academic Dean of Wheaton College Graduate School & Professor of Intercultural Studies.

[603] A. Scott Moreau, *Contextualization in World Missions: Mapping and Assessing Evangelical Models* (Grand Rapids, MI: Kregel Publishing, 2012), 228.

a functional standpoint. That is, it emphasizes the Christian agent's responsibility in the contextualization process. Where Hiebert's model seems to be weak is in not explicitly mentioning the vertical relational dimension with God during the contextualization process. We would imagine Hiebert assumed this dimension in his model. However, following Wan's Relational Paradigm, we want to make the vertical relational dimension more of a priority and to make it explicit.

In seeking a synthesis, we are actually trying to augment Hiebert's model with more of the vertical relational dimension with God. Our augmentation has five parts. First, we call for the cultivation of a kingdom[604]-covenantal[605] disposition of heart. We should pray, depend, and submit to the lordship of the King of the kingdom and the Lord of the NC. Then we should continue in that disposition throughout the rest of the contextualization process. Second, we should vertically and horizontally engage in understanding the cultural item in question. That is, we ask questions of the Lord. We ask questions of people in the culture.[606] Third, we should vertically and horizontally engage in scrutinizing the Scriptures. Here too we ask questions of the Lord, and we ask questions of the Scripture text, and we ask people in the culture. Fourth, we should vertically and horizontally engage in discussing the cultural artifact in light of the relevant Scriptures. Fifth, we should vertically and horizontally engage in determining and implementing an appropriate level and kind of contextualization. In Table 5, we have summarized the augmented model.

---

[604] The kingdom manifests itself in a Christian's life as he/she willingly submits to the joyous and peaceful rule and reign of God through Jesus in our lives. Graeme Goldsworthy, "Kingdom of God," in *New Dictionary of Biblical Theology*, ed. T. Desmond Alexander and Brian S. Rosner (Downers Grove, IL: InterVarsity Press, 2000).

[605] The covenantal relationship is all about Christians enjoying the loyal love of our God and reciprocating by giving our loyal love to God. Paul R. Williamson, "Covenant," in *New Dictionary of Biblical Theology*, ed. T. Desmond Alexander and Brian S. Rosner (Downers Grove, IL: InterVarsity Press, 2000).

[606] In this case, we seek to understand the philosophical presuppositions and beliefs of the researchers of these motivational theories.

Table 5. Relational-Critical Contextualization Model

Original Steps	Augmented Steps	Augmented Description
(No prior step)	1. Prepare by cultivating a kingdom-covenantal disposition of heart	Pray, depend, submit to lordship of King of the kingdom and Lord of the NC. Then, continue in that disposition throughout the rest of the process.
1. Exegesis of the Culture	2. Vertically and horizontally engage in exegeting the cultural item	Ask questions of the Lord...ask questions of people in the culture...
2. Exegesis of Scripture and the Hermeneutical Bridge	3. Vertically and horizontally engage in exegeting relevant Scripture	Ask questions of the Lord ... ask questions of the text...ask questions of commentators, mentors, the church community...
3. Critical Response	4. Vertically and horizontally engage in a critical response	Discuss with the relevant hermeneutical community the understanding of the cultural artifact in light of the relevant Scriptures. Also pray together seeking the ongoing help of the Spirit.
4. New Contextualized Practices	5. Vertically and horizontally engage in determining and implementing new contextualized practices	Prayerfully work with the community to devise new forms of practices that are scripturally sound and culturally appropriate. Then, put them into practice asking God's blessing.

We sought to use this model as we evaluated the four motivational theories we summarized in the previous section. What follows is our evaluation, or to use the model, our "critical response" to those theories. For most of the theories, we have both a *scriptural critique* and a *theoretical critique*.

In scripturally critiquing Maslow's theory, we consulted the analysis of other Christian researchers as well as adding our own critique. We agree in good part with Hammes'[607] Scripture-informed critique of Maslow's theory.[608] Fundamentally, Maslow has an unbiblical view of human nature. It is

---

[607] John A. Hammes was Professor of Psychology at the University of Georgia.
[608] Hammes, 724-725.

completely humanistic and naturalistic, and excludes any input from God's special revelation. Maslow says about human nature, "While it is still necessary to be very cautious about affirming the preconditions for 'goodness' in human nature...it is already possible to reject firmly the despairing belief that human nature is ultimately and basically depraved and evil."[609] As a result of Maslow's rejection of fallen human nature, he wrongly assumes that you should "trust your impulses" so long as you are a "healthy" human being.[610] This is in contrast to the Christian worldview that we need the grace of Christ to follow the Spirit and mortify the deeds of the flesh. Only by the Spirit's power can we have pure motives and actions.[611]

Koteskey agrees with this assessment of Maslow's theory. He correctly points out that Maslow's basic worldview is atheistic and naturalistic. This affects how Maslow sees human motivation. He excludes God and the biblical teaching of the image of God in humans in his consideration of human motivation. In fact, Maslow attributes all human motivation to biological reasons.[612] Yet Koteskey sees in Maslow's theory some elements of good "natural revelation" that Christians can accept from a Christian perspective. In particular, Koteskey believes that the "growth needs" in Maslow's hierarchy (i.e., the needs of belongingness and love, esteem, and self-actualization) are reflections in humans of the "attributes of God."[613]

We only partially agree with Koteskey's evaluation of Maslow's theory. It is true to say that because humans have image of God qualities, what we discover about them may give us hints of what our Creator's character is like. We believe it is scriptural to say that humans' desire for community (Maslow's belongingness and love), appreciation of being accepted (Maslow's esteem), and desire to reach one's potential (Maslow's self-actualization) are reflections of aspects of God's character. However to say, as Koteskey does, that "Maslow has discovered the attributes of God..." in these higher needs of humans is to say too much.

The Scriptures reveal the *independence or aseity* of God.[614] That is, God is not dependent upon anything, anyone, or the satisfaction of any so called "needs" in order to exist. Positively speaking, "God is self-existent, self-sufficient and self-sustaining."[615] Therefore, to say Maslow's higher needs in humans are the "attributes of God" is to imply God has these needs and must

---

[609] Maslow, xi.
[610] Maslow, 179.
[611] See Rom. 6-8.
[612] Koteskey, 9.
[613] Koteskey, 9.
[614] For instance, Ps. 90:1-4; Acts 17:23-25; John 5:26
[615] J. I. Packer, "God," in *New Dictionary of Theology*, ed. Sinclair B. Ferguson, David F. Wright, and J. I. Packer (Downers Grove: InterVarsity Press, 2000), 276.

have them fulfilled in order to move towards self-actualization. This would contradict the teaching of the Bible about God's independence.

In theoretically critiquing Maslow's theory, the first thing to point out is that Maslow himself admitted research was weak in supporting his theory. It was based more on the biographical information he had of self-actualized people and from his clinical experience. Subsequently, research has been done on the needs hierarchy theory, and yet little empirical evidence has been found to support it.[616] Other critics have pointed out that Maslow's theory does not allow for variance of needs between cultures. For instance, some people of other cultures have pursued the higher need of self-actualization though they were still living in poverty.[617] Additionally, Maslow formulated his theory in the context of individualistic Western culture where desiring one's own self-actualization is typically looked upon positively as a good goal. However, in collectivist societies people would negatively perceive such a pursuit.[618]

Adler accurately states that Maslow developed his hierarchy needs theory primarily within the context of the culture of the United States.[619] She cites various studies that generally agree "we should not assume Maslow's hierarchy to hold universally."[620] That is, the order and priority of motivating needs typically changes between cultures.

In scripturally critiquing McClelland's theory, we begin by first returning to the scriptural principle that "being" precedes "doing." We learn in Genesis 1:27 that a fundamental aspect of Adam and Eve's "being" was that they were "image of God" bearers. This preceded the command on what they should be "doing" in Genesis 1:28 of filling and subduing the earth. Viewing McClelland's theory from this biblical vantage point, the focus of his motivational research is primarily "doing" oriented. His exclusive achievement-oriented fixation in understanding human motivation seems lopsided. We are not saying it is totally wrong, yet it appears limited in scope in understanding human motivations. Also, it is obvious in his study that he believes having high nAch[621] in any culture is something to be taught and encouraged. For instance, in his research he sought to understand and promote the optimal

---

[616] Cherrington, 36-39.

[617] Kermally, 31-32.

[618] Geert H. Hofstede, Gert Jan Hofstede, and Michael Minkov, *Cultures and Organizations: Software of the Mind: International Cooperation and Its Importance for Survival*, 3rd, Kindle ed. (New York; London: McGraw-Hill, 2010), 129.

[619] Nancy J. Adler, "Cross-Cultural Motivation," in *Motivation and Work Behavior*, ed. Richard M. Steers and Lyman W. Porter, Mcgraw-Hill Series in Management (Singapore: McGraw-Hill, 1991), 320.

[620] Adler, 321.

[621] As we mentioned earlier, McClelland and associates used the abbreviation "nAch" as shorthand for the *need for achievement*.

characteristics in a father that would encourage high nAch in a son.[622] And this seemed to be done regardless of culture. McClelland has also taught and trained leaders of other cultures to be people with high achievement motivation.[623]

Critiquing McClelland's research theoretically, we perceive one factor that was very helpful was McClelland believed that a person learned how to be motived by achievement. He clearly believed it was a learned behavior. On the other hand, his theory has been criticized for not clearly specifying how one learns this behavior.[624]

McClelland's theory has received other critiques. For instance, Adler writes, "While helpful in explaining human behavior, McClelland's three motives have not been shown to be universal."[625] As we saw earlier, the important studies in motivation that McClelland is most known for is the study of the need for achievement motive. Adler cites various research findings of Geert Hofstede.[626] Hofstede has found that countries with cultures like the U.S., such as, Canada and Great Britain, typically will exhibit a high motivation for achievement. The cultural dimensions contributing to this phenomenon are a high need to produce and a great willingness to accept risk.[627] On the other hand, there are cultures, such as Chile and Portugal, that show lower motivation to achieve because they are less driven to produce and higher in risk avoidance.[628]

Turning to a scriptural critique of Vroom's theory, we underscore that Vroom is secular and humanistic in his outlook. This man-centered perspective so obviously displays itself when he suggests human motivation can be summarized in "Proposition 1" of his theory as a mathematical equation. He states, "The valence of an outcome to a person is a monotonically increasing function of the algebraic sum of the products of the valences of all other outcomes and his conceptions of its instrumentality for the attainment of these other outcomes."[629]

Vroom then goes on to provide in "equation form" his proposition. From a scriptural perspective, it seems at best too optimistic to believe we can use a

---

[622] McClelland and others, 280-283.
[623] Cherrington, 41.
[624] Noel Sheehy and Alexandra Forsythe, *Fifty Key Thinkers in Psychology* (London: Routledge, 2003), 170. http://ebookcentral.proquest.com/lib/westernseminary-ebooks/detall.action?docID=180109 (accessed 16 August 2018).
[625] Adler, 322.
[626] Geert H. Hofstede is a Dutch social psychologist and leading pioneer in researching cross-cultural dynamics in large organizations. He is also professor of organizational anthropology and international management at Maastricht University in the Netherlands.
[627] Adler, 321.
[628] Adler, 322.
[629] Vroom, 19-20.

mathematical equation to adequately describe the wonder of human motivation. The interaction of God's commands, God's providences, God's love, a person's heart and social settings, etc., all work together in motivating a person. These can hardly be squeezed into a grand unifying equation for understanding human motivation.

Theoretically critiquing Vroom's work, it is significant to mention that since the formal publication of Vroom's version of expectancy theory, various studies have tried to validate it, all without success. This has often been due to various flaws in setting up tests for such an elaborate theory.[630]

According to Adler, a simplified formula to understand Vroom's expectancy theory is $M = E \times V$.[631] "M" stands for the force of motivation. "E" means the expectancy that the person believes his/her actions will lead to desired outcomes or goals. And "V" stands for valence or the attractiveness of an outcome or goal. The research she cites finds that expectancy and valance values vary greatly between cultures. For instance, Vroom developed expectancy theory in the cultural context of the United States. American workers and managers have a relatively high expectancy value, believing that their actions can greatly control outcomes. Also, American culture has a relatively high valence for such goals like individual achievement. However, expectancy is much lower in Muslim countries that believe the will of Allah is more important than individual action in determining an outcome. Also, the valence in Latin American countries and Southern European Latin countries for individual achievement is lower, but it is higher for job security. Adler concludes that Vroom's motivational model can be considered a universal only if we contextualize expectancy and valence values to a given culture.[632]

A scriptural evaluation of prosocial motivational research needs to address a main premise of that research. From a scriptural standpoint, we do not agree with the premise that there are evolutionary natural-selection instincts that are sometimes driving people to prosocial behavior.[633] Rather, we believe we are made in the image of God. Though this image was greatly damaged in the Fall, humans still have the capacity from our Creator to show empathy and mercy so as to benefit others. Having said that, this is not to discredit all of the other helpful research in this field that does not seem to contradict biblical truth.

---

[630] Pinder, 144.
[631] Adler, 323.
[632] Adler, 323-324.
[633] "Altruism and Prosocial Behavior," in *International Encyclopedia of the Social Sciences* 88.

Integrate Motivational Theory into the Relational-Covenantal Lens

Before we go into each of the theories and point out items we integrate into the RCL to understand motivations, we need to point out two important matters. The first point is we use a *covenantal epistemology* that allows us to integrate these secular items with biblical covenantal insights. In brief, because God is covenant Lord over all things, when even secular researchers in the behavioral sciences uncover truths, those discoveries are all under the Triune God's lordship. So long as those items do not contradict the clear teaching of the Scriptures, Christians may integrate those insights into their understanding of the world. We believe we the need to go on a little "excurses" here to further develop our thinking on a covenantal epistemology.

This integration in missiology of scriptural theological truths with theories from disciplines like the behavioral sciences poses a *philosophical problem*. The problem is an *epistemological* one. The question is how can one integrate scriptural and theological knowledge with theories if their basis for knowledge are fundamentally different and even diametrically opposed?

For instance, Christian missiologist and cultural anthropologist Paul Hiebert[634] wrestled with this question. In his work *Anthropological Insights for Missionaries,* Hiebert described the dilemma of seeking to justify the integration of theology with anthropological insights. He said, "How do we integrate our theological and anthropological views of humans?... If we wish to draw upon scientific insights, we must face head on the question of how science itself relates to biblical truth."[635] Hiebert later in the book described the bridge between theology and theory through a *complementary* picture of reality. He used an illustration of two "complementary sets of blueprints" for a building. He explained, "Theology provides us with an overall picture of the building, the builder, and key events in its history." And in a complementary way, "The sciences provide us with insights into various structures of empirical reality."[636] They are two complementary *perspectives* of reality. He viewed God being the overarching giver of both perspectives of reality; therefore, Christians may accept both.

In Hiebert's later work, *Missiological Implications of Epistemological Shifts,* he engaged in a more sophisticated philosophical argument. As in the previous volume, Hiebert is seeking to find the common ground by which the missiologist can philosophically justify his/her integration of both theology

---

[634] Paul G. Hiebert was distinguished professor of mission and anthropology at Trinity Evangelical Divinity School.

[635] Paul G. Hiebert, *Anthropological Insights for Missionaries*, Kindle ed. (Grand Rapids, MI: Baker Academic, 1985; reprint, 2008), Kindle locations 151-156.

[636] Hiebert, *Anthropological Insights for Missionaries*, Kindle locations 223-224.

from the Bible and sound theory from the sciences.[637] After finding the epistemological systems of modernism and post-modernism lacking as a common bridge between Christian theology and the sciences, Hiebert settles on the epistemology of "critical realism" as the potential bridge.[638] Once more, as in his earlier volume, Hiebert believed a "complementary" relationship can exist between theology and the sciences. He wrote:

> From a critical realist perspective, science, theology, philosophy, and other knowledge systems are not antagonists but are potentially complementary. We need different knowledge systems to examine the world around us. We need theology to understand the cosmic history of all creation. We need the sciences to help us understand the material and social world around us.[639]

Hiebert recognized there could be problems and contradictions that arise between these "knowledge systems." Further examination of the data by one or several of the systems would be necessary to resolve such issues.

Therefore, we need to consider the importance of a *Christian epistemological system* in our research. We need a robust epistemology that will allow us to integrate the knowledge we gain in our research from God's special revelation (i.e., Scriptures) with the knowledge we gain in God's general revelation, particularly from secular motivational theories from the social sciences.

Ryan Gimple[640] in his very helpful missiological and philosophical dissertation finds the epistemological bridge for the integration of theology and theory from the social sciences in what he terms "covenant epistemology."[641] Gimple applies the epistemological work of Esther Meek, professor of philosophy at Geneva College.[642] Using Meek's covenant epistemology is a crucial method for Gimple to integrate Mezirow's[643]

---

[637] Hiebert, *Missological Implications of Epistemological Shifts: Affirming Truth in a Modern/Postmodern World*, xiv-xv.

[638] Hiebert, *Missological Implications of Epistemological Shifts: Affirming Truth in a Modern/Postmodern World*, 69-116.

[639] Hiebert, *Missological Implications of Epistemological Shifts: Affirming Truth in a Modern/Postmodern World*, 104.

[640] Ryan Gimple is Instructor of Christian Studies at Charleston Southern University.

[641] Ryan K. Gimple, "Integrating Transformative Learning Theory with Covenant Epistemology: An Exploration of the Missiological Implications" (PhD dissertation, Southeastern Baptist Theological Seminary, 2018), 21.

[642] "About Esther," http://www.longingtoknow.com/about-esther.html (25 August 2018). See Esther Lightcap Meek, *Loving to Know: Covenant Epistemology* (Eugene, OR: Cascade Books, 2011).

[643] Jack Mezirow was an American sociologist and educator who made famous his theory of perspective transformation.

transformational learning theory with mission theology.[644] Meek "integrated two related ideas from Frame: 'servant thinking' and a triad of the existential-situational-normative that exists in every knowing event."[645]

In Frame's Reformed covenantal epistemology, he emphasizes the covenant lordship of Jesus over everything including every human knowing event. Frame said, "What kind of knowledge is consistent with God's lordship? Above all, we must recognize that human knowledge of God is covenantal in character, as all human activities are."[646] Due to God's lordship over humankind, the proper covenantal response humans should give to God in their knowing is what Frame calls "servant thinking."[647]

Gimple and Wan in the book, *Covenant Transformative Learning: Theory and Practice for Mission*, integrated Frame's and Meek's Reformed covenant epistemology with Mezirow's transformational learning theory. One of the main ideas of Mezirow's transformational learning "challenges adult learners to critically reflect on the most basic presuppositions, our meaning perspectives, our habits of thinking, and our frame of reference."[648] By enhancing this idea with covenantal epistemology, one brings this critical reflection under the covenantal lordship of Christ so as to serve him in our thinking about reality.[649]

For our study, a form of covenant epistemology is crucial in our attempts at missiological integration. This covenant epistemology helps us integrate theological insights regarding motivations for mission with sound motivational theories in the social sciences. The *way* this covenantal epistemology helps us to *integrate* theology with sound aspects of motivational theories is by understanding the *relationship* of the different sources of knowledge. In particular, covenant epistemology emphasizes the *lordship relationship* of God over all creation including human knowledge. God as Lord gives knowledge about motivations for mission in the Scriptures and in good theology deriving from the Bible. Also, as Lord, he gives general knowledge about human motivations through research from the social sciences. Because of his lordship over these sources of knowledge, there is at least the potential of a *complementary integration*[650] of their insights so long as the theories are consistent with the special revelation of God's Word.

---

[644] Gimple, 19.
[645] Gimple, 148.
[646] Frame, *The Doctrine of the Knowledge of God*, 40.
[647] Frame, *The Doctrine of the Knowledge of God*, 21.
[648] Gimple, 157.
[649] Ryan Gimple and Enoch Wan, *Covenant Transformative Learning Theory and Practice for Mission* (Portland, OR: Western Academic Press, 2021). Appendix II.

[650] So, in a qualified way, we agree with Hiebert's complementarian epistemological perspective, but we get to that point from a covenantal lordship rationale.

The second point we need to mention before we begin the integration is we want to say that each of these items we integrate merely confirmed, sharpened, or corresponded to concepts already in the RCL. There was nothing new that we are integrating into the RCL from these theories.

From Maslow's theory, we integrate the following items into the RCL. Clayton Alderfer[651] made further refinements of Maslow's theory in at least two helpful ways.[652] First, he condensed Maslow's categories of needs into three broader categories: *existence, relatedness,* and *growth.* Existence needs include all the "material physiological desires." Relatedness needs are all those that deal with social relationships. Growth needs are the various forms of desires that involve a person being more creative and productive. It is from the first letters of these simplified categories that Alderfer gives his theory its name, the E.R.G. Theory. Second, Alderfer differed from Maslow in saying that there is no sequential order of dependency among these needs. That is, one type of need did not have to be satisfied before other needs could be satisfied (so Maslow). Instead, he asserts that simultaneously "mixtures" or a "compound" of these needs can motivate people to action. We can integrate three items from his theory.

The first item to integrate is this: Alderfer's simplified categories of needs seems to correspondence with the three-fold covenantal triperspectival grouping of motivations we mentioned earlier. Existence needs correspond to the situational covenantal motives. Relatedness needs map to the existential covenantal motives. And growth needs fit with the normative covenantal motivations. It appears the three covenantal ways God often motivates his people in part answer to his people's needs as humans.

The second item to integrate is this: Alderfer's observation that a person can simultaneously have a mixture of needs that motivate him/her is consistent with what we have already considered in the RCC. That is, the Lord often uses a combination of normative, situational, and existential motivational stimuli to motivate his covenant people.

The third and final element to integrate is as follows: we believe we can integrate the ERG Theory's proposition 6 into the RCL. The theory actually has seven major propositions. All the propositions describe the interrelatedness of the three main needs in their desire and satisfaction. Proposition 6 in particular seems relevant to our study. It states, "the more relatedness needs are satisfied, the more growth needs will be desired."[653] According to Alderfer, "relatedness needs include all the needs which involve relationships with

---

[651] Clayton P. Alderfer was with the Department of Administrative Sciences at Yale University.

[652] Clayton P. Alderfer, "The Empirical Test of a New Theory of Human Needs," *Organizational Behavior and Human Performance* 4, no. 2 (May 1969): 142-175.

[653] Alderfer, 178-179.

significant other people." He writes, "growth needs include all the needs which involve a person making creative or productive effects on himself and the environment."[654] His observation in proposition 6 seems strikingly related to what we discovered in chapter 2 that a Christian who enjoys assurance of a solid loving relationship with God (the ultimate "relatedness need") will often be motivated to go on and serve God and others, including in foreign mission (a type of "growth need").

From McClelland's theory, we integrate the following item into the RCL. There is one item from McClelland's theory in motivation that we can integrate with our covenantal understanding of motivation. As we saw earlier, according to McClelland a fundamental part of his research said that people *learn what things should motivate them.*

This idea that *motives are learned* can be integrated with the Scriptural understanding that God desires his covenant people to learn his ways which includes proper motives. Whether it is by believing parents in the family or by pastor-teachers in the local church,[655] Christians are to be disciples of Christ ever learning what should motivate them and what they should do. In our covenantal triperspectival understanding of motivations for mission from chapter 2, we would place this insight from McClelland in the *situational* motivational stimuli category.

From Vroom's theory, we integrate the following item into the RCL: all these motivational theories have as one of their basic assumptions the *hedonistic* principle. That is, people are often motivated by a desire to *maximize pleasure and minimize pain*. Though hedonism is part of each of the three theories we considered in this chapter,[656] yet it was Vroom who seemed to write most explicitly about this in his work. He wrote, "Most contemporary conceptions of motivation have their origins in the principle of hedonism…In every situation people select from alternative possibilities the course of action that they think will maximize their pleasure and minimize their pain."[657]

It seems counterintuitive to think that a Christian researcher as myself could ever integrate hedonism into a covenantal understanding of motivation. Certainly, hedonism's worse form leads to evil self-centeredness. Yet, as we studied in chapter 2, one of the fundamental motivational elements in ANE covenant treaty documents was the sanctions section that includes *blessings and curses*. Through these, God in effect was providing motivational stimuli to his people to, in a morally permissible way, maximize pleasure and minimize pain. In our covenantal triperspectival understanding of motivations for

---

[654] Alderfer, 146.
[655] See for instance Deut. 6:4-9; Eph. 6:4; Col. 2:6-7; 1 Tim. 4:12-16; 2 Tim. 3:14-15.
[656] See again the *Introduction* section to this chapter for a justification of this statement.
[657] Vroom, 11.

mission from chapter 2, we would place this insight from Vroom in the *existential* motivational stimuli category.

Finally, from prosocial motivational research, we integrate the following items into the RCL. There are at least two aspects of prosocial motivational research that we believe correspond to biblical covenantal motivational truths. The first is *prosocial personality traits and motives can be learned.* Research is showing that one can learn how to be empathic of the needs of others through the nurturing influence of authority figures like parents. Batson says, "generalized parental nurturance may provide the biological substrate for empathic emotion and altruistic motivation..."[658]

Additionally, Batson agreed with McClelland's belief that motivations are primarily a learned behavior. He wrote, "Still, were one forced to choose a single theory to explain why people do-and do not-act prosocially, social learning theory should almost certainly be the choice...Social learning theory has probably come closer to this goal than has any other theory in the history of social psychology."[659] According to Batson, this learning of motives takes place in a variety of ways such as by rewards and punishment, by relative rewards (i.e., the benefit of helping another outweighs the costs), and by observation and modelling.[660]

The second item we integrate is prosocial research's findings on the influence of the prosocial norm of *reciprocity*.[661] This is the norm in most every culture that tells people to give back to the person(s) who helped you. Gouldner has made extensive studies in this area.[662] There has also been much research to show people are motivated to follow this norm of reciprocity.[663] This reciprocity seems closely akin to that primary covenantal motivation we studied in chapter 2 of *loving gratitude* toward the gracious benevolence of the covenant Lord.

In Table 6, we summarize all the items from these motivational theories that we integrate into the RCL. Also in the table, we indicate where particularly in the RCL we integrate each item.

---

[658] Batson, 257.
[659] Batson, 246.
[660] Batson, 244-245.
[661] Batson, 246.
[662] A. W. Gouldner, "The Norm of Reciprocity: A Preliminary Statement," *American Sociological Review* 25, (1960).
[663] K. J. Gergen and others, "Obligation, Donor Resources, and Reactions to Aid in 3 Cultures," *Journal of Personality and Social Psychology* 31, (1975); D. G. Pruitt, "Reciprocity and Credit Building in a Labratory Dyad," *Journal of Personality and Social Psychology* 8, (1968).

Table 6. Integrating motivational theory into the Relational-Covenantal Lens

Motivational Theory	Theoretical Element to Integrate	Integrate with which Area in the RCL
1. Alderfer's E.R.G. Theory (an improvement of Maslow's Hierarchy of Needs)	3 simplified categories of motivational needs (i.e., *existence, relatedness, growth*)	Corresponds with Covenantal Triperspectivalism's categories (i.e., *situational, existential, normative*).
	A *mixture* of needs can work *simultaneously* to motivate	Corresponds with Covenantal Triperspectivalism's notion God simultaneously uses various motivational stimuli.
	Proposition 6: "the more relatedness needs are satisfied, the more growth needs will be desired."[664]	Corresponds with Covenantal Triperspectivalism's *existential* motivational stimuli arousing desire to accomplish *normative* commands.
2. McClelland's Achievement Theory	Motivations are *learned*	Corresponds with Covenantal Triperspectivalism's *situational* motivational stimuli. This learning is an instance of situational stimulus.
3. Vroom's Valence-Instrumentality-Expectancy Theory	*Hedonistic* principle at work in motivations	Corresponds with Covenantal Triperspectivalism's *existential* motivational stimuli. This hedonism is an instance of existential stimulus.
4. Prosocial motivational research	Empathic traits and motives can be *learned*	Corresponds with Covenantal Triperspectivalism's *situational* motivational stimulus. This learning is an instance of situational motivational stimulus.
	Reciprocity is a norm in most every culture	Corresponds with Covenantal Triperspectivalism's *situational* motivational stimulus. This reciprocity is an instance of situational motivational stimulus.

---

[664] Alderfer, 148, 151-152.

Examine Motivations for Mission with an Augmented Relational-Covenantal Lens

In the previous section, we integrated selected elements from the motivational theories into our RCL to understand motivations. Here in this section we seek to briefly examine how these elements can enhance our understanding of motivations for mission. The further practical out workings of these elements must wait until chapter 4 when we consider implications of our research.

From *Alderfer's refinement of Maslow's theory*, we observe two things. First, we are confirmed in our belief that we must pay careful attention to the mixed motivational stimuli God gives to his people to engage in mission. He gives normative, relational, and situational stimuli. Second, we should see the importance and power of the existential or relational stimuli God gives his people for mission. As with the Apostle Paul in 2 Corinthians 5:14, 15 and Ephesians 3:14-21, the felt sense of Christ's assuring love for him compelled him in his mission.

McClelland helpfully reminds us that motives are learned behavior. The Church needs to take pains to intentionally instruct the people God, through teaching, rewarding, and modeling, the high value of being passionately involved in mission.

Vroom's work reminds us to take seriously covenantal sanctions which God has calculated to motivate his people. We need to teach to Christians both the blessings of obedience to mission as well as the detriments of disobedience to the call to mission.

The *research in prosocial motivation* helps us to see the powerful influence Christian parents, pastors, and missionaries can have in teaching Christians to have altruistic mission motivations. The research also confirms that a reciprocating love to God, who first loved us, is a powerful and universal motive for mission.

Summary

"*What are some aspects of motivational theories that correspond with covenantal motivations for mission?*" This is the key question we have sought to answer in this chapter. We first surveyed three influential motivational theories (i.e., Maslow's Hierarchy of Needs, McClelland's Need for Achievement, Vroom's Expectancy Theory) along with prosocial motivational research. Second, we evaluated these theories using a scriptural Relational-Critical Contextualization Model. Third, using a covenantal epistemology, we integrated some elements of the motivational theories into the RCL. Fourth and finally, we used this augmented RCL to briefly examine motivations for mission.

CHAPTER 4

MISSIOLOGICAL IMPLICATIONS FROM RELATIONAL-COVENANTAL MOTIVATIONS FOR MISSION

Introduction

Our third and final key question is, "*What are some missiological implications that come from this study?*" We answer that question in this chapter. These implications are not detailed applications. It is our hope and prayer that this study will be helpful to future readers, and that they will more fully develop applications from this research to benefit the Church's mission work.

In this chapter then, we use the RCL we constructed in chapter 2 and augmented in chapter 3 to derive several possible missiological implications for mission motivations. Again, these implications are more suggestive than comprehensive. We limit ourselves to six implications. We have organized them in three categories – personal, pastoral and ecclesiastical, and intercultural.

Personal Implications

Towards Cultivating a Balanced Spirituality

As we saw in chapter 2, there appears to be a correlation between a healthy spirituality and strong motivations for mission. The triperspectival covenantal framework can guide us in cultivating a balanced spirituality.[665] As we have seen, the Lord's *control*, *authority*, and *presence* are fundamental parts of a covenant relationship with him. In the Christian life, we believe these parts translate to *structure*, *doctrine*, and *experience* in our lives, respectively. Each is very important in cultivating a balanced covenantal spirituality.

It has been our experience that in some, perhaps many, churches, *structure* and *doctrine* have been heavily emphasized while *experience* has been minimized or neglected altogether. It is good and right that we teach proper biblical structure in the family, church, and society. It is also good and right that we teach proper biblical doctrine. Yet, we have noticed some ministries seem to believe that reform in structure and doctrine is all we need to bring in a healthy individual and corporate spirituality. However, in these ministries the cultivation of an intimate experiential relationship with God

---

[665] See the following sections in chapter 2 entitled, *Covenantal Triperspectivalism* and *A New-Covenant Spirituality*.

appears minimized or simply neglected. Perhaps this is because, in Church history and in our own times, segments of the Church have abused religious experience. Nevertheless, if a biblical covenantal relationship includes experiencing God's presence, then such a model of spirituality is lacking.

Ministers and theologians through the years have shared this concern. Men such as Francis Schaeffer, Richard Lovelace, and J. I. Packer have in their own words voiced similar concerns. Schaeffer wrote of his spiritual crisis as a result of a scandal in his denomination that prided itself in its biblical structure and doctrine. He became disillusioned. He spent months praying and rethinking his theology. He wrote:

> I went further and wrestled deeper and asked, "But then where is the spiritual reality, Lord, among most of that which calls itself orthodoxy?" And gradually I found something. I found something that I had not been taught, a simple thing but profound. I discovered the meaning of the work of Christ, the meaning of the blood of Christ, moment-by-moment in our lives after we are Christians-the moment-by-moment work of the whole Trinity in our lives because as Christians we are indwelt by the Holy Spirit. That is true spirituality."[666]

Schaeffer found the importance of an on-going experiential walk of faith and obedience with his covenant God. He said later that many in traditional denominations were never taught the meaning of Christ's work in their daily life. He wrote of the things such Christians may be ignorant of: "He may never have been taught that there is a reality of faith *to be acted on consciously* after justification. This last point is the point of ignorance of many who stand in the orthodox and historic stream of the Reformation."[667]

Lovelace also found in his study of Church revival and renewal history that God used "doctrinal and structural reformation" as well as "spiritual revitalization" to bring vitality to individuals and churches.[668] All of these elements must be in balance. He wrote, "We must aim at building the structures of God's kingdom but recognize that we will only create these through the transformation of our experience. Concentration on reformation without revival leads to skins without wine; concentration on revival without reformation soon loses the wine for want of skins."[669]

During the First Great Awakening, the Spirit moved mightily among many different denominations and movements. Lovelace observed that there were

---

[666] Francis A. Schaeffer, *25 Basic Bible Studies and Two Contents Two Realities* (Wheaton, IL: Crossway Books, 1996), 134.
[667] Schaeffer, *True Spirituality*, 75.
[668] Lovelace, *Dynamics of Spiritual Life: An Evangelical Theology of Renewal*, 16.
[669] Lovelace, *Dynamics of Spiritual Life: An Evangelical Theology of Renewal*, 16.

common denominators to what was preached and taught and which the Spirit blessed:

> Each sought to balance carefully the two thrusts of the Puritan and Pietist synthesis of "live orthodoxy" ... *doctrine ... experience* [italics ours] ... This balance varied in its application according to the needs of the church in the different sectors of the awakening. Among the American Puritans, where *Calvinistic doctrine* [italics ours] was fairly well known-often in the form of a conceptual "dead orthodoxy"-there was a considerable stress on the *illuminating and assuring work of the Spirit in transforming head knowledge into heart experience, and sanctification* [italics ours] was more emphasized than justification.[670]

Lovelace observed further the contrast between a Puritan and Pietist "live orthodoxy" versus some stagnant forms of Protestant orthodoxy:

> Both Puritans and Pietists, however were concerned to guard against the subjectivism which might result from a unilateral emphasis on the Spirit, and they balanced that emphasis with a stress on the objective Word. ... The Pietism of Spener and Francke stressed also the primacy of biblical revelation over confessional doctrinal structures, holding that another cause of dead orthodoxy was reliance on purely manmade objective formulations rather than on the God-inspired objectivity of Scripture. The complicated system building of some forms of *Protestant scholasticism* [italics ours], which asked the Bible questions it is not designed to answer and extrapolated great leaning towers of theory from a few scriptural loci, was alien to the practical spirituality of the Pietists. ... *We may conclude therefore that the key to live orthodoxy offered by the Puritan and Pietist traditions is the proper balance between the Spirit and the Word with appropriate attention given to the role of each* [italics ours].[671]

Added to this are the similar observations of J. I. Packer. In cultivating a balanced spirituality, we naturally must include the process of sanctification. Packer compared many different "versions of holiness" among Protestants. He insightfully wrote:

> The historical conclusion is that Wesleyan and Keswick teachings about holiness have been influential mainly because they offer *what all Christians long for: fuller deliverance from sin and closer fellowship with Christ than any yet experienced.* [italics ours] In situations where *Reformed*

---

[670] Lovelace, *Dynamics of Spiritual Life: An Evangelical Theology of Renewal*, 43-44.
[671] Lovelace, *Dynamics of Spiritual Life: An Evangelical Theology of Renewal*, 278, 279.

Augustinianism [italics ours] was stressing the Christian's continuing sinfulness, as part of its testimony against justification by works, a vacuum was felt to exist in relation to hopes of holiness, and these doctrines stepped in to fill it. . . . The *theological conclusion* [italics ours] is that Scripture supports Augustinianism against the other positions, where they diverge from the Augustinian path, *but censures many Augustinians* [italics ours] for making too much of our continuing sinfulness and too little by comparison of the scriptural expectation of ongoing moral change into Christ's image through the Holy Spirit. The *devotional conclusion* [italics ours] is that when Christians ask God to make them more like Jesus, through the Spirit's power, he will do it, never mind what shortcomings appear in their theology.[672]

We need to cultivate a balanced spirituality that gives appropriate attention to the three areas of covenantal life – *structure, doctrine*, and *experience*. When we do so, under the blessing of the Spirit, many wonderful things may happen to us and our churches. One of those things we believe is a spontaneous increase of mission zeal, to which we now turn in our next implication.

Towards Fueling a Missionary Zeal

As with the previous implication, the covenantal triad of *structure, doctrine*, and *experience* can guide us in motivating the Church to engage in mission. Earlier in this book, we saw the Lord of the covenant of grace often uses all three types of motivational stimuli.[673] Though structural[674] and doctrinal[675] motivational stimuli are legitimate and needed when we seek to stir people to engage in mission, yet our research has found the important connection between experiential motivational stimuli and motivation for mission.

Can we really expect to cultivate an experience of the "love of Christ" like Paul's in 2 Corinthians 5:14, 15 and Ephesians 3:14-21 that will lead to spontaneous zeal for mission? We believe, by God's grace, to some extent we

---

[672] Packer, *Keep in Step with the Spirit: Finding Fullness in Our Walk with God*, 133.
[673] See the following sections in chapter 2 entitled, *Covenantal Motivational Stimuli* and *Motivation in the New Covenant*.
[674] For example: appreciating God's sovereignty in history that makes mission possible, organizing our churches to effectively send and care for missionaries, going on short-term mission trips to do evangelism, etc.
[675] For example: teaching we are loving God and others when we engage in mission, preaching people are lost without the gospel of Christ, understanding what Christ meant when he said, "teaching them to observe all that I have commanded you," etc.

can. We have already written about the elements of covenantal assurance.[676] With two of the three essential elements, faith and obedience, we can take pains to positively affect our lives and the lives of other Christians. However, the work of the Spirit in assurance is something we cannot control. It is his sovereign, mysterious, and gracious work.

There are many things we can do to encourage *faith* in Christ and his promises. Paul said in Romans 10:17 that, "faith comes from hearing, and hearing through the word of Christ." Preaching and teaching the narrative sections of the Bible are designed by God to build up faith in him. Encouraging the practice of meditation upon the Word of God will tremendously help. The Puritans were firm believers in the spiritual discipline of meditation.[677] One of the choicest truths to meditate upon is the love of Christ displayed upon his cross. This is what Paul said he did in 2 Corinthians 5:14, 15, and this is what he prayed for in Ephesians 3:14-21 that the believers would do. Edmund Clowney[678] has said, "Until we meditate on the price he paid, we cannot know the meaning of the love of God."[679] Furthermore, we can take Lovelace's advice and ensure our preaching of the gospel includes preaching to believers that Christ is not only our hope in justification but in sanctification as well.[680]

Likewise, there are a multitude of things we can do to cultivate *obedience* to Christ. Matthew records Christ saying in the GC in Matthew 28:20, "teaching them to observe all that I have commanded you." Christ wants obedience, and Matthew seems to have structured his gospel around five major blocks of Jesus' teaching that he expected his disciples to obey.[681] So teaching through those blocks would be helpful. All the while, we should encourage the people with Jesus' promise in John 14:21 that he would reward obedience with the experience of his presence: "Whoever has my commandments and keeps them, he it is who loves me. And he who loves me will be loved by my Father, and I will love him and manifest myself to him."

Though the third element in a biblical experience of assurance is the sovereign work of the *Spirit* witnessing to our souls, yet we can do something to even encourage this. That is, pray for this work of the Spirit. As we saw in our analysis of Ephesians 3:14-21, Paul prayed that very assurance for the Ephesian brothers and sisters.

---

[676] See the sections in chapter 2 entitled, *Covenantal Assurance* and *Assurance in the New Covenant*.
[677] Beeke, *Puritan Reformed Spirituality*, 73-100.
[678] Edmund P. Clowney was professor of practical theology and former president of Westminster Theological Seminary in Philadelphia, Pennsylvania.
[679] Clowney, 50.
[680] Lovelace, *Dynamics of Spiritual Life: An Evangelical Theology of Renewal*, 72-80.
[681] Chamblin, "A Commentary on the Gospel According to Matthew," 5.

If God were to bless our efforts to promote biblical assurance in ourselves and in the people of our churches, we believe it could result in a new day of spontaneous zeal for mission dawning upon us.

Pastoral and Ecclesiastical Implications

Reading Matthew 28:18-20 through the Relational-Covenantal Lens

Jesus famously said in Matthew 28:18-20, "All authority in heaven and on earth has been given to me. Go therefore and make disciples of all nations, baptizing them in the name of the Father and of the Son and of the Holy Spirit, teaching them to observe all that I have commanded you. And behold, I am with you always, to the end of the age."

Using the RCL, we can detect a covenantal triperspectival pattern[682] in the motivations Jesus gives to his Church to engage in cross-cultural mission. First, in verse 18, Jesus as the NC Lord, uses a *situational* motive to urge his Church into mission. Namely, in all the universe he has complete sovereign authority. Therefore his people need not be afraid to "go...make disciples of all the nations."[683]

Second, the Lord uses a *normative* motive to stir up his people to go on mission. That is, in verse 19, he gives them a clear command, "go...make disciples of all the nations." This is the main imperative of the GC, and Jesus explains the main imperative by three participles – going, baptizing, and teaching.[684] Jesus as the NC Lord, motivates his people by giving them clear direction for their mission.

Third, the Lord uses the *existential/experiential* motive to powerfully encourage his people to go on mission. There is nothing they will face alone when they are on mission. Jesus will always be with his people.

Pastors, teachers, missionaries can use these three categories of motives to stir up the Lord's people to engage in mission.

Evaluating a Church's Attempt to Motivate Members to Mission through the Relational-Covenantal Lens

The RCL can help us identify strengths and weaknesses in the Church's attempt to motivate members to go or to remain on mission. For example, if a church is almost purely doctrinal and rationalistic in its ministry, it is possible it will follow that pattern and merely emphasize *normative perspective*

---

[682] For an explanation of Covenantal Triperspectivalism, refer again to the section by the same title in chapter 2.

[683] We want to qualify this statement by underscoring what we said in chapter 2 under the section entitled the *Great Commission*. In that section, we acknowledged that the Church's mission includes the Matthew 28:19 GC command to "make disciples," but it includes more relational elements as well.

[684] Hesselgrave, *Planting Churches Cross-Culturally: North America and Beyond*, 20-21.

motives that stress the command of Christ. If motivation for mission is low among the members, such a church should prayerfully consider adding contextually relevant *situational perspective* motivations. These could include short-term mission trips, exposure trips to help inner-city multi-ethnic churches, and corporate reading and discussion of missionary biographies of devout and diligent missionaries. Such a church should also consider increasing *experiential perspective* motives. These could include some of the same ideas mentioned above under situational perspective motivations, and could include sessions of prayer and fasting for a fresh filling of the Spirit and increase in the experience of assurance. Restudying and implementing the truths found in Figure 2 about biblically cultivating the experience of assurance, could be of tremendous help to increase the members' motivations for mission.

Another example could be using the RCL to see if church members are placing *vertical relational* priorities before *horizontal* concerns. Pastors may detect members being more *horizontally* focused. The people may be ignoring or forgetting the *vertical* encouragements of the Lord regarding their identity as servants who are to be on mission with him. If this is the case, pastors can take appropriate steps to remedy the situation with factors such as repentance, teaching on mission, and prayer to greater experience the "love of Christ" that should "compel" them to service in mission.

A final example is that we could use the RCL, to help *identify deficiencies in the members' understanding about and living from a relational-covenantal worldview.* In chapter 2, as part of the RCL, we considered many facets in the RCC between the Triune God and his people. All those features are parts of a relational-covenantal worldview. One important part of that worldview is that we are to live under his loving lordship. As we have seen, another part of that worldview is our Triune God's *commands, redemption*, and *presence* are supposed to all stimulate us to reciprocal, faithful loving obedience to him. If this worldview is properly grasped by members and applied to their daily life, then enormous mission-related covenantal promises like those found in the Abrahamic Covenant in Genesis of his people living *to be a blessing to the nations* would be enormously motivating to them.[685] *Contrariwise, a deficiency in a biblical relational-covenantal worldview would be a significant reason for weak motivations for mission.* Ministers who find these deficiencies in their members' worldview can pray, trust the Spirit, and then work to help *transform their worldview.* For instance, the ministers could address three

---

[685] The idea of this final example came to me while I, Chris, was in Kairos training in October 2018 at Team Expansion headquarters in Louisville, Kentucky. See *Kairos: God, the Church, and the World - Reader*, 4th ed. (Living Springs International, 2011). In particular, the last devotional entitled, "Pursuing a Biblical Worldview" was instrumental in giving me this idea.

areas – *understanding, situation,* and *experience.* We have made some suggestions in Table 7.

Table 7. Suggestions in addressing areas of deficiencies in relational-covenantal worldview

1.	Understanding
	   a. Knowing God
	      i. Kingdom-covenant mentality
	      ii. *Missio Dei*
	   b. Knowing ourselves
	      i. Kingdom-covenant identity
	      ii. Priests/Servants on mission with their God
	      iii. Seeds of Abraham
	      iv. Multiethnic corporate identity of the Church according to Scriptures[686]
	   c. Knowing covenantal relationship dynamics
	      i. Fundamental RCC values taught and emphasized such as, "faithful loyal love" of God to us and us to God; RCC motivations[687]
	      ii. NC "blessings"; summary and application of them

2.	Situation
	   a. The leadership models in word and life a relational-covenantal worldview
	   b. Provide situations for members to serve short-term in domestic or foreign mission work

3.	Experience[688]
	   a. Paul's prayers in Ephesians 1 and 3 for experience of HS to know the love of God
	   b. Experience the Lord's Supper as a covenantal renewal ceremony[689]

Intercultural Implications

Cross-Culturally Communicating Relational-Covenantal Motivations for Mission

If, by his grace, an implication of this study is that it is practically helpful to some and they desire to teach it cross-culturally, then the following suggestions may be helpful in doing that.

---

[686] *Diaspora Missiology: Reflections on Reaching the Scattered Peoples of the World*, ed. Enoch Wan and Michael Pocock, Kindle ed., Evangelical Missiological Society Series, vol. 23 (Pasadena, CA: William Carey Library, 2015), Kindle locations 2554-2567.

[687] See Figure 4 and Tables 1 through 3 for a quick summary of RCC motivational findings.

[688] Smith believed that "experience" is the closest layer to emotionally-based worldview core. Therefore, to affect change at this core it might be very effective to use biblical experiences to transform the worldview. See Donald K. Smith, *Creating Understanding: Christian Communication across Cultural Landscapes*, Kindle ed. (Books On Creating Understanding, 2014), Kindle locations 4955-4968.

[689] Geerhardus Vos, *Biblical Theology: Old and New Testaments* (Grand Rapids: William B. Eerdmans Publishing Co., 1948; reprint, Edinburgh: Banner of Truth, 2004), 300. Like the

Some Principles of Intercultural Communication

We seek to keep before us the following principles as we make our cross-cultural communication suggestions. The sub-sections below consist of two things: a brief summary of the principles, and a brief application of them.

Wan's Creator and Creatures in Relation to Each Other

Wan's diagram that we reproduce in Figure 5 addresses the presence of the oft forgotten cultures of the Triune God and of angels.[690] We should consider them as cultures because as Wan informs us culture should be defined as "patterned interaction of personal Beings/beings."[691]

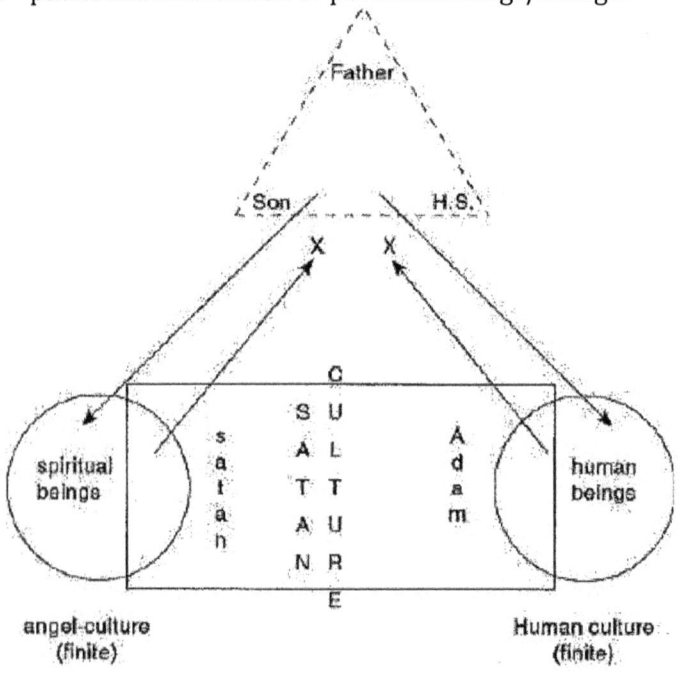

Figure 5. Creator and creatures in relation to each other

"historical prologue" in ANE treaty documents, the Lord's Supper is a visual reminder of the historical redemption at Christ's cross. And, like the historical prologue, it should cause believers to remember the great salvation won for us by our Lord, and in turn motivate us to new loving obedience to him. Also, like biblical covenantal renewal ceremonies, the Lord's Supper is meant to motivate us to loyal love shown in obedience to our Lord.

[690] Enoch Wan, "The Theological Application of the Contextual-Interaction Model of Culture," *His Dominion* 9, no. 1 (1982): 2.

[691] Wan, "A Critique of Charles Kraft's Use/Misuse of Communication & Social Sciences in Biblical Interpretation & Missiological Formulation," 122.

We therefore observe that the communication that flows between the Triune God and humans is one flowing between two cultures. Thus, communications between God in a perfect Trinitarian RCC with humans in a God-to-human RCC are always intercultural communications.[692] Therefore, when we communicate RCC motivations for mission to a Christian audience, we are engaging in cross-cultural communication. We are seeking to communicate truths from a biblical RCC to Christians whose native human cultures may not have these ideas.

Hedinger's and Wan's Relationships within Intercultural Ministry

Hedinger's[693] and Wan's diagram in Figure 6 seeks to show that in any human to-human intercultural communication, we must remember there is always the vertical involvement in some way of the Triune God.[694] The line numbers in the diagram have the following meaning:

1. Relationship between the Members of the Trinity
2. Relationship between God and the gospel messenger (vertical)
3. Relationship between God and the audience (vertical)
4. Relationship between the messenger and the audience (horizontal)
5. Relationship between the gospel messenger and his/her home culture (horizontal)
6. Relationship between the audience and his/her home culture (horizontal)
7. Demonic interaction with all other relationships

---

[692] We mentioned this in chapter 1 under the section *Definition of Key Terms* in particular under the definition of "RCC."

[693] Mark Hedinger is Executive Director of CultureBound in Portland, Oregon. He is also adjunct professor of Intercultural Studies at Western Seminary.

[694] Wan and Hedinger, 41.

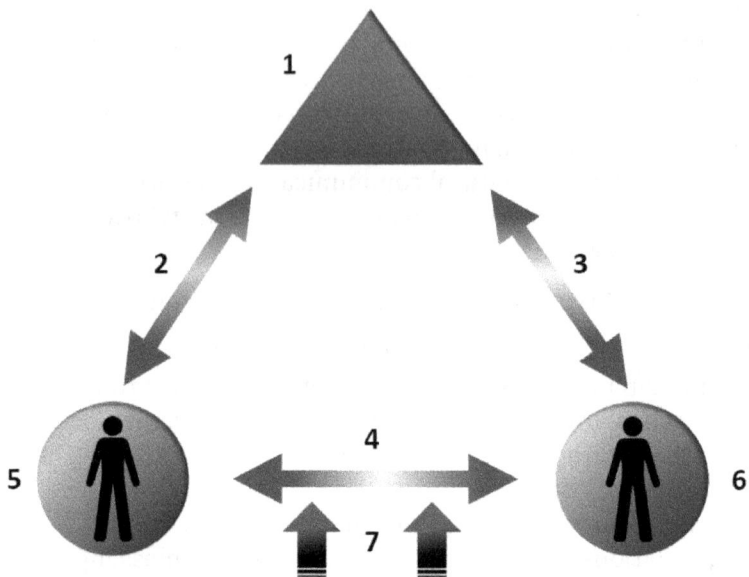

Figure 6. Relationships within intercultural ministries

Therefore, when we communicate the material of RCC motivations for mission to Christians, we must know the Triune God is also involved in this communication.

Hesselgrave's Three-Culture Model of Communication

In Figure 7,[695] Hesselgrave has a similar diagram to that of Wan's (see Figure 5). However, there are differences. Wan's diagram is focusing on the different personal Beings/beings of culture and their interaction. Hesselgrave's diagram is showing the different cultural contexts in communication. So, by "Bible culture," he is saying the Bible's message is steeped in the culture of the human authors of the Bible, God being the ultimate Author.

---

[695] Hesselgrave, *Communicating Christ Cross-Culturally*, 108.

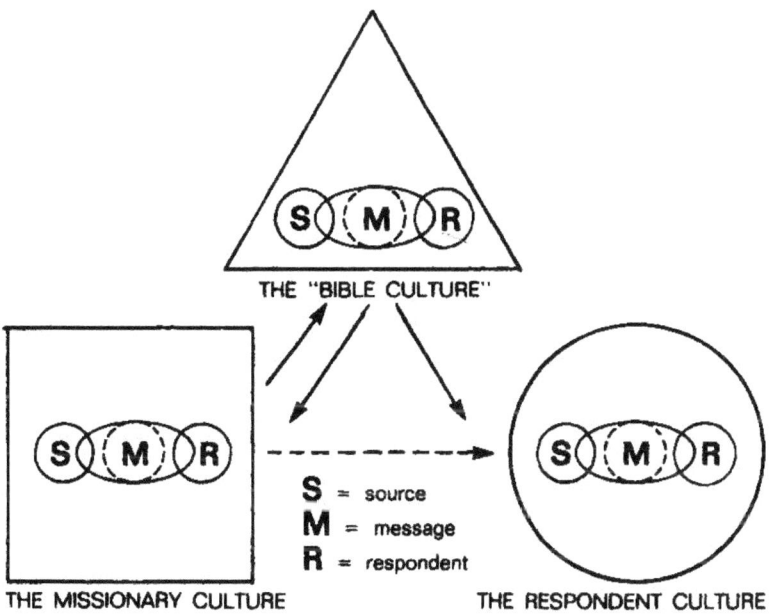

Figure 7. Three-culture model of communication

In our objective to cross-culturally communicate RCC motivations for mission material to Christians of various cultures, we must realize our task actually involves navigating three cultures. First, we are taking biblical RCC concepts from biblical culture. Second, we take that information through our native culture. Finally, we endeavor to communicate those truths to our audience in his/her native culture.

Smith's Framework for Understanding Intercultural Communication

In Figure 8, Smith's[696] diagram shows, in *process* form, major steps in intercultural communications, from a horizontal human level.[697] He admits that this model is oversimplifying the rather complex realities of intercultural communication; nonetheless, it is a helpful framework to discuss the process.[698]

---

[696] Donald K. Smith was professor of international communication at Western Seminary in Portland, Oregon. He was a missionary in southern and eastern Africa. He was also director of the International Institute for Christian Communication now called CultureBound in Portland, Oregon.
[697] Smith, Kindle locations 256-270.
[698] We also think Smith's model is weak in that the vertical dimension of the Triune God's involvement in the process is not explicitly stated in the model. However, in Smith's explanations it is more evident.

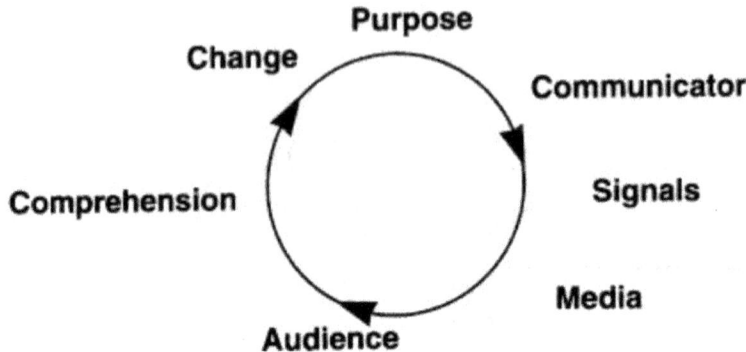

Figure 8. Framework for understanding intercultural communication

In the next section, we integrate Smith's framework with another model to produce a general approach to guide us as we think through suggestions on how to interculturally communicate the RCC motivations for mission material.

A General Approach

There are many possible approaches to help us organize our suggestions for cross-culturally communicating RCC motivations for mission. *The approach we have devised is to integrate two frameworks into a matrix.* The first is *Smith's framework for understanding intercultural communication* (see above).[699] The reason we want to use Smith's framework is because it is based on the reasonable premise that intercultural communication is a *process* with key steps to consider.

The second framework we use for this integrated matrix is *Hesselgrave's framework*, or "schema" as he calls it, for "motivation and cultural patterns."[700] The reason we choose this schema is because it notably takes into consideration *how various cultural elements affect the kind of motivations that a given culture finds persuasive*. We also appreciate the *four cultural categories* he puts forth because they seem to span various Eastern and Western cultures. We should note that we realize the original context in which Hesselgrave presented his material was in regards to sharing the gospel cross-culturally so as to persuade unbelievers to believe. However, the insights he carefully gleans from "ethnopsychology" regarding the effects of culture on motivations are pertinent to our book. In Figure 9, we reproduce

---

[699] Smith, Kindle locations 256-270.
[700] Hesselgrave, *Communicating Christ Cross-Culturally*, 590-611.

his original schema that represents a composite picture of various schemas in this field of study.[701]

---

[701] Hesselgrave, *Communicating Christ Cross-Culturally*, 595, 603.

COLLECTIVISTIC-DEPENDENCY CULTURES AND INDIVIDUALISTIC-INDEPENDENCY CULTURES

	COLLECTIVISTIC-DEPENDENCY CULTURES		INDIVIDUALISTIC-INDEPENDENCY CULTURES	
	ANCESTOR ORIENTATION	PEER-GROUP ORIENTATION	SUBJECTIVITY ORIENTATION	OBJECTIVITY ORIENTATION
Values	Traditional: "It has always been done this way."	Popular: "Everyone is doing it."	Intuitional: "Follow the gleam."	Lawful: "It is written...." "The evidence shows...."
Avoidance Goal	Shame of dishonoring the ancestors	Shame of disappointing the peer group	Guilt of disregarding the "vision"	Guilt of disobeying the "laws"
Attainment Goals	Acquiescence to the will of the ancestors leads to harmony.	Conformance to the expectations of peers leads to acceptance.	Attention to inner self leads to identity	Obedience to requirements leads to reconciliation.
Models	"Great men" of the tribe or clan	"Good guys" of the gang or club	Gurus and "tycoons"	Lawmakers and prophets
Media	Myths and legends	Interviews and opinion polls	Arts, poetry, reports of "visions" or success	Lawbooks, sermons, and scientific treatises
Decision Type	Group decision expected rather than individual	Group decision or individual decision expected to reflect group expectations	Individual decisions expected	Individual decisions expected
Decision Timing	Time is required for either group or individual.	Time may be required to ascertain "group mind."	Time may be required. Decisions should be immediate when the way becomes known.	The time for decision is now. The way is known. Any decision is better than none.
Decision Strength	Group decision is binding; individual decision tends to be risky and tentative	Group decision binding, but both group and individual decisions subject to change with mood or fashion	Group decision regarded with some suspicion; individual decision binding but subject to change with new "light"	Group decision regarded with some suspicion; individual decision expected to be followed through
Example	China	Modern United States	India	United States in the past

Figure 9. Collectivistic-dependency cultures and Individualistic-independency cultures

Notice Hesselgrave uses two general classifications for cultures (i.e., collectivistic-dependency and individualistic-independency). Then, he further subdivides each of those categories into two more sub-categories for a total of four culture categories.

We integrate Smith's framework and Hesselgrave's schema by using Smith's process steps as our vertical axis and Hesselgrave's four cultural categories as our horizontal axis. We use Hesselgrave's four cultural "psychosociological" categories of Ancestor Orientation (**A-O**),[702] Peer-Group Orientation (**PG-O**), Subjectivity Orientation (**S-O**), and Objectivity Orientation (**O-O**).[703] In the next seven sections below, we consider Smith's seven broad steps in the communication process using insights from Hesselgrave's original vertical cultural-motivational attributes to inform our intercultural communication suggestions. For each of the seven steps, we first review Smith's meaning of that step in the communications process. Second, we make our suggestions. At the end of these seven steps, we will present Table 8 that summarizes our suggestions in matrix form.

Purpose

Effective intercultural communication starts with the communicator having a *clear understanding of the material* he/she wants to communicate to the respondent. Also, the communicator must have clear *goals* in the communication.[704]

Chapters 2 and 3 give a clear understanding of the materials regarding motivations for mission from a relational-covenantal perspective. As for goals, for all four cultural categories, our communication goals are the same. *By God's grace and help one communicates so that the Christian respondent will change by, 1) more clearly understanding ("head") RCC motivations for mission, 2) more enthusiastically feeling ("heart") RCC motivations for mission, and 3) more willingly engaging ("hands") in mission.*

Communicator

The communicator's message, his/her personality, his/her perception of the audience, and the various audiences he/she communicates with, all interact with each other to affect the communication process. Also, how the audience perceives the communicator will influence the effectiveness of the communicator.[705]

A wise communicator will pay attention to what kind of person an audience perceives as a "model." Such a model person communicating to people in that culture will more likely effectively communicate a message.

---

[702] Regarding the A-O category, though we assume all in our respondent audience are Christians, it may seem strange we retain the "Ancestor Orientation" cultural category. We do not mean to imply Christians can worship ancestors. Rather, it is a recognition that Christians who came from A-O cultures may still have cultural patterns of motivation from their native culture.

[703] Hesselgrave, *Communicating Christ Cross-Culturally*, 595, 603.

[704] Smith, Kindle locations 270-288.

[705] Smith, Kindle locations 270-288.

Hence, the communicator of RCC motivations for mission material would be wise to pay attention that people from *A-O cultures perceive a "great man" to be the model. In PG-O cultures, it is a "good guy." In S-O cultures, it is the "guru." And in O-O cultures, it is the "prophet."*[706]

Signals

Smith observes, "All human communication occurs through the use of twelve signal systems."[707] This is true of all cultures. The twelve systems are verbal, written, numeric, pictorial, artifactual, audio, kinesic, optical, tactile, spatial, temporal, and olfactory.[708] Smith further observes, "Because culture and signals are inseparable, effective intercultural communication begins with learning how signals are used in different cultures."[709]

There appears to be a relationship between the four cultural categories Hesselgrave uses with "three cognitive approaches to reality" that these cultures seem to prefer. The three cognitive approaches are the *conceptual*, the *concrete relational*, and the *intuitional/psychical*.[710] It appears to us that A-O and PG-O cultures tend to be primarily concrete relational in cognitive approach. S-O cultures are more intuitional/psychical. And O-O cultures are more conceptual. If the communicator considers the preferred cognitive style of the audience's culture when he/she encodes the message, it will likely result in the communicator more successfully communicating that message. It will also likely result in the communicator being more able to motivate the audience if he/she is calling them to change. *Therefore, in cross-culturally communicating RCC motivations for mission materials, use the twelve signal systems in culturally appropriate ways to make the message's form more concrete relational for A-O and PG-O cultures, more intuitional/psychical for S-O audiences, and more conceptual for O-O cultures.*

Media

Media extends the spatial and chronological reach of a message. Media can also influence the form of a message. Yet the effectiveness of communication is due to more than simply the media itself.[711]

Hesselgrave has found that for people in the A-O cultural category they often use the medium of "myth and legends" to communicate important information. People in the PG-O category often use the media of "interviews and opinion polls." People in the S-O category show a greater affinity to the

---

[706] Hesselgrave, *Communicating Christ Cross-Culturally*, 590-596, 603.
[707] Smith, Kindle locations 288-306.
[708] Smith, Kindle locations 2746-2764.
[709] Smith, Kindle locations 288-306.
[710] Hesselgrave, *Communicating Christ Cross-Culturally*, 302.
[711] Smith, Kindle locations 280-313.

media of "arts, poetry, reports of 'vision' or success." Those in O-O cultures prefer communications in the form of "law books, sermons, and scientific treaties."[712] The communicator of the material regarding RCC motivations for mission should consider these cultural preferences when contemplating the use of appropriate media to communicate and to stir his/her audience in RCC motivations for mission.

Audience

The "cultural onion"[713] is an analogy to describe the different "layers" of any culture. There is the outer layer of visible *behaviors*. They are affected by the middle cultural layers of various *values, beliefs,* and *experiences*. At the deepest layer of culture, the core of the culture, is the *worldview* with its unspoken fundamental presuppositions and allegiances. These layers of culture will affect the audience's perception and response to a message.[714]

The one who wants to communicate and to incite their audience in RCC motivations for mission, needs to pay attention to the following cross-cultural insights from Hesselgrave. Those in A-O cultures are often motivated *by tradition, by avoiding bringing shame to the group, and by seeking to achieve harmony for the group.* People from PG-O cultures will be greatly motivated *by doing what is popular to everyone in the group, by avoiding the shame of disappointing the group, and by seeking to achieve the acceptance of the group.* Those in S-O cultures will tend to be motivated *by visions, by avoiding the guilt of disregarding a vision, and by achieving a clear personal identity.* Finally, people in O-O cultures often are motivated *by acting in ways consistent with law and rules, by avoiding the guilt of disobedience, and by seeking to achieve reconciliation through obedience to laws.*[715]

Comprehension

A person's collective culture as well as his/her individual personal experiences, rationality, and emotions will all affect how he/she comprehends and responds to a message. Furthermore, the person's collective and individual sense of "felt needs" will affect his/her comprehension.[716]

We apply something here that we first observed in the above Signals section. It seems that Christians who come from A-O and PG-O cultures *will tend to have the "felt need" for a communicator to communicate a message in a concrete-relational form.* Those from S-O cultures *will have a felt need for an intuitional/psychical formed message.* People from O-O cultures *will have a felt*

---

[712] Hesselgrave, *Communicating Christ Cross-Culturally*, 590-596, 603.
[713] Smith, Kindle locations 4741-4955.
[714] Smith, Kindle locations 296-313.
[715] Hesselgrave, *Communicating Christ Cross-Culturally*, 590-596, 603.
[716] Smith, Kindle locations 306-325.

need for a more conceptual message. Therefore, to effectively communicate and to motivate using the RCC motivations for mission material, a good communicator will make use of these various felt needs in his/her Christian audience.[717]

Change and Feedback

Regarding the final steps of the communication process, Smith observes, "Change therefore requires the use of channels reaching both the group and the individual. The message originator monitors signals from participants in the communication process, adjusting form and content so the message will be more clearly perceived by both the group and the individual."[718]

Regarding the motivation to change, Hesselgrave observes various factors about change and decisions among the people in the four cultural categories. People in *A-O and PG-O cultures prefer to follow a group decision and want plenty of time to make that decision. Those in S-O cultures prefer to make an individual decision with little time provided the right choice is very clear. People in O-O cultures want to make an individual decision without prolonged deliberation.*[719] Once again, a wise communicator of the RCC motivations for mission material will take these things into consideration when he motivates his/her audience to change and to be more engaged in mission.

In Table 8, we summarize all our suggestions from the above seven steps of the communication process. Again, the framework for this intercultural communication approach is a combination of insights from both Smith and Hesselgrave.

---

[717] Hesselgrave, *Communicating Christ Cross-Culturally*, 590-596, 603.
[718] Smith, Kindle locations 306-325.
[719] Hesselgrave, *Communicating Christ Cross-Culturally*, 590-596, 603.

Table 8. Suggestions for interculturally communicating RCC motivations for mission

Cultural Categories[720] / Comm. process steps[721]	Collectivistic-Dependency Cultures		Individualistic-Independency Cultures	
	Ancestor-Orientation (A-O)	Peer-Group Orientation (PG-O)	Subjectivity Orientation (S-O)	Objectivity Orientation (O-O)
Purpose	• "Head"- Clearly understanding RCC motivations for mission • "Heart"- Enthusiastically feeling it • "Hands"- Willingly engaging in mission	• "Head"- Clearly understanding RCC motivations for mission • "Heart"- Enthusiastically feeling it • "Hands"- Willingly engaging in mission	• "Head"- Clearly understanding RCC motivations for mission • "Heart"- Enthusiastically feeling it • "Hands"- Willingly engaging in mission	• "Head"- Clearly understanding RCC motivations for mission • "Heart"- Enthusiastically feeling it • "Hands"- Willingly engaging in mission
Communicator	Model is the "great man"	Model is the "good guy"	Model is the "guru"	Model is the "prophet"
Signals	More "concrete relational"	More "concrete relational"	More "intuitional / psychical"	More "conceptual"
Media	Like "Myths and legends"	Like "Interviews and opinion polls"	Like "Arts, poetry, reports of vision or success"	Like "Law books, sermons and scientific journals"
Audience	Motivated by tradition, by avoiding shame to group, and by achieving harmony	Motivated by doing what is popular with group, by avoiding shame of disappointing group, and achieving group acceptance	Motivated by having a vision, by avoiding guilt of disregarding vision, and by achieving clear identity	Motivated by acting in ways consistent with rules, by avoiding the guilt of disobedience, and by achieving reconciliation by obedience to rules
Comprehension	Felt need for a "concrete-relational" formed message	Felt need for a "concrete-relational" formed message	Felt need for an "intuitional / psychical" formed message	Felt need for a "conceptual" formed message
Change and Feedback	Likes group decision with time	Likes group decision with time	Likes individual decision with little time if way is clear	Likes individual decision made without much deliberation

---

[720] Hesselgrave, *Communicating Christ Cross-Culturally*, 595, 603.
[721] Smith, Kindle locations 256-270.

Comparing Hiebert's Critical Contextualization Model with Relational-Covenantal Motivations

Another implication from our study's findings is that RCM can help with the contextualization of motivations for mission. We agree with Moreau's definition of contextualization: "The process whereby Christians adapt the forms, content, and praxis of the Christian faith so as to communicate it to the minds and hearts of people with other cultural backgrounds. The goal is to make the Christian faith as a whole – not only the message but also the means of living out of our faith in the local setting – understandable."[722] As we mentioned in the previous section, between cultures there can be differences in what people find persuasive to motivate them to action.[723] Christians in their native culture may find one set of motivational stimuli powerful in inciting them to engage in mission. However, other Christians from another culture may find those same stimuli not very powerful to motivate them towards mission. What contextualization process can a pastor, teacher, or missionary use to help in determining which motivations for mission in a culture are scripturally allowable and which are not? Which motives that are allowable need some reprioritizing? We propose an answer to these and other similar contextualization questions regarding mission motivations. In Table 9, we propose one could use Hiebert's Critical Contextualization Model that we mentioned in Table 4 as a basic process, then use the RCM for mission that we summarized in Table 3 to *enhance* the contextualization process.

---

[722] Moreau, 36.
[723] See the discussion associated with Figure 9.

Table 9. Comparing Hiebert's Critical Contextualization Model with Relational-Covenantal Motivations

Step	Hiebert's Critical Contextualization Model	RCM Contextualization Model
Exegesis of the Culture	To exegete some cultural item (e.g., physical artifact, behavior, value, belief) so as to ascertain its meaning in that culture context	Similar to Hiebert's step 1.
Exegesis of Scripture and the Hermeneutical Bridge	To exegete the Scripture to gain insight on God's view of that cultural item	• It is primarily here where the RCM for mission can enhance Hiebert's model. The enhancements come from Table 3. • Regarding motivational dimensions, the RCM for mission perspective informs us to look for vertical "love to God" and horizontal "love to others" dimensions. • Regarding motivational stimuli, the RCM for mission perspective informs us to analyze the motives in the command, redemption, and presence categories. • Regarding motivational responses, priority should be given to motives that are expressions of gratitude to God for his redemptive work in the life. However, as the RCM for mission understanding shows, there are other motivations that can be encouraged.
Critical Response	To discuss with local Christians how to understand this cultural item scripturally	The RCM for mission perspective can help inform the discussion with local Christians.
New Contextualized Practices	To guide local Christians and allow them to decide on new attitudes and practices that honor the Scriptures and yet are sensitive to the culture. Note: At times the scriptural response is to shun a cultural item because it clearly violates God's Word.	The RCM for mission perspective can help inform the decision of the local Christians.

Summary

"What are some missiological implications that come from this study?" is the key question we have sought to answer in this chapter. We derived six missiological implications of using the RCL. We organized them under the categories of *personal*, *pastoral and ecclesiastical*, and *intercultural*. Under the personal category, we placed the first and second implications. In both, we considered some ideas on how to increase spirituality so as to correspondingly increase zeal for mission. Under the pastoral and ecclesiastical category, we placed the third and fourth implications. We suggested a relational-covenantal reading of an important missionary text like Matthew 28:18-20. We then mentioned how ministers can use our findings to evaluate the mission motivational health of those they serve and take corrective action if needed. Lastly, under the intercultural category, we put the fifth and sixth implications. We proposed an approach to cross-culturally communicate these findings on RCM for mission. We then briefly compared Hiebert's contextualization model with RCM.

CHAPTER 5

CONCLUSION

Colin Grant wrote about the lessons we might learn from the Moravian Brethren's zeal for Christ that motivated their mission endeavors. He wrote, "Today, *we need a full theological formulation of our motivation in mission* [italics ours] and an adequate grasp of what we believe. But if there is no passionate love for Christ at the center of everything, we will only jingle and jangle our way across the world, merely making a noise as we go."[724]

In chapter 2, we made a humble attempt from a covenantal perspective to approach a "theological formulation of our motivation in mission." We have but scratched the surface. It is merely one approach to study motivations for mission. Yet it is an important approach as there seems to be a deficiency in the missiological literature in studying motivations for mission from this perspective. We sought to analyze the Apostle Paul's motivations for mission from a relational-covenantal framework that we distilled down into the RCL.[725] In analyzing passages such as 2 Corinthians 5:14, 15, Galatians 2:20, Ephesians 3:14-21, and Romans 15:14-24 from this framework, we sought to understand what moved Paul, using the triad of covenantal *motivational stimuli – command, redemption,* and *presence*.[726] Additionally, we saw that *command, redemption,* and *presence* stimuli correspond with the virtues of *faith, hope,* and *love.* We primarily studied the *vertical motivational dimension* (i.e., God to his people) of these stimuli.[727] In the *command* of Christ in the GC and in his personal call to be an apostle to the Gentiles, Paul had faith, and this motivated him. In historical *redemption*, Paul cognitively understood and relished the theological and personal significance of Christ's love on the cross for him. Paul had hope in Christ's on-going redemptive work in and through him. These also deeply motivated him. The experienced *presence* of Christ's love for him by the NC Spirit's work of assurance seemed especially powerful to motivate Paul in all his missionary work.[728] We also sought to understand Paul's motivations, using a collection of covenantal *motivational responses*.[729] In response to the stimulus of Christ's redemptive love at the cross, we found that a mixture of loving "gratitude to God" and "enjoying God" appears to be Paul's main motivations for mission in 2 Corinthians 5:14, 15 and Ephesians

---

[724] Colin Grant, 275.
[725] See Figure 4.
[726] See Table 1.
[727] See Tables 2 and 3.
[728] See Figure 2 and Table 3.
[729] See Table 3.

3:14-21. Paul as a missionary was motivated by love *for* Christ because he had first wonderfully experienced the love *of* Christ. We found that Paul in Romans 15:14-24 had a mixture of "obedience to God" and "gratitude to God" as motivational responses for mission. Paul's faith and hope in Christ, in Christ's word, and in Christ's work motivated him. Additionally, we further focused on the spiritual dynamic of how the motivational stimulus of *experiencing God's presence* as covenantal *assurance* often leads to the motivational response of loving *enjoyment of God* in service. Furthermore, we sought to show that a healthy NC spirituality legitimately includes such important experiences of Christ's love, and that it often leads to spontaneous zeal in mission.

We demonstrated from Church history that Paul was not alone in this. Others, like the Moravian Brethren, experienced and/or wrote about how this spiritual dynamic of experiencing the assurance of Christ's love made them passionate to obey and serve their Lord.

In chapter 3, we surveyed several important motivational theories from the behavioral sciences. After evaluating them, we integrated those acceptable parts of the theories into the RCL. Then we examined motivations for mission through this augmented RCL.

Finally, in chapter 4, we derived six missiological implications from this study. We grouped them into three categories.

Many Christians from around the world sing a hymn by Isaac Watts. The hymn calls believers to remember *the Lord Jesus' magnificent display of faithful loyal love for his people upon the cross*, and it calls us to respond with a life of *grateful reciprocating faithful loyal love towards our Lord*. The hymn elegantly captures the essence of one of the important covenantal motivations that should motivate us to love, obey, trust, and serve Jesus all around the world and throughout all time.

When I survey the wonderous cross[730]
On which the Prince of glory died...
Love so amazing, so divine,
Demands my soul, my life, my all.

> **14** For the *love of Christ* controls us, because we have concluded this: that one has died for all, therefore all have died; **15** and he died for all, that those who live might no longer live for themselves but for him who for their sake died and was raised. 2 Corinthians 5:14, 15 (emphasis His)

---

[730] *Trinity Hymnal.* Hymn number 186.

APPENDIX

Detailed Outline of Book Contents

00. Introduction
    00.01.   Purpose of the book
    00.02.   Background of book
    00.03.   The researchers
    00.04.   Statement of the problem
    00.05.   Key questions
    00.06.   Definition of key terms
    00.07.   Potential significance of the book
    00.08.   Organization of the book
01. Explore motivations for mission theologically
    01.01.   Introduction
    01.02.   Analysis based on biblical theology
        01.02.01.   Selection criteria for texts
        01.02.02.   2 Corinthians 5:14, 15
            01.02.02.01.   Original context, structure, and meaning
            01.02.02.02.   Observations on Paul's spirituality
        01.02.03.   Galatians 2:20
            01.02.03.01.   Original context, structure, and meaning
            01.02.03.02.   Observations on Paul's spirituality
        01.02.04.   Ephesians 3:14-21
            01.02.04.01.   Original context, structure, and meaning
            01.02.04.02.   Observations on Paul's spirituality
        01.02.05.   Romans 15:14-24
            01.02.05.01.   Original context, structure, and meaning
            01.02.05.02.   Observations on Paul's spirituality
        01.02.06.   Summary of biblical theology analysis
    01.03.   Analysis based on systematic theology
        01.03.01.   Considering relational-covenantal truths
            01.03.01.01.   Covenantal Triperspectivalism
                01.03.01.01.01.   Control
                01.03.01.01.02.   Authority
                01.03.01.01.03.   Presence
            01.03.01.02.   Relational Paradigm
                01.03.01.02.01.   A covenantal connection
            01.03.01.03.   Other covenantal truths
                01.03.01.03.01.   Structure of biblical covenants
                01.03.01.03.02.   Responses in biblical covenants

                01.03.01.03.02.01. Faith
                01.03.01.03.02.02. Obedience as love
                01.03.01.03.02.03. Worship
          01.03.01.03.03.   Spirituality of biblical covenants
                01.03.01.03.03.01. Covenantal communion
                      01.03.01.03.03.01.01. God is personal
                      01.03.01.03.03.01.02. Humans are personal
                      01.03.01.03.03.01.03. Broken and restored communion with God
                      01.03.01.03.03.01.04. Covenant motto
                      01.03.01.03.03.01.05. Motivated by love
                01.03.01.03.03.02. Covenantal motivational stimuli
                      01.03.01.03.03.02.01. Redemption
                      01.03.01.03.03.02.02. Command
                      01.03.01.03.03.02.03. Presence
                01.03.01.03.03.03. Covenantal assurance
                      01.03.01.03.03.03.01. Assurance as covenantal presence
                      01.03.01.03.03.03.02. Promoted by covenantal elements
                01.03.01.03.03.04. Connection between covenantal assurance and motivation
     01.03.01.04.   Integration of a Relational-Covenantal Lens
          01.03.01.04.01.   Parts of the Relational-Covenantal Lens
          01.03.01.04.02.   The Relational-Covenantal Lens
          01.03.01.04.03.   Applied to motivations for mission
01.03.02.   Analysis using the Relational-Covenantal Lens
     01.03.02.01.   Relational Paradigm perspective
          01.03.02.01.01.   Use this RCL aspect to analyze Paul's experience
     01.03.02.02.   A New-Covenant spirituality
          01.03.02.02.01.   Structure of the New Covenant
                01.03.02.02.01.01. Similar to other biblical covenants
                      01.03.02.02.01.01.01. Name of the Lord
                      01.03.02.02.01.01.02. Historic Prologue
                      01.03.02.02.01.01.03. Stipulations
                      01.03.02.02.01.01.04. Sanctions
                01.03.02.02.01.02. Promised blessings
                01.03.02.02.01.03. Use this RCL aspect to analyze Paul's experience
          01.03.02.02.02.   Communion in the New Covenant
                01.03.02.02.02.01. Personal aspects of the New Covenant

                01.03.02.02.02.02. Foundation is union with Christ
                01.03.02.02.02.03. Use this RCL aspect to analyze Paul's experience
            01.03.02.02.03.   Motivation in the New Covenant
                01.03.02.02.03.01. Similar to other biblical covenants
                    01.03.02.02.03.01.01. Redemption
                    01.03.02.02.03.01.02. Command
                    01.03.02.02.03.01.03. Presence
                01.03.02.02.03.02. Great Commission
                    01.03.02.02.03.02.01. Prologue
                    01.03.02.02.03.02.02. Stipulations
                    01.03.02.02.03.02.03. Sanctions
                01.03.02.02.03.03. Use this RCL aspect to analyze Paul's experience
            01.03.02.02.04.   Assurance in the New Covenant
                01.03.02.02.04.01. Experienced as presence of Christ and his love
                01.03.02.02.04.02. Experienced by faith
                01.03.02.02.04.03. Use this RCL aspect analyze Paul's experience
        01.03.03.   Summary of systematic theology analysis
01.04.   Analysis based on historical theology
    01.04.01.   Analysis using the Relational-Covenantal Lens focusing on the existential motivation of assurance
    01.04.02.   Former theologians
        01.04.02.01.   John Calvin
        01.04.02.02.   Puritans
        01.04.02.03.   Pietists
        01.04.02.04.   Moravians
        01.04.02.05.   First and Second Great Awakenings
        01.04.02.06.   Pentecostals and charismatics
    01.04.03.   Foreign missionaries
        01.04.03.01.   Hudson Taylor
        01.04.03.02.   John G. Paton
        01.04.03.03.   Roland Allen
        01.04.03.04.   Andrew Murray
        01.04.03.05.   J. O. Fraser
        01.04.03.06.   Roger Greenway
    01.04.04.   Contemporary theologians
        01.04.04.01.   J. I. Packer
        01.04.04.02.   Tom Wells
        01.04.04.03.   Michael Haykin

    01.04.04.04. Douglas Kelly
    01.04.04.05. David McKay
    01.04.04.06. Richard F. Lovelace
  01.04.05. Summary of historical theology analysis
 01.05. Summary
02. Examine motivations for mission with motivational theories
 02.01. Introduction
 02.02. Survey of motivational theories
  02.02.01. Abraham Maslow's Hierarchy of Needs
  02.02.02. David McClelland's Need for Achievement
  02.02.03. Victor Vroom's Expectancy Theory
  02.02.04. Prosocial Motivational Research
 02.03. Evaluate the motivational theories
  02.03.01. Evaluate using the Relational-Critical Contextualization Model
 02.04. Integrate motivational theory into the Relational-Covenantal Lens
 02.05. Examine motivations for mission with an augmented Relational-Covenantal Lens
 02.06. Summary
03. Derive missiological implications from Relational-Covenantal Motivations for mission
 03.01. Introduction
 03.02. Personal implications
  03.02.01. Towards cultivating a balanced spirituality
  03.02.02. Towards fueling a missionary zeal
 03.03. Pastoral and ecclesiastical implications
  03.03.01. Reading Matthew 28:18-20 through the Relational-Covenantal Lens
  03.03.02. Evaluating a church's attempt to motivate members to mission through the Relational-Covenantal Lens
 03.04. Intercultural implications
  03.04.01. Cross-culturally communicating Relational-Covenantal Motivations for mission
   03.04.01.01. Some Principles of Intercultural Communication
    03.04.01.01.01. Wan's Creator and Creatures in Relation to Each Other
    03.04.01.01.02. Hedinger's and Wan's Relationships within Intercultural Ministry
    03.04.01.01.03. Hesselgrave's Three-Culture Model of Communication

03.04.01.01.04. Smith's Framework for Understanding Intercultural Communication
03.04.01.02. A general approach
03.04.01.02.01. Purpose
03.04.01.02.02. Communicator
03.04.01.02.03. Signals
03.04.01.02.04. Media
03.04.01.02.05. Audience
03.04.01.02.06. Comprehension
03.04.01.02.07. Change and feedback
03.04.02. Comparing Hiebert's Critical Contextualization Model with Relational-Covenantal Motivations
03.05. Summary
04. Conclusion

BIBLIOGRAPHY

"About Esther." http://www.longingtoknow.com/about-esther.html (25 August 2018).

Adam, Peter. *Hearing God's Words: Exploring Biblical Spirituality*, New Studies in Biblical Theology, Edited by D.A. Carson. Downers Grove: InterVarsity Press, 2004.

Adler, Nancy J. "Cross-Cultural Motivation." In *Motivation and Work Behavior*, edited by Richard M. Steers and Lyman W. Porter, 320-326. Fifth, International ed., Mcgraw-Hill Series in Management. Singapore: McGraw-Hill, 1991.

Akin, Daniel L., Benjamin L. Merkle, and George G. Robinson. *40 Questions About the Great Commission*, 40 Questions Series, Edited by Benjamin L. Merkle. Grand Rapids, MI: Kregel Academic, 2020.

Alderfer, Clayton P. "The Empirical Test of a New Theory of Human Needs." *Organizational Behavior and Human Performance* 4, no. 2 (May 1969): 142-175.

Alexander, James W. *The Life of Archibald Alexander, D.D. First Professor in the Theological Seminary, at Princeton*. New York: Charles Scribner, 1854.

Allen, Joseph L. "A Covenantal Model of the Moral Life." In *Love and Conflict: A Covenantal Model of Christian Ethics*, 15-48. Nashville: Abingdon Press, 1984.

_____. *Love and Conflict: A Covenantal Model of Christian Ethics*. Nashville: Abingdon Press, 1984.

Allen, Roland. *Missionary Methods: St. Paul's or Ours?* Grand Rapids, MI: Wm B. Eerdmands Publishing Co., 1962. Reprint, 2002.

_____. *The Spontaneous Expansion of the Church*. Grand Rapids: Wm. B. Eerdmans, 1962. Reprint, Eugene, OR: Wipf and Stock Publishers, 1997.

Allison, Gregg R. "Assurance of Salvation." In *Evangelical Dictionary of World Missions*, edited by A. Scott Moreau, Harold Netland and Charles Van Engen, 92. Logos ed. Grand Rapids: Baker Reference Library, 2000.

"Altruism and Prosocial Behavior." In *International Encyclopedia of the Social Sciences*, 2nd ed., edited by William A. Darity, Jr. Vol. 1, 88-89: Gale, 2016. https://go-gale-com.westernseminary.idm.oclc.org/ps/retrieve.d...E%7CCX3045300068&searchId=R4&userGroupName=s4556763&inPS=true (accessed 30 September 2019).

Ames, William. *The Marrow of Theology*, Edited by John D. Eusden. Grand Rapids, MI: Baker Books, 1997.

Anderson, Gerald H. "Introducing Missiology." *Missiology* 1, no. 1 (1973): 3-5.

Archer, G. L. "Covenant." In *Evangelical Dictionary of Theology*, edited by Walter A. Elwell, 300-301. Second ed. Grand Rapids: Baker Academic, 2001.

Bancroft, J. David. *Overflowing: Love of the Triune God as the Motive for Global Missions*. Bloomington, IN: WestBow Press, 2015.

Barnett, Paul W. "Opponents of Paul." In *Dictionary of Paul and His Letters*, edited by Gerald F. Hawthorne, Ralph P. Martin and Daniel G. Reid, 644-652. Downers Grove: InterVarsity Press, 1993.

Batson, C. Daniel. "A History of Prosocial Behavior." In *Handbook of the History of Social Psychology*, edited by Arie W. Kruglanski and Wolfgang Stroebe, 243-264. New York: Psychology Press, 2012.

Batson, C. Daniel, Stephanie L. Anderson, and Elizabeth Collins. "Personal Religion and Prosocial Motivation." In *Motivation and Religion*, edited by Stuart A. Karabenick and Martin L. Maehr, 151-185. Bingley, United Kingdom: Emerald Publishing Limited, 2005.

Bavinck, Herman. *Doctrine of God*. Translated by William Hendriksen. Grand Rapids: Wm B. Eerdmans Publishing Company, 1951. Reprint, Edinburgh, Scotland: The Banner of Truth Trust, 2003.

Bavinck, J. H. *Inleiding in De Zendingswetenschap (an Introduction to the Science of Missions)*. Translated by David H. Freeman. Kampen: J. H. Kok, 1954. Reprint, Phillipsburg, NJ: Presbyterian and Reformed Publishing Co., 1962.

"Bavinck, Johan Herman (1895-1964) | History of Missiology." http://www.bu.edu/missiology/missionary-biography/a-c/bavinck-johan-herman-1895-1964/ (21 September 2018).

Beaver, R. Pierce. "American Missionary Motivation before the Revolution." *Church History* 31, no. 2 (1962): 216-226.

Beeke, Joel R. *Puritan Reformed Spirituality*. Grand Rapids: Reformation Heritage Books, 2004.

_____. *The Quest for Full Assurance: The Legacy of Calvin and His Successors*. Carlisle, PA: Banner of Truth Trust, 1999. Reprint, 2000.

Berkhof, Louis. *Systematic Theology*. New combined ed. Grand Rapids: Eerdmans, 1996.

Blackaby, Henry T., and Avery T. Willis. "On Mission with God." In *Perspectives on the World Christian Movement: A Reader*, edited by Ralph D. Winter and Steven C. Hawthorne, 55-58. Third ed. Pasadena: William Carey Library, 1999.

Block, Daniel I. *How I Love Your Torah, O Lord!: Studies in the Book of Deuteronomy*. Google Books ed. Eugene, OR: Cascade Books, 2011.

_____. "Reading the Decalogue Right to Left: The Ten Principles of Covenant Relationship in the Hebrew Bible." In *How I Love Your Torah, O LORD!: Studies in the Book of Deuteronomy*, Google Books ed., 21-55. Eugene, OR: Cascade Books, 2011.

Bolt, M. "Motivation." In *Baker Encyclopedia of Psychology & Counseling*, edited by David G. Brenner and Peter C. Hill, 766-768. Second and Logos ed., Baker Reference Library. Grand Rapids, MI: Baker Books, 1999.

Borgman, Brian S. *Feelings and Faith: Cultivating Godly Emotion in the Christian Life*. Wheaton, IL: Crossway Books, 2009.

Bosch, David J. *Transforming Mission: Paradigm Shifts in Theology of Mission*. 20th Anniversary, Kindle ed. Maryknoll, NY: Orbis Books, 2011.

Breen, Mike. *Covenant and Kingdom: The DNA of the Bible*. Google Books ed. Pawleys Island, SC: 3D Ministries, 2010.

Brooks, Brent T. "A Biblical Theology of Motivation in the Pauline Epistles." Th.M. thesis, Dallas Theological Seminary, 1984. Theological Research Exchange Network, 001-0187, http://www.tren.com/e-docs/search.cfm?001-0187.

Brooks, Thomas. *Heaven on Earth*, 1654. Reprint, Carlisle, PA: Banner of Truth Trust, 2008.

_____. *Works*. Vol. II. Edinburgh: James Nichol, 1867.

Bruce, F. F. *Paul: Apostle of the Heart Set Free*. Paperback ed. Grand Rapids: Eerdmans, 2000.

Bruner, Frederick Dale. *A Theology of the Holy Spirit: The Pentacostal Experience and the New Testament Witness*. Grand Rapids: William B. Eerdmans, 1970.

Burgess, Anthony. *Spiritual Refining: Or a Treatise of Grace and Assurance*. London: A. Miller for Thomas Underhil, 1652. Reprint, Ames IA: International Outreach, 1990.

Calhoun, David B. "The Last Command: Princeton Theological Seminary and Missions (1812-1862)." Ph.D. dissertation, Princeton Theological Seminary, 1983.

_____. *Princeton Seminary. Vol. 1, Faith and Learning 1812-1868*. Edinburgh: Banner of Truth Trust, 1994.

_____. *Princeton Seminary. Vol. 2, the Majestic Testimony 1869-1929*. Edinburgh: Banner of Truth Trust, 1996.

Calvin, John. *Christianae Religionis Institutio (Institutes of the Christian Religion)*. Translated by Ford Lewis Battles. Vol. 1. 2 vols., The Library of Christian Classics, Edited by John T. McNeill, 1559. Reprint, Louisville, KY: Westminster John Knox Press, 2006.

_____. *Christianae Religionis Institutio (Institutes of the Christian Religion)*. Translated by Ford Lewis Battles. Vol. 2. 2 vols., The Library of Christian Classics, Edited by John T. McNeill, 1559. Reprint, Louisville, KY: Westminster John Knox Press, 2006.

———. *Commentary on the Epistle to the Romans.* Translated by John Owen. Rio, WI: AGES Software, 2000. DVD.

Carson, D. A. *A Call to Spiritual Reformation: Priorities from Paul and His Prayers.* Grand Rapids: Baker Academic, 1992.

Carson, D. A., and Douglas J. Moo. *An Introduction to the New Testament.* Second ed. Grand Rapids: Zondervan, 2005.

Chamblin, J. Knox. "A Commentary on the Gospel According to Matthew." Charlotte, NC: Reformed Theological Seminary-Virtual Campus, 2003.

———. *Paul and the Self: Apostolic Teaching for Personal Wholeness.* Grand Rapids: Baker Books, 1993. Reprint, Eugene, OR: Wipf and Stock Publishers, 2002.

———. "Pauline Epistles." Charlotte, NC: Reformed Theological Seminary-Virtual Campus, 2003.

Chan, Simon. *Spiritual Theology: A Systematic Study of the Christian Life.* Downers Grove, IL: InterVarsity Press, 1998.

Chapell, Bryan. *Holiness by Grace: Delighting in the Joy That Is Our Strength.* Wheaton: Crossway Books, 2001.

Cherrington, David J. "Need Theories of Motivation." In *Motivation and Work Behavior*, edited by Richard M. Steers and Lyman W. Porter, 31-44. Fifth, International ed., Mcgraw-Hill Series in Management. Singapore: McGraw-Hill, 1991.

Clowney, Edmund P. *Christian Meditation.* 2002 ed. Vancouver, BC: Regent College Publishing, 1979.

The Compact Guide to World Religions. Edited by Dean C. Halverson. Minneapolis: Bethany House Publishers, 1996.

Consolation in Discourses on Select Topics, Addressed to the Suffering People of God. reprint ed. Ligonier, PA: Soli Deo Gloria, 1992.

Creasman, Ron. "Why Do Missions? A Probe of Wesley's Life and Ministry in Search of Motivational Resources for Missions in the Twenty-First Century." *Wesleyan Theological Journal* 38, no. 1 (2003): 210-225.

Cummings, James E. "Paul's Theological Motivation for Mission." Th.M. thesis, Fuller Theological Seminary, 1974.

Dabney, R. L. *Systematic Theology*. Carlisle, PA: Banner of Truth, 1985. Reprint, Simpsonville, SC: Christian Classics Foundation, 1996.

Diaspora Missiology: Reflections on Reaching the Scattered Peoples of the World. Vol. 23. Kindle ed. Evangelical Missiological Society Series, Edited by Enoch Wan and Michael Pocock. Pasadena, CA: William Carey Library, 2015.

Dictionary of Biblical Imagery, Logos electronic ed., Edited by Leland Ryken, James C. Wilhoit and Tremper Longman III. Downers Grove: InterVarsity Press, 2000.

Douglas, J. D., Philip Wesley Comfort, and Donald Mitchell. *Who's Who in Church History*. Wheaton, IL: Tyndale House, 1992.

Duncan, J. Ligon. "Systematic Theology III." Charlotte, NC: Reformed Theological Seminary-Virtual Campus, 2003.

Dunn, James D. G. *Word Biblical Commentary: Romans 9-16*. Vol. 38b, Word Biblical Commentary, Edited by Bruce M. Metzger, David A. Hubbard, Glenn W. Baker, John D. W. Watts and Ralph P. Martin. Dallas: Word, Incorporated, 2002.

Eckman, David. *神的接纳与我的感恩 (Acceptance and Gratitude)*, Disc 1. BC101 Spiritual Life Formation. Pleasanton, CA: Becoming What God Intended Ministries, 2015. DVD.

Edwards, Jonathan. "A Divine and Supernatural Light Immediately Imparted to the Soul, by the Spirit of God, Shown to Be Both a Scriptural and Rational Doctrine." In *The Works of Jonathan Edwards*. Vol. 4, 585-603. Rio, WI: AGES Software, 2000. DVD.

Foster, Stuart J. "The Missiology of Old Testament Covenant." *International Bulletin of Missionary Research* 34, no. 4 (2010): 205-208.

Frame, John M. *The Doctrine of God*. Vol. 2. 4 vols., A Theology of Lordship. Phillipsburg: P&R Publishing, 2002.

———. *The Doctrine of the Christian Life*. Vol. 3. 4 vols., A Theology of Lordship. Phillipsburg: P&R Publishing, 2008.

———. *The Doctrine of the Knowledge of God*. Vol. 1. 4 vols., A Theology of Lordship. Phillipsburg: P&R Publishing, 1987.

———. *The Doctrine of the Word of God*. Vol. 4. 4 vols., A Theology of Lordship. Phillipsburg: P&R Publishing, 2010.

———. "Pastoral and Social Ethics." Charlotte, NC: Reformed Theological Seminary-Virtual Campus, 2008.

France, R. T. *Matthew: An Introduction and Commentary*. Vol. 1, Tyndale New Testament Commentaries, Edited by Leon Morris. Downers Grove: InterVarsity Press, 1985.

Gentry, Peter J., and Stephen J. Wellum. *Kingdom through Covenant: A Biblical-Theological Understanding of the Covenants*. Kindle ed. Wheaton, Illinois: Crossway, 2012.

George, Timothy. "Evangelical Revival and the Missionary Awakening." In *The Great Commission: Evangelicals and the History of World Missions*, edited by Martin Klauber and Scott M. Manetsch, 44-63. Nashville, TN: B&H Academic, 2008.

———. *Theology of the Reformers*. Nashville, TN: Broadman & Holman Publishers, 1988.

Gergen, K. J., P. Ellsworth, C. Maslach, and M. Seipel. "Obligation, Donor Resources, and Reactions to Aid in 3 Cultures." *Journal of Personality and Social Psychology* 31, (1975): 390-400.

Gimple, Ryan K. "Integrating Transformative Learning Theory with Covenant Epistemology: An Exploration of the Missiological Implications." PhD dissertation, Southeastern Baptist Theological Seminary, 2018.

Gimple, Ryan, and Enoch Wan. *Covenant Transformative Learning Theory and Practice for Mission*. Portland, OR: Western Academic Press, 2021.

Gloer, Hulitt. "2 Corinthians 5:14-21." *Review & Expositor* 86, no. 3 (1989): 397-405.

Golding, Peter. *Covenant Theology: The Key of Theology in Reformed Thought and Tradition*. Tain, Ross-shire: Christian Focus Publications, 2004.

Goldsworthy, Graeme. "Kingdom of God." In *New Dictionary of Biblical Theology*, edited by T. Desmond Alexander and Brian S. Rosner. Electronic ed. Downers Grove, IL: InterVarsity Press, 2000.

Gonzalez, Justo L. *The Story of Christianity Volume II: The Reformation to the Present Day*. Vol. 2. Second ed. New York: HarperCollins Publishers, 2010.

Goodwin, Thomas. *Works*. Vol. I, Edited by J. Miller. London: James Nichol, 1861.

Gorman, Michael J. *Apostle of the Crucified Lord: A Theological Introduction to Paul & His Letters*. Grand Rapids: Eerdmans, 2004.

Gouldner, A. W. "The Norm of Reciprocity: A Preliminary Statement." *American Sociological Review* 25, (1960): 161-179.

Grant, Colin A. "Europe's Moravians: A Pioneer Missionary Church." In *Perspectives on the World Christian Movement: A Reader*, edited by Ralph D. Winter and Steven C. Hawthorne, 274-276. Third ed. Pasadena: William Carey Library, 1999.

Green, Michael. *Evangelism in the Early Church*. Revised edition, Kindle ed. Grand Rapids, MI: Wm. B. Eerdmans Publishing, 2003.

Greenway, Roger S. "My Pilgrimage in Mission." *International Bulletin of Missionary Research* 30, no. 3 (2006): 144-147.

Greenway, Roger S., and Timothy M. Monsma. *Cities: Missions' New Frontier*. Second ed. Grand Rapids, MI: Baker Books, 2000.

Greidanus, Sidney. *The Modern Preacher and the Ancient Text: Interpreting and Preaching Biblical Literature*. Grand Rapids: Eerdmans, 1988.

Grudem, Wayne. *Systematic Theology: An Introduction to Biblical Doctrine*. Grand Rapids: Zondervan, 1994.

Hammes, J. A. "Maslow, Abraham Harold." In *Baker Encyclopedia of Psychology & Counseling*, edited by David G. Brenner and Peter C. Hill, 724-725. Second and Logos ed., Baker Reference Library. Grand Rapids, MI: Baker Books, 1999.

Haykin, Michael A. G. *The God Who Draws Near: An Introduction to Biblical Spirituality*. Webster, NY: Evangelical Press, 2007.

Hendriksen, William, and Simon J. Kistemaker. *Exposition of Paul's Epistle to the Romans*. Vol. 12-13, New Testament Commentary. Grand Rapids: Baker Book House, 1953-2001.

Henry, Matthew. *Matthew Henry's Commentary on the Whole Bible: Complete and Unabridged in One Volume*. Peabody: Hendrickson, 1996.

Hesselgrave, David J. *Communicating Christ Cross-Culturally*. 2nd ed. Grand Rapids: Zondervan, 1991.

_____. *Planting Churches Cross-Culturally: North America and Beyond*. Second ed. Grand Rapids: Baker Books, 2002.

Hiebert, Paul G. *Anthropological Insights for Missionaries*. Kindle ed. Grand Rapids, MI: Baker Academic, 1985. Reprint, 2008.

_____. *Anthropological Reflections on Missiological Issues*. Grand Rapids, MI: Baker Books, 1994.

_____. *Missological Implications of Epistemological Shifts: Affirming Truth in a Modern/Postmodern World*, Christian Mission and Modern Culture, Edited by Alan Neely, H. Wayne Pipkin and Wilbert R. Shenk. Harrisburg, PA: Trinity Press International, 1999.

Hoehner, Harold W. *Ephesians: An Exegetical Commentary*. Grand Rapids: Baker Academic, 2002. Reprint, 2007.

Hoffecker, Andrew. *Piety and the Princeton Theologians*. Phillipsburg, NJ: Presbyterian and Reformed Publishing Co., 1981.

Hofstede, Geert H., Gert Jan Hofstede, and Michael Minkov. *Cultures and Organizations: Software of the Mind: International Cooperation and Its Importance for Survival*. 3rd, Kindle ed. New York; London: McGraw-Hill, 2010.

Houston, J. M. "Spirituality." In *Evangelical Dictionary of Theology*, edited by Walter A. Elwell, 1138-1143. Second ed. Grand Rapids: Baker Academic, 2001.

Hughes, P. E. *Paul's Second Epistle to the Corinthians*. Vol. 47, New International Commentary on the New Testament. Grand Rapids, MI: Eerdmans, 1962.

Johnson, Ben. *An Evangelism Primer: Practical Principles for Congregations*. Atlanta: John Knox Press, 1983.

Kairos: God, the Church, and the World - Reader. 4th ed. Living Springs International, 2011.

Kaiser, Walter C. *The Christian and the "Old" Testament*. Pasadena: William Carey Library, 1998.

Kelly, Douglas. *Systematic Theology I*. Charlotte, NC: Reformed Theological Seminary-Virtual Campus, 2003. 12 Sys I - Lesson 7.mp3. MP3.

———. "Systematic Theology I." Charlotte, NC: Reformed Theological Seminary-Virtual Campus, 2003.

Kermally, Sultan. *Gurus on People Management*. London: Thorogood Publishing, 1999. http://ebookcentral.proquest.com/lib/westernseminary-ebooks/detail.action?docID=308965 (accessed 17 August 2018).

Kistemaker, Simon J., and William Hendriksen. *Exposition of Galatians*. Vol. 8, New Testament Commentary. Grand Rapids: Baker Book House, 1953-2001.

———. *Exposition of the Second Epistle to the Corinthians*. Vol. 19, New Testament Commentary. Grand Rapids: Baker Book House, 1953-2001.

Klein, William W., Craig L. Bloomberg, and Robert L. Hubbard, Jr. *Introduction to Biblical Interpretation*. Revised and Expanded ed. Nashville: Thomas Nelson Publishers, 2004.

Kline, Meredith G. *The Structure of Biblical Authority*. 2nd; Google Books ed. Eugene, OR: Wipf and Stock Publishers, 1997.

_____. *Treaty of the Great King: The Covenant Structure of Deuteronomy: Studies and Commentary*. Grand Rapids, MI: William B. Eerdmans, 1963.

Kohls, L. Robert, and Herbert L. Brussow. *Training Know-How for Cross-Cultural and Diversity Trainers*. Duncaville, TX: Adult Learning Systems, Inc., 1996.

Koschade, Alfred. "Luther on Missionary Motivation." *Lutheran Quarterly* 17, no. 3 (1965): 224-239.

Kostenberger, Andreas J., and Peter T. O'Brien. *Salvation to the Ends of the Earth: A Biblical Theology of Mission*. Vol. 11, New Studies in Biblical Theology, Edited by D. A. Carson, 2001.

Koteskey, Ronald L. "Toward the Development of a Christian Psychology: Motivation." *Journal of Psychology & Theology* 7, no. 1 (1979): 3-12.

Kruse, Colin G. *2 Corinthians: An Introduction and Commentary*. Vol. 8, Tyndale New Testament Commentary, Edited by Leon Morris. Downers Grove: InterVarsity Press, 1987.

Ladd, George Eldon. *A Theology of the New Testament*. Revised ed., Edited by Donald A. Hagner. Grand Rapids: Eerdmans, 1974. Reprint, 1993.

Latourette, Kenneth Scott. *A History of Christianity Volume II: A. D. 1500 - A. D. 1975*. Vol. 2. 2 vols. New York: Harper & Row, 1975.

Little, Christopher R. "In Response to 'the Future of Evangelicals in Missions.'" In *Missionshift: Global Mission Issues in the Third Millennium*, edited by David Hesselgrave and Ed Stetzer, 203-222. Nashville, TN: B&H Academic, 2010.

London Baptist Confession of Faith. 1689.

Longenecker, Richard N. *Word Biblical Commentary: Galatians*. Vol. 41, Word Biblical Commentary, Edited by David A. Hubbard, Glenn W. Baker, John D. Watts and Ralph P. Martin. Dallas: Word, Incorporated, 2002.

Longman III, Tremper, and Raymond B. Dillard. *An Introduction to the Old Testament*. Grand Rapids, Mich.: Zondervan, 2006.

Lovelace, Richard F. *Dynamics of Spiritual Life: An Evangelical Theology of Renewal*. Downers Grove: InterVarsity Press, 1979.

_____. *Renewal as a Way of Life: A Guidebook for Spiritual Growth*. Downers Grove: InterVarsity Press, 1985. Reprint, Eugene, OR: Wipf and Stock Publishers, 2002.

Lowrie, Walter M. *Memoirs of the Rev. Walter M. Lowrie*, Edited by Walter Lowrie. New York: Board of Foreign Missions of the Presbyterian Church, 1851.

Malone, Fred A. *The Baptism of Disciples Alone: A Covenantal Argument for Credobaptism Versus Paedobaptism*. Cape Coral, FL: Founders Press, 2003.

Martin, Ralph P. *Word Biblical Commentary: 2 Corinthians*. Vol. 40. Second ed., Word Biblical Commentary, Edited by David A. Hubbard, Glenn W. Baker, John D. Watts and Ralph P. Martin. Dallas: Word, Incorporated, 1998.

Maslow, Abraham H. *Motivation and Personality*. 2nd ed. New York, NY: Harper & Row, 1970.

McClelland, David C., John W. Atkinson, Russell A. Clark, and Edgar L. Lowell. *The Achievement Motive*. East Norwalk, Conn.: Appleton-Century-Crofts, 1953. https://search-proquest-com.dtl.idm.oclc.org/publication/177429 (accessed 10 June 2019).

McKay, David. *The Bond of Love: God's Covenantal Relationship with His Church*. Tain, Ross-shire: Christian Focus Publications, 2001.

Meek, Esther Lightcap. *Loving to Know: Covenant Epistemology*. Eugene, OR: Cascade Books, 2011.

Mendenhall, George E. *Law and Covenant in Israel and the Ancient near East*. Pittsburgh: The Biblical Colloquium, 1955.

Miner, John B. *Organizational Behavior 1 : Essential Theories of Motivation and Leadership*. Armonk, NY: M.E. Sharpe, 2005. http://ebookcentral.proquest.com/lib/westernseminary-ebooks/detail.action?docID=302474 (accessed 17 August 2018).

Mohrlang, R. "Love." In *Dictionary of Paul and His Letters*, edited by Gerald F. Hawthorne, Ralph P. Martin and Daniel G. Reid, 575-578. Downers Grove: InterVarsity Press, 1993.

Moreau, A. Scott. *Contextualization in World Missions: Mapping and Assessing Evangelical Models*. Grand Rapids, MI: Kregel Publishing, 2012.

Morris, Leon. *The Epistle to the Romans*, The Pillar New Testament Commentary. Grand Rapids: Eerdmans 1988.

"Motivation." In *The Gale Encyclopedia of Psychology*, 3rd ed., edited by Jacqueline L. Longe. Vol. 2, 778-780: Gale, 2016. http://link.galegroup.com.westernseminary.idm.oclc.org/apps/doc/CX3631000520/GVRL?u=s4556763&sid=GVRL&xid=51e456a4. (accessed 8 May 2019).

Murray, Andrew. *The Believer's New Covenant*. Minneapolis: Bethany House Publishers, 1984.

_____. *The Key to the Missionary Problem*. Fort Washington, PA: CLC Publications, 2001.

Murray, John. *The Covenant of Grace*. London: Tyndale Press, 1954. Reprint, Phillipsburg, NJ: Presbyterian and Reformed Publishing Company, 1988.

_____. *Principles of Conduct*. Grand Rapids: Eerdmans, 1957. Reprint, 1984.

_____. *Redemption Accomplished and Applied*. Grand Rapids: Wm. B. Eerdmans, 1955.

"National Director Commissioning Celebration | Omf." http://www.omf.org/omf/us/about_omf_international/news/national_director_commissioning_celebration (14 August 2011).

Neill, Stephen. *A History of Christian Missions*. Second ed. New York: Penguin Putnam Inc., 1986. Reprint, 1990.

New Bible Commentary: 21st Century Edition. 4th ed., Edited by D. A. Carson, R. T. France, J. A. Motyer and G. J. Wenham. Downers Grove, IL: Inter-Varsity Press, 1994.

Nichols, Greg. *Covenant Theology: A Reformed and Baptistic Perspective on God's Covenants*. Vestavia Hills, AL: Solid Ground Christian Books, 2011.

Noll, Mark A. *Turning Points: Decisive Moments in the History of Christianity*. Second ed. Grand Rapids: Baker Academic, 1997. Reprint, 2005.

O'Brien, Peter T. *The Letters to the Ephesians*, The Pillar New Testament Commentary. Grand Rapids: Eerdmans 1999.

Owen, John. *Communion with God: Abridged and Made Easy to Read by R.J.K. Law*, Puritan Paperbacks. Edinburgh: Banner of Truth, 2000.

_____. *The Works of John Owen*. Vol. 2. 23 vols., Edited by William H. Goold. Rio, WI: AGES Software, 2000. DVD.

Packer, J. I. "God." In *New Dictionary of Theology*, edited by Sinclair B. Ferguson, David F. Wright and J. I. Packer, 274-277. Downers Grove: InterVarsity Press, 2000.

_____. *Keep in Step with the Spirit: Finding Fullness in Our Walk with God*. Revised and Enlarged ed. Grand Rapids: Baker Books, 1984. Reprint, 2005.

_____. *Knowing God*. Downers Grove: InterVarsity Press, 1973.

_____. *A Quest for Godliness: The Puritan Vision of the Christian Life*. Wheaton: Crossway Books, 1990.

Paton, John G. *John G. Paton: Missionary to the New Hebrides*, Edited by James Paton, 1891. Reprint, Edinburgh, Scotland: The Banner of Truth Trust, 1994.

Pieratt, Jason. "Calling to the Missionary Vocation: A Study of the Lived Experience of American and Majority World Missionaries of Children's Relief International." D.Int.St. dissertation, Western Seminary, 2018. Theological Research Exchange Network, 002-0949.

Pierson, Paul E. "Great Century of Missions." In *Evangelical Dictionary of World Missions*, edited by A. Scott Moreau, Harold Netland and Charles Van Engen. Logos ed. Grand Rapids: Baker Reference Library, 2000.

Pinder, Craig C. "Valence-Instrumentality-Expectancy Theory." In *Motivation and Work Behavior*, edited by Richard M. Steers and Lyman W. Porter, 144-

164. Fifth, International ed., Mcgraw-Hill Series in Management. Singapore: McGraw-Hill, 1991.

Pink, Arthur W. *Spiritual Union and Communion*. Lafayette, IN: Sovereign Grace Publishers, Inc., 2002.

Pratt, Richard L. "Genesis through Joshua." Charlotte, NC: Reformed Theological Seminary-Virtual Campus, 2003.

Pruitt, D. G. "Reciprocity and Credit Building in a Labratory Dyad." *Journal of Personality and Social Psychology* 8, (1968): 143-147.

Ramsay, William M. *St. Paul the Traveller and Roman Citizen*. London: Hodder & Stroughton, 1907.

Reymond, Robert L. *A New Systematic Theology of the Christian Faith*. Nashville: Thomas Nelson Publishers, 1997.

_____. *Paul: Missionary Theologian*. Tain, Ross-shire: Christian Focus Publications, 2000.

Ridderbos, Herman. *Paulus: Ontwerp Van Zijn Theologie (Paul: An Outline of His Theology)*. Paperback ed. Kampen: J. H. Kok N. V., 1966. Reprint, Grand Rapids: Eerdmans, 1997.

Roberts, Maurice. *Union and Communion with Christ*. Grand Rapids, MI: Reformation Heritage Books, 2008.

Robertson, O. Palmer. *The Christ of the Covenants*. Phillipsburg: Presbyterian and Reformed Publishing, 1980.

Ryle, J. C. *Holiness*. 1979 ed. Hertfordshire: Evangelical Press, 1879. Reprint, 1985.

Sanders, E. P. *Paul and Palestinian Judaism: A Comparison of Patterns of Religion*. Philadelphia: Fortress, 1977.

Schaeffer, Francis A. *25 Basic Bible Studies and Two Contents Two Realities*. Wheaton, IL: Crossway Books, 1996.

_____. *True Spirituality*. Wheaton: Tyndale House Publishers, 1971. Reprint, Carol Stream: Tyndale House Publishers, 2001.

Schreiner, Thomas R. *Paul, Apostle of God's Glory in Christ: A Pauline Theology*. Downers Grove: InterVarsity Press, 2001.

Sheehy, Noel, and Alexandra Forsythe. *Fifty Key Thinkers in Psychology*. London: Routledge, 2003. http://ebookcentral.proquest.com/lib/westernseminary-ebooks/detail.action?docID=180109 (accessed 16 August 2018).

Sills, M. David. *Changing World, Unchanging Mission: Responding to Global Challenges*. iBooks ed. Downers Grove, IL: InterVarsity Press, 2015.

Smith, Donald K. *Creating Understanding: Christian Communication across Cultural Landscapes*. Kindle ed.: Books On Creating Understanding, 2014.

Smith, Gordon T. "Spirituality." In *Evangelical Dictionary of World Missions*, edited by A. Scott Moreau, Harold Netland and Charles Van Engen, 904-905. Logos ed. Grand Rapids: Baker Reference Library, 2000.

Smith, Ralph. *Paradox and Truth: Rethinking Van Til on the Trinity*. Moscow, ID: Canon Press, 2002.

Sproul, R. C., Jr. *Knowing Scripture*. Second ed. Downers Grove: InterVarsity Christian Fellowship, 1977. Reprint, Downers Grove: InterVarsity Press, 2009.

Stackhouse, Max L. *Covenant and Commitments: Faith, Family, and Economic Life*. Louisville: Westminster John Knox Press, 1997.

Steers, Richard M., and Lyman W. Porter. *Motivation and Work Behavior*. Fifth, International ed., Mcgraw-Hill Series in Management. Singapore: McGraw-Hill, 1991.

Swanson, James. "1182 Γινώσκω (Ginōskō)." In *Dictionary of Biblical Languages with Semantic Domains : Greek (New Testament)*. Electronic ed. Oak Harbor: Logos Research Systems, Inc., 1997.

Taylor, Howard, and Mrs. Howard Taylor. *Hudson Taylor's Spiritual Secret*. PDF ed.: OMF International, 2002. http://www.missionstomilitary.org/discipleship/lessons/Hudson Taylors Spiritual Secret.pdf (accessed 14 August, 2011).

Taylor, Mrs. Howard. *Behind the Ranges: Fraser of Lisuland Southwest China*. London: China Inland Mission, Lutterworth Press, 1944. Reprint, 1956.

Terry, John Mark, and Robert L. Gallagher. *Encountering the History of Missions (Encountering Mission): From the Early Church to Today*. Google Books ed.: Baker Academic, 2017.

Trinity Hymnal. Philadelphia: Great Commission Publications, 1961. Reprint, 1982.

Van Den Berg, Johannes. *Constrained by Jesus' Love: An Inquiry into the Motives of the Missionary Awakening in Great Britain in the Period between 1698 and 1815*. Kampen: J.H. Kok, 1956.

Van Engen, Charles. "'Mission' Defined and Described." In *Missionshift: Global Mission Issues in the Third Millennium*, edited by David Hesselgrave and Ed Stetzer, 7-29. Nashville, TN: B&H Academic, 2010.

Van Gelder, Craig. "The Covenant's Missiological Character." *Calvin Theological Journal* 29, no. 1 (1994): 190-197.

Varg, Paul A. "Motives in Protestant Missions, 1890-1917." *Church History* 23, no. 1 (1954): 68-82.

Verkuyl, Johannes. *Contemporary Missiology: An Introduction*. Translated by Dale Cooper. Grand Rapids, MI: Eerdmans, 1978.

"Verkuyl, Johannes (1908-2001) | History of Missiology." http://www.bu.edu/missiology/missionary-biography/t-u-v/verkuyl-johannes-1908-2001/ (21 September 2018).

Vincent, Thomas. *The True Christian's Love to the Unseen Christ*. Reprint, Morgan, PA: Soli Deo Gloria Publications, 1994.

Vine's Complete Expository Dictionary of Old and New Testament Words, Edited by Merrill F. Unger and William Jr. White. Nashville: Thomas Nelson, 1996.

Von Rohr, John R. "Covenant and Assurance in Early English Puritanism." *Church History* 34, no. 2 (1965): 195-203.

Vos, Geerhardus. *Biblical Theology: Old and New Testaments*. Grand Rapids: William B. Eerdmans Publishing Co., 1948. Reprint, Edinburgh: Banner of Truth, 2004.

Vroom, Victor H. *Work and Motivation*, Jossey-Bass Management Series. San Francisco, CA: Jossey-Bass Publishers, 1995.

Waldron, Samuel E., and Richard G. Barcellos. *A Reformed Baptist Manifesto: The New Covenant Constitution of the Church*. Palmdale, CA: Reformed Baptist Academic Press, 2004.

Walvoord, John F., and Roy B. Zuck. *The Bible Knowledge Commentary: An Exposition of the Scriptures*. Logos ed. Wheaton, IL: Victor Books, 1985.

Wan, Enoch. "A Critique of Charles Kraft's Use/Misuse of Communication & Social Sciences in Biblical Interpretation & Missiological Formulation." In *Missiology and the Social Sciences: Contributions, Cautions, and Conclusions*, edited by Edward Rommen and Gary Corwin. Vol. 4, 121-147, Evangelical Missiological Society Series. Pasadena, CA: William Carey Library, 1996.

_____. "Diaspora Missiology and International Student Ministry (ISM)." In *Diaspora Mission to International Students*, edited by Enoch Wan, 11-42, Diaspora Studies. Portland, OR: Center of Diaspora and Relational Research-Western Seminary Press, 2019.

_____. "Introduction." In *Missions from the Majority: Progress, Challenges, and Case Studies*, edited by Enoch Wan and Michael Pocock. Vol. 17, i-vi, Evangelical Missiological Society Series. Pasadena, CA: William Carey Library, 2013.

_____. "'Mission' and *Missio Dei*: Response to Van Engen's 'Mission Defined and Described.'" In *Missionshift: Global Mission Issues in the Third Millennium*, edited by David Hesselgrave and Ed Stetzer, 41-50. Nashville, TN: B&H Academic, 2010.

_____. "The Paradigm of 'Relational Realism.'" *Occasional Bulletin* 19, no. 2 (Spring 2006): 1-8.

_____. "The Theological Application of the Contextual-Interaction Model of Culture." *His Dominion* 9, no. 1 (1982): 1-7.

Wan, Enoch, and Mark Hedinger. *Relational Missionary Training: Theology, Theory, and Practice*, Urban Ministry in the 21st Century, Edited by Kendi Howells Douglas and Stephen Burris. Skyforest, CA: Urban Loft Publishers, 2017.

Waters, Guy Prentiss. *Justification and the New Perspective on Paul: A Review and Response*. Phillipsburg, NJ: P&R Publishing Company, 2004.

Watson, Thomas. *A Body of Divinity*, 1890. Reprint, Edinburgh: The Banner of Truth Trust, 1997.

Wells, Tom. *A Vision for Missions*. Carlisle, PA: The Banner of Truth, 1985.

Wells, Tom, and Fred Zaspel. *New Covenant Theology: Description, Definition, Defense*. Frederick, MD: New Covenant Media, 2002.

Wenham, Gordon J. *Word Biblical Commentary : Genesis 16-50*. Vol. 2, Word Biblical Commentary, Edited by David A. Hubbard, Glenn W. Baker, John D. Watts and Ralph P. Martin. Dallas: Word, Incorporated, 2002.

The Westminster Confession of Faith. The Westminster Assembly, 1647.

The Westminster Shorter Catechism. The Westminister Assembly, 1647.

Williamson, J. R. *From the Garden of Eden to the Glory of Heaven*. United States: Calvary Press Publishing, 2008.

Williamson, Paul R. "Covenant." In *New Dictionary of Biblical Theology*, edited by T. Desmond Alexander and Brian S. Rosner. Electronic ed. Downers Grove, IL: InterVarsity Press, 2000.

_____. *Sealed with an Oath: Covenant in God's Unfolding Purpose*. Downers Grove, IL: IVP Academic, 2007.

Winter, Ralph D. "The Future of Evangelicals in Mission." In *Missionshift: Global Mission Issues in the Third Millennium*, edited by David Hesselgrave and Ed Stetzer, 164-191. Nashville, TN: B&H Academic, 2010.

Wright, Christopher J. H. *The Mission of God: Unlocking the Bible's Grand Narrative*. Downers Grove: InterVarsity Press, 2006.

www.ingramcontent.com/pod-product-compliance
Lightning Source LLC
Chambersburg PA
CBHW070849050426
42453CB00012B/2105